Praise for the Foundations for Spirit-Filled Christianity Series

"I am amazed at how North American and European Christians continue to ignore the dramatic changes in global Christianity. These changes are not insignificant. They call for serious revisions in the Christian mission, ecumenism, and theological training. One of the most dramatic shifts has been the rapid rise of Pentecostal/Charismatic spirituality. It is safe to say that in all forms of the global church—Protestant, Roman Catholic, and Orthodox—people are increasingly seeing themselves as Spirit-filled believers. Unfortunately, colleges and seminaries often lack textbooks that address these changes. This series, Foundations for Spirit-Filled Christianity, is a timely intervention, one that will certainly help to fill this gap."

—**Cheryl Bridges Johns**, Global Pentecostal House of Study, United Theological Seminary

"The Foundations for Spirit-Filled Christianity series rightly identifies the pivotal role of Pentecostal and Charismatic Christianity in shaping tomorrow's global Christianity and addresses the shortage of resources for training future leaders. The titles of the series will serve this Christian family's continuing growth by providing textbooks for its theological education."

—**Wonsuk Ma**, College of Theology and Ministry, Oral Roberts University

"The church and academy are finally ready for Foundations for Spirit-Filled Christianity, which relays the insights and perspectives of mature Pentecostal and Charismatic theologians and biblical scholars on a broad array of important theological topics, doctrinal loci, and practical realities. Pentecostal theologians from around the world are now ready to speak in their own accents in ways that will benefit the church catholic."

—**Amos Yong**, Fuller Theological Seminary

FOUNDATIONS FOR SPIRIT-FILLED CHRISTIANITY

SERIES EDITORS

Jerry Ireland, chaplain, US Navy

Paul W. Lewis, professor of historical theology and intercultural studies, Assemblies of God Theological Seminary at Evangel University, Springfield, Missouri

Frank D. Macchia, professor of systematic theology, Vanguard University, and associate director of the Centre for Pentecostal and Charismatic Studies at Bangor University, Wales, United Kingdom

ADVISORY BOARD

Kim Alexander, director of academics and RSM online, Ramp School of Ministry

Roli Dela Cruz, Assemblies of God (USA) World Missions missionary serving as Greek and New Testament instructor at Asia Pacific Theological Seminary, Baguio, Philippines

Sarita Gallagher Edwards, practitioner-scholar and frequent speaker and writer on global Christianity, biblical theology of mission, and mission history

Robert L. Gallagher, professor of intercultural studies emeritus, Wheaton College Graduate School

Byron Klaus, professor of intercultural leadership studies, Assemblies of God Theological Seminary

Andy Lord, minister at All Saints' Didcot in the diocese of Oxford and visiting lecturer at the London School of Theology

Gary Tyra, professor of biblical and practical theology, Vanguard University

Nimi Wariboko, Walter G. Muelder Professor of Social Ethics, Boston University

Introduction *to* Biblical Interpretation

PARTICIPATING IN GOD'S STORY
OF REDEMPTION

JACQUELINE GREY
AND PAUL W. LEWIS

B
Baker Academic
a division of Baker Publishing Group
Grand Rapids, Michigan

© 2024 by Jacqueline Grey and Paul W. Lewis

Published by Baker Academic
a division of Baker Publishing Group
Grand Rapids, Michigan
www.BakerAcademic.com

Printed in the United States of America

Library of Congress Cataloging-in-Publication Data
Names: Grey, Jacqueline, author. | Lewis, Paul W., author.
Title: Introduction to biblical interpretation : participating in God's story of redemption / Jacqueline Grey and Paul W. Lewis.
Description: Grand Rapids, Michigan : Baker Academic, a division of Baker Publishing Group, [2024] | Series: Foundations for Spirit-filled Christianity | Includes bibliographical references and index.
Identifiers: LCCN 2023049248 | ISBN 9781540963369 (paperback) | ISBN 9781540967732 (casebound) | ISBN 9781493445998 (ebook) | ISBN 9781493446001 (pdf)
Subjects: LCSH: Redemption—Biblical teaching. | Bible—Hermeneutics. | Bible—Criticism, interpretation, etc. | Bible—Reading.
Classification: LCC BT775 .G76 2024 | DDC 220.601—dc23/eng/20240116
LC record available at https://lccn.loc.gov/2023049248

Baker Publishing Group publications use paper produced from sustainable forestry practices and postconsumer waste whenever possible.

24   25   26   27   28   29   30   7   6   5   4   3   2   1

For our parents,
John and Nancye Grey
and
Terrance and Ruth Lewis,
from whom we learned our love of God and his Word

CONTENTS

PART 3: Reading and Living

SERIES PREFACE

The demographics of Christianity, along with those of the general world population, have changed and expanded significantly over the past few centuries. A key aspect of this expansion has been the influence and growth of the church internationally, especially in the Global South, which is largely composed of believers within Pentecostal and Charismatic streams of Christianity. Consequently, the changing face of global Christianity is becoming increasingly diverse and characterized by Pentecostal and Charismatic beliefs and praxis. Despite the massive increase in Pentecostal churches and educational institutions, there still exists a lacuna of textbooks that incorporate perspectives from Pentecostal and Charismatic streams of Christianity. The Foundations for Spirit-Filled Christianity series attempts to fill that void by offering high-quality introductory textbooks that include both global and Pentecostal streams of thought. These textbooks will explore primary topics of interest in the fields of biblical studies, church ministries and practical theology, church history, theology, and missions.

The global aspect of Christianity is reflected in the diversity and breadth of the series advisory board, and global perspectives have been intentionally highlighted by the series editors, who have been immersed in other cultural settings throughout their lives. Jerry Ireland and his wife, Paula, lived and worked in Africa, including in educational entities, for well over a decade; Paul Lewis and his wife, Eveline (a native Chinese Indonesian), lived and worked in East Asia, primarily in academic institutions, for almost two decades; and Frank Macchia and his wife, Verena (a native of Switzerland), lived in Europe while Frank studied at the University of Basel.

Each book in the series will also reflect the increasingly Pentecostal nature of global Christianity. The various authors will offer robust discussions and balanced appraisals of their topics while simultaneously situating Pentecostal perspectives alongside those traditionally showcased in introductory text-books for evangelical Bible colleges and seminaries. These textbooks will also help students navigate the sometimes-controversial arguments surrounding some Pentecostal and Charismatic themes and concerns. Further, while remaining global in perspective, authors will locate their themes within a theologically conservative framework.

In summary, what distinguishes this series is, first, its primary focus on providing high-quality introductory college and seminary textbooks and, second, its resonance with contemporary students who are fully in tune with global Pentecostal and Charismatic theology and perspectives. Ultimately, the goal is to provide tools for the global church that represent the vast array of church expressions in order to set the stage for the next generation to continue to effectively and responsibly advance the good news of the gospel.

To God be the glory!

PREFACE

The journey of developing this volume was an involved one. When the series Foundations for Spirit-Filled Christianity was established by Baker Academic, the basics were set for the audience and goals of the respective volumes, including the notion that each volume was to be a textbook for freshman- and sophomore-level students in college or the equivalent in a local church, with a lens toward Pentecostal and Charismatic theological sensibilities that have been neglected in many other textbooks. One of the agreed-upon topics in the series editors' discussions (Paul W. Lewis being one of those editors) was for a volume on biblical interpretation. It was decided that Paul would work on this volume. From the very earliest days, Paul interacted with Jacqueline N. Grey of Alphacrucis College, Sydney, Australia, about coauthoring this book. The two of us, Jacqui and Paul, had known each other for quite a while and had worked together on other projects. Jacqui had also previously published on biblical interpretation. It was agreed that we would work together on this project and would divide the writing according to our strengths and interests. Paul contributed most significantly to part 1, while Jacqui focused mainly on part 2, with subsequent collaborative work to blend the overall volume into a cohesive whole.

From the beginning, there was both an excitement about the volume and a sense of the overwhelming task in front of us. Both of us were aware of a lack of beginning textbooks fitting the niche described above. The opportunity was never lost on us. The overwhelming aspect was that there are literally thousands of books, articles, and essays on biblical interpretation and biblical hermeneutics and related topics, which are too numerous to mention, and we both have been teaching on this topic for many years. Paul has been teaching graduate-level hermeneutics (at both master's and doctoral levels) since the late 1990s. Jacqui, similarly, has been teaching both undergraduate and graduate biblical interpretation since the early 2000s. So the question was, What should we include or not include? Further, there is a fine line between adequately representing the field and related issues and getting into the detailed or technical side of the issues and positions. Equally true is that after teaching this for so many years, as well as reading hundreds of sources, we cannot always remember where some perspectives originally come from. With all of this in mind, we have tried to minimize the number of footnotes in this book and cite only key resources for each discussion, should the reader want to follow up for further research. This means that for every source cited, there are a hundred or so more sources that could be named.

Why this volume on biblical interpretation? This topic is so fundamental to the Christian faith that the volume's need seems self-explanatory. However, our day and time, on a global scale, seems to highlight the neglect of sound biblical interpretation. Thus, in chapter 1 we start with the question, Why biblical interpretation? Yet we are also mindful that we live in a multicultural world, so the issue of how to engage cross-culturally in our biblical hermeneutics is addressed in chapter 14. At the end of the day, learning about biblical hermeneutics is learning about God, having his Spirit guide us into a solid Christlike walk, applying his Word to our lives, and proclaiming his gospel to every person, no matter their cultural background.

ACKNOWLEDGMENTS

From Paul Lewis

As with any project of this type, there are many people behind the scenes who helped bring this volume to fruition. First, I would like to thank my coauthor, Jacqui Grey, whose collaborative effort strongly aided the process of completing this volume. Second, I would like to thank my friends and colleagues who looked over the manuscript and gave valuable insight, Drs. Robert Eby and James Railey, and I thank other friends and colleagues who actively talked about related topics, such as Drs. Roger Cotton, William Griffin, Gary Martindale, Marty Mittelstadt, Meghan Musy, and Rick Wadholm (and many others who did not even know I was asking questions pertinent to this project). Yet all the failings in the text are my own. Third, I would like to express my appreciation to my master's and doctoral students whom I have had in hermeneutics classes at Asia Pacific Theological Seminary, Baguio, Philippines; Asia Theological Centre, Singapore; and Assemblies of God Theological Seminary, Springfield, Missouri, from the 1990s to the present. Their questions and requests for clarification aided me in refining my understanding of biblical interpretation and hermeneutics, particularly in a cross-cultural context.

I would like to especially thank my wife, Eveline, who encouraged and supported me throughout this project and also allowed for my absence at times so I could research, write, and edit. I would also like to express appreciation to my daughter Anastasia (Ana), for helping look over the manuscript and making sure it suited the appropriate audience. Also, I need to mention my other daughter, Rachel, her husband, Josh, and their two daughters (my granddaughters), Seraphina and Gloria, were blessed distractions when I needed a break.

From Jacqui Grey

As Paul notes above, there are many people who have encouraged and assisted us along this journey. I would like to first thank Paul for inviting me into this project. He could have written this on his own, but he included me as part of the team, each of us bringing our strengths. I think the result is a richer reading experience for students and a potent example of collegial collaboration.

Second, I would especially like to thank my sister, Brooke Pipes, who read, edited, and offered suggestions and encouragement for each chapter. She even provided wording for many of the prayers at the ends of the chapters. I am so appreciative of her love and support. I am also thankful for my parents, John and Nancye Grey, who provided much prayerful and practical support—such as meals when I was up late writing, and shopping when I was buried in manuscripts.

The process of writing and editing requires many hours, so I want to thank my colleagues at Alphacrucis University College in Australia for allowing me the time and space to work on this project. As with Paul, many of these colleagues (particularly Matt Jarlett) helped me clarify my ideas without realizing they contributed to this project. Other friends, including Pastor Kristy Rigg, Pastor Kay Dohle, and Dr. Serene Paul, provided moral support and feedback and walked with me through the moments of despair and joy that so often accompany enterprises like this.

Finally, we would like to thank our delightful editor, Brandy Scritchfield, as well as the team at Baker Publishing. It really does take a village to raise a book.

Yet all glory, honor, and praise go to our Lord Jesus Christ, to whom this volume points in every word. Praise the Lord!

1

MAKING BIBLICAL
INTERPRETATION PERSONAL

In this chapter, you should expect to learn the following:

- ▶ Why biblical interpretation is important
- ▶ The PERSONAL method of biblical interpretation
- ▶ The layout of this book
- ▶ The layout of the chapters

> I meditate on your precepts
> and consider your ways.
> I delight in your decrees;
> I will not neglect your word.
> —Ps. 119:15–16

Why Biblical Interpretation?

On the one hand, the answer to the question "Why biblical interpretation?" seems glaringly obvious. As the above psalm emphasizes, meditating on and studying God's Word is central for the development of our faith. On the other hand, the task of interpreting the Bible can seem quite daunting and complex.

The Metropolitan Museum of Art, Rodgers Fund, 1966

Figure 1.1. *Reading the Scriptures,* by Thomas Waterman Wood

Yet Psalm 119 reminds us not to neglect God's Word. Studying the Bible is of essential importance in our Christian discipleship; therefore, we need to take seriously the interpretive enterprise. As these verses and the painting in figure 1.1 convey, the study of Scripture is important for numerous reasons. First, it helps us know God's ways. By studying God's Word, we learn about God and his plan for redemption. We grow in our faith as we further our knowledge of God through prayer and studying his Word. Second, reflecting on the Scriptures also aids us in getting to know God relationally, not just getting to know *about* him. The Bible helps to reveal God and his character to us. Third, the Bible informs who we are—our identity, purpose, and self-understanding. As the psalmist declares, studying God and God's ways through his Word is both a delight and life giving. The goal of this volume is to assist you in the best ways to meditate on God's "ways" and "decrees" (Ps. 119:15–16). By pursuing this task, we can better know God and Jesus Christ personally and see ourselves more clearly. The study of Scripture demands intentionality; we need to purposefully spend time meditating on, considering, reading, and studying God's Word.

Psalm 119 can help us see why reading the Bible is so important. This psalm was written by an ancient Israelite as part of Israel's worship, but its words can be read by all people in all times. This psalm is also a prayer that encourages us to seek revelatory knowledge of God. It models for us this intentionality to know God's Word and the longing to fulfill God's commands.[1] Psalm 119 has 176 verses that are divided into twenty-two sections of 8 verses each. Each section begins with a consecutive letter of the Hebrew alphabet, composing what is called an acrostic poem and highlighting the poem's sense of completeness (from *a* to *z*). In the same way, the Bible is complete. That is, the Bible contains all that we need for salvation and faithful living. This desire to live faithfully is reflected in these verses of Psalm 119, as the writer joyfully meditates on God's law (torah). Studying the Bible is an act of worship. This is also the aim of this book: that you would apply the message of the Bible in your own life, that you would join the story of God's redemption and live the Bible faithfully in your location and context. However, whereas the psalmist reveals *why* they study Scripture, they don't show us how to interpret the biblical text.

So how do we pursue this task of studying Scripture? The Bible is unique. It is different from any other piece of literature. Throughout this book we will explore the uniqueness of Scripture. Yet the biblical text is still a written communication using the conventions of human language. So just as we use interpretive techniques to understand different literary texts, from classical literature to newspapers, so we also use similar techniques when we interpret the Bible. The appropriate techniques and lenses aid the interpreter to understand and apply the biblical message. However, the church has historically distinguished between sacred and secular texts. This is why the Bible is referred to as "holy" (meaning "set apart"). Therefore, the Bible is seen as set apart from other literature and, as such, is unique. While there are some small differences in the content of the Bible across Christian traditions (which we will discuss later), our focus will be on the sixty-six books of the Protestant Bible.

One of the main reasons for the uniqueness of the Bible is captured with the term "inspiration." While we will discuss in detail the concept of inspiration in chapter 2, essentially it means that the Holy Spirit superintended the writing and development of the Bible. So while we might read and be "inspired" by other literature, such as *The Hobbit* by J. R. R. Tolkien, the Bible is fundamentally different from these other texts. Instead, as the psalmist reflects, the Bible is God's Word, which provides guidance for our life and faith as we "consider [God's] ways" (119:15). So then, as we approach the task of biblical

---

1. Federico G. Villanueva, *Psalms 73–150*, Asia Bible Commentary Series (Cumbria, UK: Langham, 2022), 329.

interpretation, we do so as an expression of faith in God and his Word. It is an act of worship and should be approached accordingly. To understand the Bible both as sacred and as significant for our lives is why we engage in the venture of biblical interpretation. We want to be genuine followers of God and become more like Jesus—thus, we study God's Word.

Historically, many schools in the US have emphasized studying the Bible in English, most notably due to the Bible school movement of the late nineteenth and early twentieth centuries. This movement emphasized the importance of "Bible study methods," which were primarily geared toward devotional and personal benefit. Such methods tend to dismiss the importance of understanding the historical context and the insight gained from studying the original languages of the biblical text. We encourage reading the Bible for personal benefit (see part 3), while acknowledging that biblical interpretation is much more than a devotional exercise.[2] Biblical interpretation must incorporate a broader understanding of the hermeneutical process, including the historical and cultural context of a passage and the particular genre (or type of writing) by which an author chose to communicate their message.

Ultimately, the goal of biblical interpretation is to determine what the text meant to its original audience and to apply the meaning to our lives today. That is, we take the meaning from a biblical author (or editor), who was writing to an original audience (an audience in a different place, time, and culture), and using all the tools possible for understanding this original message, we then "translate" how that meaning is significant to us today in our contemporary context. The first part of studying and articulating the message for the original context (the ancient audience) is called *exegesis* or the *exegetical process*.[3] However, we are also concerned with what the message means for us today—the discovery of which is called *application*. So the exegetical process plus the application to our context is called the *hermeneutical process*. The appropriate use of tools for good exegesis and the whole hermeneutical process are part of the art and science of biblical interpretation. It is this whole

---

2. Over the last century or so, and even today in many schools of ministry or the like, "biblical interpretation" or "biblical hermeneutics" courses have been taught that are actually courses on Bible study methods (how to study the Bible in English—or whichever local vernacular) for personal and/or devotional benefit. Over the years, many of my students have said they took "biblical interpretation" as an undergraduate student, only to find out they never talked about theological foundations, original contextual issues (or our contexts), or interpretive issues and concerns.

3. For the beginner, two very good works on exegesis are Gordon D. Fee, *New Testament Exegesis: A Handbook for Students and Pastors*, 3rd ed. (Louisville: Westminster John Knox, 2002), and Douglas Stuart, *Old Testament Exegesis: A Handbook for Students and Pastors*, 5th ed. (Louisville: Westminster John Knox, 2022).

process of exegesis and application that this book will teach you. Accordingly, the theological reflection on and the practical steps for biblical interpretation set out in this book will provide formative guidance for the beginning student. This can be seen in what we will call being "PERSONAL" in biblical study.

The PERSONAL Approach to Biblical Interpretation

There are many aspects to interpreting the Bible. As we noted earlier, interpretation can seem complex and overwhelming. To provide an overview and to ready our hearts for the task, we have adopted a macro approach using the acronym PERSONAL. This approach lays out the steps we can follow as we seek to interpret the biblical text. It gives the big picture of the overall task of studying Scripture. It is a tool that beginning students of hermeneutics can use to come away with a deeper understanding of God and his Word.[4] As Psalm 119:15–16 reminds us, reading the Bible should not be a chore but personally enriching. Although it requires effort to follow these steps, it is a life-giving activity that engages our whole person. Being PERSONAL means:

P – Pray

Before opening our Bible, we start by opening our hearts to God. Prayer is the beginning point of studying the Bible. By dedicating our task to the Lord, we center ourselves on God and open ourselves to the sensitivity of his Spirit. While we need to always start with prayer, prayer should also be present throughout our study, as we ask the Lord to help us cement the ideas we learn into our minds, our actions, and our lives. If you are unsure how to pray, you can use the words from Psalm 119 as a guide.

E – Evaluate Yourself

Next, as we begin to approach the biblical text, we need to take stock of our distances from the biblical text.[5] We recognize that we are not operating

---

4. There are several other guidelines available that can help teachers guide students in beginning hermeneutics and help students visualize the process; three different types are Larry Caldwell, *Doing Bible Interpretation!* (Sioux Falls, SD: Lazy Oak, 2016), 29–30; J. Scott Duvall and J. Daniel Hays, *Grasping God's Word: A Hands-On Approach to Reading, Interpreting, and Applying the Bible*, 4th ed. (Grand Rapids: Zondervan, 2020); and John Goldingay, *Models for Interpretation of Scripture* (Grand Rapids: Eerdmans, 1995), 283–87.

5. See William W. Klein, Craig L. Blomberg, and Robert L. Hubbard Jr., *Introduction to Biblical Interpretation*, 3rd ed. (Grand Rapids: Zondervan, 2017), 53–59. For "gaps," see Bernard Ramm, *Protestant Biblical Interpretation* (Grand Rapids: Baker, 1970), 4–7.

in the same language. Nor are we located in the same history, culture, or geo-political entities of any of the biblical books. Our context today is not the same as the context of the Bible. We are distant from the Scriptures in various ways. By analogy, readers today are distant historically from Jane Austen's *Pride and Prejudice* (originally published in 1813) and the works of William Shakespeare. Note how movie adaptations of these literary works highlight the historical differences by re-creating the clothing, music, language, culture, and so forth of the original era. Similarly, readers today are historically distant from the world of the Bible.

This distance can also be seen linguistically. The biblical languages—Greek, Hebrew, and Aramaic—have words and syntax differing from English. Even good translations cannot completely replicate the exact details of the language in the original text (especially if there are intentional puns or wordplays that do not translate). So the linguistic differences between our world today and the biblical world are significant.

There is a geographical distance as well. For us Western readers, our geography and environment are very different from the biblical lands (that is, of course, unless you live in Israel or the surrounding areas). Furthermore, the terrain of the Holy Land, as well as the significance of that landscape, may be different. For instance, frequently in the Old Testament the statement "Come, let us go up to the mountain of the Lord" is made (Isa. 2:3; Mic. 4:2; cf., e.g., Ps. 122:1; Jer. 31:6). In Hebrew, to "go up" refers to elevation, including spiritual elevation. To "go up" to the mountain of the Lord is to pilgrimage to the temple and engage in worship. In English, we can use this phrase to refer to elevation, but if I state that "I will go up to Chicago," the reference is to going north. It has no spiritual significance. This example highlights both the difference of the geography and the descriptive significance attached to the locations of the Bible.

Furthermore, there are a lot of cultural differences. The biblical cultures tended to be corporate and honor-shame oriented. In contrast, the cultures of the Western world today tend to be individualistic and guilt oriented.[6] So the biblical writers and their ancient audiences presupposed cultures very differ-ent from many cultures today. It is important, then, to approach the task of biblical interpretation with this awareness of our cultural distance. This is so

---

6. For dealing with this distance and the danger of presupposing Western cultural lenses when reading the Bible, see E. Randolph Richards and Brandon J. O'Brien, *Misreading Scripture with Western Eyes: Removing Cultural Blinders to Better Understand the Bible* (Downers Grove, IL: IVP Books, 2012), and E. Randolph Richards and Richard James, *Misreading Scripture with Individualist Eyes: Patronage, Honor and Shame in the Biblical World* (Downers Grove, IL: IVP Academic, 2020).

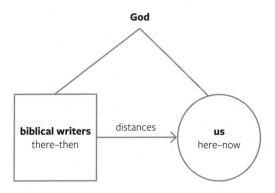

Figure 1.2. From there-then to here-now / Paul Lewis

we don't "cut and paste" our cultures onto the cultures of the Bible, thinking wrongly that they are the same. By evaluating ourselves and seeing how we live in a different culture, world, and time, we can better understand the message given to the original audience. As can be seen in figure 1.2, we recognize the distance between the biblical authors ("there-then") and us today ("here-now"), and then we seek to close that gap by understanding their world and what their message meant to them.

In a similar way, we should evaluate ourselves regarding our "preunderstanding." This term refers to our presuppositions—that is, those assumptions, prejudices, and preformed ideas that we bring to the text, often without even realizing it. By recognizing our presuppositions, we can truly be open to what God is saying in the Bible and not just jump to our own conclusions or preconceived assumptions. We will discuss this further in chapter 5.

R – Read in Context

This discussion leads to the importance of reading in context. This step includes reading the Bible and other useful resources that help us identify the situation a Bible passage is addressing. There are primarily two contexts that the interpreter needs to be concerned about. One is *the cultural-sociohistorical context*, which we have already discussed to an extent in the previous section.[7] This refers to the world of the audience originally hearing the message—that is, the "there-then" (as noted above). Identifying the context of the original

7. This context can include what Craig S. Keener calls the "spiritual context," as well as economic, political, and other contexts (*Spirit Hermeneutics: Reading Scripture in Light of Pentecost* [Grand Rapids: Eerdmans, 2016], 43–45). Throughout the rest of this book, these various elements will generally be represented by the phrase "historical context."

hearers helps us understand the occasion of the original text and what the writers were addressing. Sometimes, the context of a biblical passage is clear. However, other times the context is not obvious and thus tricky to identify. This is where other tools and resources help us in this task. That is, often we need to read other books and resources to help us in the task of interpretation. Some great resources for exploring the original context of a passage are Bible dictionaries, wordbooks, handbooks, and Bible or Holy Land atlases. These resources, plus appropriate technical monographs, textbooks, and commentaries, can give us a lot of information concerning the cultural and social environments of the biblical writers.[8] Also of note, you should be using a suitable translation of the Bible for this task of reading. If you don't or if you're unsure if you do, jump down to chapter 2 for the discussion on selecting a Bible translation.

The second context is *the literary context*. This refers to specific passages in view and how those passages fit into their surrounding chapter(s) and book(s). However, before we look closely at the literary context, we need to recognize that every literary text generally fits a *type* of writing. This is called the "genre" of a text. It's the category and writing style of a passage. By analogy, movies can be classified as action, horror, comedy, drama, musical, or documentary. These categories can be identified by the characteristics movies share. Action movies are generally fast paced and include a lot of fight scenes, stunts, and car chases—usually ending in the hero (or superhero) defeating the villain. The genre of a movie or literary piece establishes its expectation, style, and content. In the same way, biblical genres share particular features in common. Some examples of genres in the Bible include narrative, poetry, letter, prophecy, and law. Identifying the genre and its characteristics is such an important topic that we dedicate part 2 of this book to its study. But for now, we simply highlight that each biblical passage takes a form that is consistent with its genre.

What is more, literary context involves two levels. The first is the grammatical structure of a passage. We might use the verses of Psalm 119:15–16, quoted above, as an example. The first level of literary context, then, is the study of the words and grammar of this passage. These verses emphasize the study of the torah, God's law. They don't use the word "torah," but they do use

---

8. Helpful resources include Craig S. Keener, *The IVP Bible Background Commentary: New Testament*, 2nd ed. (Downers Grove, IL: IVP Academic, 2014), and John H. Walton, Victor H. Matthews, and Mark W. Chavalas, *The IVP Bible Background Commentary: Old Testament* (Downers Grove, IL: IVP Academic, 2000). Be aware, however, that a note of caution is needed insofar as sometimes (other) contemporary writers are more influenced by their own philosophical or ideological agendas than by the biblical text itself.

synonyms, such as "precepts," "ways," and "decrees," which all refer to torah. We dig into the immediate literary context of a passage by unpacking the words, sentences, and paragraphs of the text in view.

The second level of literary context focuses on how the passage fits into the larger structure of the chapter and book at hand. As noted above, Psalm 119:15–16 is part of an acrostic poem, which means that the poem follows the Hebrew alphabet, like from *a* to *z*. To fully appreciate this passage, then, we have to read these verses in light of the whole chapter. In doing so, we realize that Psalm 119 is part of the book of Psalms, which functioned as something of a worship songbook for ancient Israel. The Psalms teach us to worship in all circumstances, whether in good times or bad. To read Psalm 119—which is a happy psalm and is quite distinct from, say, the lament of Psalm 22—without due attention to where it fits within the grand scheme of things is to miss the richness, diversity, and purpose of the book. Therefore, we read each passage in its immediate literary context (focusing on its words and syntax) as well as in its larger literary context (focusing on the broader chapter and book).

As we have emphasized so far, identifying the historical context and literary context are foundational for biblical interpretation. We need to understand these to *read well*. This leads to the basic building blocks for analyzing the literary context of a passage. But before we unpack these building blocks, let's consider some helpful resources.

Interlude: What Are Some Relevant Resources?

There is a plethora of good Bible dictionaries, wordbooks, handbooks, and Bible or Holy Land atlases available.[9] Bible dictionaries aid the student by defining biblical characters, places (sometimes with archaeological updates), concepts, key words, and the like, in alphabetical order. There are even different types of biblical dictionaries—some focusing on places, others on persons, and still others on cultural matters. Wordbooks concentrate on words themselves, which helps to clarify their meaning(s). Depending on which context(s) or word(s) you are studying, an appropriate dictionary or wordbook can assist you greatly.[10]

9. A good survey of these resources is John Glynn, *Commentary and Reference Survey: A Comprehensive Guide to Biblical and Theological Resources*, 10th ed. (Grand Rapids: Kregel Academic & Professional, 2007).

10. For a survey of Bible dictionaries, see Glynn, *Commentary and Reference Survey*, 232, 235–37; see also "Selected Bibliography for Biblical and Theological Research: Appendix 18," in *Missiological Research: Interdisciplinary Foundations, Methods, and Integration*, ed. Marvin Gilbert, Alan R. Johnson, and Paul W. Lewis (Pasadena, CA: William Carey Library, 2018), 351–68.

As for Bible handbooks, they tend to focus on cultural, thematic, and book-level aspects of the biblical text. So they comprise more of an overview than a series of detailed analyses. This type of resource aids the student in looking at macrocontextual features of the text (e.g., the book of Nehemiah as a whole or the Persian period, more broadly).[11]

Several quality Bible or Holy Land atlases are also available. These focus on the geographical and topographical aspects of the land of the Bible, both Old and New Testaments.[12] They can assist you in comprehending locations, distances, and elevations. It is noted that the advent of digital technology has simplified research tremendously;[13] however, not all online resources are well researched or equally reliable. Traditional types of resources are still helpful and should continue to be consulted.

Having considered some relevant resources, we turn to our exploration of the basic building blocks that unpack the literary context of "seeking" to understand biblical texts.

S – Seek Meaning

Studying the Bible requires us to "seek" to understand the meaning of a passage through the close study of the words, sentences, paragraphs, and discourse of the text. This process continues the focus on the literary context of the passage. As the psalmist says, we are to "meditate on [the Lord's] precepts" (Ps. 119:15). This requires us to look closely at and reflect deeply on the words and the construction of the passage.

Seeking Meaning through Words

The basic components of any written communication are words.[14] Words are the first building blocks one should look at when seeking to understand the meaning of a biblical passage. However, one of the challenges (as noted above) is that these basic units, the words of the biblical text, are translated from another language. Therefore, issues and considerations concerning the translation

11. E.g., J. Daniel Hays and J. Scott Duvall, eds., *The Baker Illustrated Bible Handbook* (Grand Rapids: Baker Books, 2014); Craig A. Evans and David Mishkin, eds., *Handbook on the Jewish Roots of the Christian Faith* (Peabody, MA: Hendrickson, 2019). See Glynn, *Commentary and Reference Survey*, for a wide array of resources along this line.

12. E.g., Adrian Curtis, *Oxford Bible Atlas*, 4th ed. (Oxford: Oxford University Press, 2009). See Glynn, *Commentary and Reference Survey*, 233, 237–39.

13. For a wide range of digital (computer, e-version, and online) resources, see Glynn, *Commentary and Reference Survey*, 343–68. Some helpful online resources include The Bible Project (https://bibleproject.com) and Bible Odyssey (https://www.bibleodyssey.org).

14. See, on word studies, Duvall and Hays, *Grasping God's Word*, 165–90.

of the Bible into our target languages (such as English) come into play. This is important to remember as we seek to understand the meaning of a passage for its original hearers. Translations must deal with *semantic range*, or the range of what a word can mean when used. Frequently, a translation decision has to be made about the most appropriate word to select in the target language. For example, in English the word "love" can be used to translate three different Greek words: *agapē*, *philia*, and *erōs*. In Greek, they do have slight variations in meaning; however, the differences are not always clear-cut, although *erōs* is mostly distinct from the other two meanings. For instance, *agapē* highlights a self-sacrificial and life-giving type of love, whereas *philia* refers to brotherly love and *erōs* to romantic and erotic love. Yet the English language uses just one word for these three Greek words. So we need good approaches to word studies.[15] While there is value in word studies, especially in reference to the biblical languages, it is generally the literary context that will provide the most guidance for understanding the meaning and best translation of a word.[16]

Seeking Meaning through Sentences and Syntax

The next building block is combining the words together into a coherent thought, which is a sentence (including clauses).[17] These sentences make statements, declare truths, display dialogue, and so on. Syntax is the structure of the phrases and words that coherently communicate within a language. In English, word order is the primary way by which coherent communication takes place in a sentence. Other languages, such as Greek, modify words themselves to show parts of speech, tense, and the like. For instance, in English we can say, "The dog bit the man." Clearly, the word order helps to convey the action. In Greek, though, the order can be switched, with the equivalents of "dog" and "man" having different endings to convey the same action. This is also why some very literal translations of the Bible can seem disjointed, while much looser translations can read more easily in English. So sentences and syntax are important in seeing clearly the flow of thought and the direction of the texts, especially theologically. However, we also need to keep in mind

15. Helpful summaries on doing word studies are appendices 19–20, in Roger D. Cotton and James D. Hernando, in Gilbert, Johnson, and Lewis, *Missiological Research*, 369–76. Glynn, *Commentary and Reference Survey*, offers a wide variety of quality resources, both print and electronic, for word studies in the biblical languages.

16. See especially D. A. Carson, *Exegetical Fallacies*, 2nd ed. (Grand Rapids: Baker, 1996), 27–64. An example of pushing word study too far is insisting that *agapē* must always refer to God's love, even where, in the Septuagint and the New Testament, the verb form is used for decidedly nondivine aspects of love; see Carson, *Exegetical Fallacies*, 28, 47–53, esp. 31–32.

17. On sentences, see Duvall and Hays, *Grasping God's Word*, 37–56; a helpful example of what analyzing sentences can look like is on p. 50.

that for the most part, punctuation does not come from the original texts but was added over the centuries by scribes and scholars.

Seeking Meaning through Paragraphs

Paragraphs are very important; they combine sentences into a unit of thought. Each paragraph usually captures a new idea as part of the discussion. It helps move the discussion forward and informs broader thinking on the topic.[18] However, we must note that the oldest manuscripts of the Greek and Hebrew (and Aramaic) texts of Scripture did not have paragraphs. Instead, the lines were written tight together without breaks to conserve the writing material. Therefore, paragraphing in modern translations is the product of scholars who spent many years studying the text to determine its flow of thought and argumentation. While paragraphs are very helpful and reflect scholars' best guesses, the paragraphing in our Bibles may still be inexact. Likewise, chapter and verse separations are late additions to the originals. So keep in mind that paragraphs may bridge chapters at times and that verse separations may be awkward. However, paragraphs do help us look at the structure and flow of ideas in a passage.

Seeking Meaning through Discourse

Together, all of these building blocks combine into discourse.[19] How is the message (with its parts) communicated? In the Bible, there are various types (or genres) of discourse: narrative, epistle (letter), prophecy, and others. (The second part of this book will explore these in more detail.) But mostly, the study of discourse seeks to understand the message the biblical author is seeking to communicate.

So we can see that words, sentences (and syntax), paragraphs, and discourse are the building pieces for exegetical study. Each contributes toward greater understanding of the meaning of the text. Therefore, in our overall task of biblical interpretation, we seek to understand the components of the biblical text and discover the meaning of a passage in its original, there-then context.

O - Observe

After exploring the text within its contexts, we can now make key observations. We observe on two levels. First, we observe what the passage would

18. On paragraphs, see Duvall and Hays, *Grasping God's Word*, 57–80.
19. On discourses, see Duvall and Hays, *Grasping God's Word*, 81–106.

have meant for its original hearers. Based on what we have seen in our study so far, what did this passage mean to the original audience there-then? What stands out to you from this passage as a key message? What important details do you notice? This is the exegetical process. This process recognizes that God spoke to the original audience through this text for a particular reason. Exegesis is about identifying that reason.

However, second, we also believe that God speaks to us through the Bible today. God's Word has relevancy beyond its original audience; it is significant for us as well in the here-now. This is the process of application. We will explore these processes of exegesis and application further in the book. However, for now, we want to observe what God might be speaking to us about from the biblical passage at hand. What speaks to you? What are important personal and devotional highlights for you? It takes time and energy to reflect on the passage and observe these key items.

N – Note

Once you have observed the text, what are your takeaways? Note your thoughts by writing them down in your own words. Now is the opportunity to look at the works of other scholars on your passage—notably commentaries. A commentary is essentially a collection of comments about a specific book or set of books.[20] Preferably, a commentary should be written by a learned scholar whose life work was or is on the language(s) and contexts of the texts involved, and it should be up to date, reflecting the many advances in biblical studies due to recent linguistic, historical, and archaeological findings.

For many students, the tendency is to plunge into commentaries immediately when studying a biblical passage. However, in Bible study, if a student does their research well on a biblical passage (as outlined in the "Read in Context" and "Seek Meaning" sections above), and if they use quality study resources such as Bible dictionaries, wordbooks, handbooks, and atlases, they will already have a good understanding of the passage. However, a quality commentary can reinforce what the student has found already. Yet there are many times when a scholar, as a result of their yearslong or lifelong process of investigation, articulates insights about the language(s), literary context, and historical context of a passage that greatly enhance our understanding of that passage's meaning.

20. In addition to Glynn, *Commentary and Reference Survey*, see also D. A. Carson, *New Testament Commentary Survey*, 7th ed. (Grand Rapids: Baker Academic, 2013); John F. Evans, *A Guide to Biblical Commentaries and Reference Works*, 10th ed. (Grand Rapids: Zondervan, 2016); and Tremper Longman III, *Old Testament Commentary Survey*, 5th ed. (Grand Rapids: Baker Academic, 2013).

Yet there should also be a note of caution: commentators' own blind spots can also come through. Theological, ideological, and philosophical perspectives can distort a commentator's interpretations. As an example, over a decade ago, I (Paul) attended a conference where a key speaker gave a postcolonial interpretation of the book of Joshua. He stated that, from his perspective, the Canaanites were the heroes and that Joshua and the Israelites were the oppressors. In a careful reading of Joshua (and the Bible as a whole), the biblical text clearly sees Joshua and the Israelites as learning to be obedient to God (albeit they did have issues along the way). They were following the guidance of a holy and righteous God. The Canaanites are not the heroes of the story.[21] So commentators can allow their personal biases to inform their work.

With this caution in mind, the student should, with good analytical skill, engage commentaries after they have already done their own reading, seeking, and observing. Further, especially when you are starting out, I recommend using three or four quality commentaries, comparing and contrasting the findings to mitigate individual bias. Yet at the end of your research, good commentaries should be seen as an aid rather than the first place to go in a study.

A - Apply

Biblical hermeneutics is not just learning about the there-then (original context) but also bringing the message into our here-now (present). This means that theological reflection is necessary after we engage the biblical text. The steps of the interpretive task move from *reading, seeking, observing,* and *noting* to a "call to action." This makes the interaction with Scripture both practical and devotional. This area will be discussed in more detail in chapter 13.

As was noted in the first section above (i.e., "Pray"), prayer should permeate the whole interpretive process. The application part of the hermeneutical process is especially important and needs God's guidance. We pray for divine enablement and empowerment; we pray that this application of the biblical text will be not just a one-time occurrence but an ongoing dynamic in our lives.

The application has both internal and external elements. It deals with both the inner person and the outward expression, including proclamation (see chap. 13). However, in our global context, this application and proclamation are not isolated to our own situations but occur in all the various cross-cultural environments of global Christianity (see chap. 14). All are important in applying Scripture.

21. For further reading on this, see Paul Copan, *Is God a Moral Monster? Making Sense of the Old Testament God* (Grand Rapids: Baker Books, 2011).

L - Live and Share

While applying the biblical text is a crucial step, sometimes the ongoing application is lost or neglected. That is, we can focus on applying individual passages and miss the bigger picture of personal transformation. The ultimate goal of reading the Bible is to become more like Christ and to participate in God's story of redemption. Yet this macrotransformation can be hampered if we simply trade one microapplication this week with a different one next week—for example, if I focus on applying humility this week, only to abandon it to focus on applying patience the following week. The goal is cumulative application that leads to holistic change. I add patience to the humility I am already applying. What we learn and implement this week becomes an ongoing habit, and we add another next week, and so on. Paul says in 2 Corinthians 3:18 that we "are being transformed into his image with ever-increasing glory, which comes from the Lord, who is the Spirit." The goal, as we live in accordance with and apply God's Word, is to become Christlike.

Further, we do not apply the Bible to our personal lives apart from others; we are part of a community. We are to share with others what we have learned from the Bible. This is a form of teaching—teaching can happen not only in a classroom but also when we share with one another through our daily lives. By teaching, we take ownership of what we have learned, and this ownership solidifies the learned truth in our lives. Sharing cements these lessons in our mind and helps us be accountable to others in our community.

The Layout of This Book

This book has been constructed so that you, the reader, can develop an understanding of the basics of biblical interpretation. To aid in this process, this book has been divided into three parts.

The first part is titled "The Purpose and Passion of Reading." This section provides the foundational pieces of biblical interpretation. The first chapter of this section is chapter 2, "Trusting the Word of God," which explores the principles of inspiration and authority and the process of canonization. This chapter provides key theological affirmations about the Bible so that we have a strong understanding of why the Bible is sacred and trustworthy. Chapter 3 focuses on lessons about biblical interpretation throughout history. This chapter summarizes key interpretive schemes from the late Old Testament and early New Testament periods to today. Chapter 4 explores the role of the Holy Spirit (and the triune God) in the whole interpretive and formational process.

Further, a basic understanding of communication theory (à la David Berlo) is delineated in order to better comprehend the complexity of interpretation and associated issues. While chapters 2–4 work through the science of biblical interpretation, chapter 5 emphasizes the art of biblical interpretation. This chapter looks at the beauty of God and his Word. This also leads into the significance of the interpreter in the process of biblical interpretation, including the role of preunderstanding.

The second part of the book is titled "Transformational Reading." It is within this section that the basics of reading various biblical genres are unpacked. Chapter 6 highlights the role of narrative in our lives. Further, it notes how our personal narrative connects with God's overall narrative of creation and redemption, specifically as we enter into *his*-story. Chapter 7 then focuses on the narrative texts found in the Bible. This chapter also explores how lessons from narratives can be applied today. Chapter 8 highlights the purpose of the Old Testament law and notes the connections of law with the Spirit in the New Testament. Of concern is how lessons from the law are relevant for New Testament believers. Chapter 9 focuses on the role of poetry in the Old Testament and the value of poetry in the Bible. Emphasis is on different types of poetry and their applicability in our contemporary circumstances. In chapter 10, the prophetic literature and biblical prophecy are considered in detail. Old Testament and New Testament prophecy are compared, and the importance of prophetic discernment today is underscored. The final chapter of this section, chapter 11, centers on the key features of New Testament letters (epistles). This includes a discussion of the ancient situations these letters addressed and their significance for our contexts today.

The final part is titled "Reading and Living." This section takes the first two parts and moves them into a discussion of what we do now. Chapter 12, "Daily Bread," highlights the ways in which we, as believers, are to daily read the Bible devotionally. The method of *lectio divina* is put forward as an aid for devotional reading and personal implementation with an awareness of the Spirit's role. Chapter 13 unpacks how the interpretation of Scripture needs to move into application. The engagement of personal application internally and externally is examined. Chapter 14 is concerned with our present situation and the need for global, cross-cultural, or missional hermeneutics.[22] It considers how to do hermeneutics in a multicultural context.

---

22. For this book, "missional" means focused on following the mission of God and reaching out to a lost and dying world, particularly in a cross-cultural situation. As such, "missional" is more aligned with divine purpose than is the common usage of the term in the contemporary world.

The final chapter brings the whole volume together. We will revisit the goal of being PERSONAL in the task of biblical interpretation and conclude with some reflections on joining God's story of redemption.

The Layout of the Chapters

To aid the student, all the chapters share a few features in common. First, each chapter includes a painting or visual representation for the student to observe. This is intended to help the student visualize the main topic of the chapter. Second, tied to the art, a verse or set of verses that similarly reflect the topic appear as epigraphs. The visual representation and the biblical text jointly allow the student to engage the topic in memorable ways. After the body of the chapter unpacks the topic, the chapter will have a "What Do I Do Now?" section, which helps the student move forward in their implementation of the chapter's theme and ideas. A prayer is provided to aid students in cementing their learning in their minds and hearts. It provides a model of praying for God's empowerment and enablement in this enterprise of biblical interpretation. After that, as below, a review section contains some questions for collaborative learning.

PRAYER

Lord, we thank you for your Word.
  Let us be sensitive to what you would have us learn.
  Help each of us to be open to your Spirit, and use our thoughts and affections to help us understand your Word.
  Let me not fail to worship you through the study of your Word. Amen.

TOPICS FOR REVIEW

1. Why is biblical interpretation important?
2. In what ways are you distant from the time and place of Old and New Testament contexts and the biblical texts themselves?
3. What is your process for studying a passage? What version(s) and resources would you use? What would be your order of usage?

PART ONE

The Purpose and Passion of Reading

2

TRUSTING THE WORD OF GOD

In this chapter, you should expect to learn the following:

- ► The foundations of trusting the Word of God
- ► The development of the biblical canon
- ► Core theological affirmations about the Bible
- ► Considerations for selecting a translation of the Bible

All Scripture is God-breathed and is useful for teaching, rebuking, correcting and training in righteousness.

—2 Tim. 3:16

Second Timothy 3:16 highlights that all Scripture is God breathed or, as translated by the NASB, "inspired by God." Scripture is tied to the Spirit (the word "breath" being the same as the word for "S/spirit" in Greek). This truth emphasizes the divine origins of Scripture, which reflect the life-giving and creative activity of the Holy Spirit.[1] The Bible originates with and was providentially directed by the triune God. The Bible is God's revelation of himself and of his redemptive purposes for creation. This self-revelation of God in Scripture draws us into relationship with the triune God and the Christian community. As the art in figure 2.1 illustrates, the biblical text is

---

1. Gordon D. Fee, *1 and 2 Timothy, Titus*, New International Biblical Commentary (Peabody, MA: Hendrickson, 1988), 279.

Figure 2.1. Grotto on the exterior of Holy Trinity Church, Pastuh, Bulgaria

Spirit invested; the inspired Scripture first demonstrates the authority of the Bible but also leads to action (see chap. 13).

The Bible aids us in our ministry work and discipling of others. Timothy is the young pastor addressed in 2 Timothy. The writer, most likely Paul, lists here the various tasks expected of Timothy in his pastoral work, including teaching, rebuking, correcting, and training. In this passage, Timothy is reassured that the Bible not only contains truth to keep him and his community on track in their faith but that it also contains the resources needed for avoiding the error of false teachings. He is also encouraged that the Bible provides the tools for him to live out the truth of God's Word in his daily life and ministry. Today, we can take courage from these same words about the Bible for our own faith and work. When starting to look at biblical interpretation, we foundationally ask, Why should we trust the biblical text? Only then can we look at how the collection of the books of the Bible (i.e., the canon) came about. Based on this foundation, we will offer key theological affirmations about the Bible to cement our convictions concerning the authority and trustworthy nature of the biblical text.

The Foundation of Trusting the Word

A major question relating to biblical interpretation is, Why can we trust the Bible? Throughout church history, Scripture has been affirmed as reliable.[2] However, defining what trusting Scripture means can differ from person to person or group to group. There are diverse implications for the authority of Scripture—and therefore a need for a whole conversation about issues of inerrancy and infallibility. To say Scripture in inerrant is to say it is without error. Similarly, the term "infallible" means incapable of leading astray. However, misunderstandings about these terms abound and have led to sharp debates, disagreements, and divisions among Christian groups, particularly within the evangelical community. These terms raise questions such as What does "error" mean? and In what way can we say the biblical text is without error or infallible? For some groups, inerrancy and infallibility mean that every detail contained in the Bible (including historical and factual information) is true and correct. For other groups, though, inerrancy and infallibility mean that the Bible is true and without error in all it affirms, particularly in all matters pertaining to our salvation.[3] To say this another way, since the Bible is given for the purpose of knowing God as revealed through Jesus Christ, then all that Scripture reveals to us about knowing God and the salvation made possible through Christ is true and without error. So we can agree that the Bible is infallible but differ in the way we consider it truthful and without error.

Unless we can place a text in its historical and literary contexts, we can misunderstand its purpose. This is why accurate interpretation is so crucial. For example, the purpose of the book of Joshua is arguably about teaching obedience through a historical narrative, and so it presents its history of events according to this purpose. This is not to undermine the historical reliability of the Bible; there is plenty of external evidence from archaeology that verifies the biblical data. However, we recognize that the historical documents of the ancient world did not provide the same kind of material we would expect of

2. Two noted volumes on the reliability of Scripture are F. F. Bruce, *The New Testament Documents: Are They Reliable?*, 6th ed. (Grand Rapids: Eerdmans, 2003), and K. A. Kitchen, *On the Reliability of the Old Testament* (Grand Rapids: Eerdmans, 2003). On the reliability of the Gospel accounts about Jesus, see also Craig S. Keener, *Christobiography: Memory, History, and the Reliability of the Gospels* (Grand Rapids: Eerdmans, 2019).

3. Millard J. Erickson, *Christian Theology*, 3rd ed. (Grand Rapids: Baker Academic, 2013), 191–93. Erickson notes a continuum: the range can go from the text being useful and without error in every way (a position held by Harold Lindsell), to the text being without error in some areas (e.g., history) but primarily consisting of a spiritual book (a view held by Roger Nicole), to the Bible being without error in the spiritual arena (a perspective held by Daniel Fuller), to the Bible being without error in what it purposes (the view of Jack Rogers). There are other perspectives that could be noted, but the point is that there is a range of definitions.

a history text today. We must read the biblical text according to its purpose and recognize that the data and perspectives the Bible sometimes presents are limited to and by human knowledge of the world of that time.

Yet while the terms "inerrancy" and "infallibility" are regularly used in doctrinal statements about the Bible, neither of these terms adequately captures the claims the Bible itself makes about its nature and purpose. In addition, as noted, the discussion around inerrancy is often highly charged with emotion, and therefore misunderstandings often abound when Christians use this term. In a recent meeting, for instance, I (Jacqui) was discussing the topic of inerrancy with some senior pastors when all of them asserted their commitment to this doctrine. But when asked what the term "inerrancy" actually meant, none of the pastors could say. So we understand that many believers are passionate about inerrancy and infallibility because they treasure the Bible and want to uphold its authority and sacredness. However, we propose that a more helpful approach to understanding the nature and purpose of Scripture is to adopt the terminology used in the Bible itself, which is the language of "inspiration."

Scripture Is Inspired

The standard verse, quoted above, is 2 Timothy 3:16: "All Scripture is inspired by God" (NASB), or "All scripture is given by inspiration of God" (KJV), or "All Scripture is God-breathed" (NIV). This passage highlights that Scripture describes itself as God breathed or inspired.[4] That is, all the books of the Bible were written by people who were inspired by the Holy Spirit to record what God wanted them to write. Each writer was influenced by the prompting and direction of the Holy Spirit in their thinking and writing. The words of the biblical text therefore reflect both the thoughts and mind of God and the particular personalities and contexts of the human authors. As God superintended the process of writing, this means that God is the ultimate author of the Bible; hence, Scripture is the "Word of God." It is this God-given origin that makes it sacred (or holy) and gives it authority. As no other book is given this status in the Christian tradition, the Bible is unique.

---

4. See Erickson, *Christian Theology*, 174–75. Note how Erickson paints the continuum of inspiration in terms of "inspired text": from purely human understanding (e.g., James Martineau); to a slightly modified version that is mostly human and slightly divine (e.g., Auguste Sabatier); to a mediating understanding of inspiration with equal divine and human dynamics (e.g., Augustus Strong); to a strong understanding of divine inspiration down to the actual wording, albeit with human style and usage (also called verbal inspiration; e.g., James I. Packer); to full divine dictation (thus, any apparent differences in grammar, style, etc. between authors are provided by God; e.g., John Rice). Many mainline groups lean toward the first two categories; evangelicals tend to fit with Strong and Packer, while fundamentalists lean toward Rice's position.

The terminology of inspiration is also reflected in 2 Peter 1:19–21. This text highlights the same influence of the Spirit on the Old Testament prophets. It essentially tells us that the prophecies recorded in Scripture never had their origin in the human will or imagination but that the prophets, even though they were human, were moved to speak (and write) God's words as they were carried along by the Spirit. Likewise, while primarily referring to what is now called the Old Testament, 2 Peter 3:15–16 puts some of Paul's letters on par with "the other Scriptures."[5] Inspiration is seen as something God's Spirit invested into the writing process (including the selection and act of writing), which makes the biblical authors' works qualitatively different from other texts. This is why the Christian community historically has recognized the Bible as distinctly different from other literature. This leads us to now consider the authority of the Bible and ask two questions: Does the Bible have authority over our lives? And if so, on what basis?

Scripture Is Authoritative and Trustworthy

The divine origins of Scripture and the affirmations of the historic church emphasize the authority of the Bible over believers. Scripture testifies of itself that it is authentic and true. As the psalmist says, "All [the Lord's] words are true; all [his] righteous laws are eternal" (Ps. 119:160). The authority of the Bible is asserted through its own claims. The Bible provides the standard by which we evaluate ideas, doctrines, philosophies, ethical issues, and activities. We are to assess a doctrine in light of the biblical text, which provides the standard of truth. In this way, the Bible functions as our highest authority. All other sources of knowledge (tradition, reason, experience) are subservient to Scripture.

But do we accept the Bible as authoritative and trustworthy just because it tells us that it is? Isn't that circular reasoning? There are five main reasons, we propose, why the Bible is trustworthy. First, the Bible is reliable because it can stand alone as a coherent text that provides a comprehensible and consistent worldview. That is, the biblical text overall makes sense of our world. As Amy Orr-Ewing notes, Scripture accurately diagnoses the human condition.[6] This includes the rationale for the dignity of all people—namely, that God made humanity in his image (Gen. 1:27). Scripture gives an intelligible reason for

---

5. Paul also apparently refers to some of Jesus's words in 1 Cor. 9:14 and 1 Tim. 5:18 that are found in Luke 10:7. Similarly, Paul cites the traditional words of Jesus passed down about the Lord's Supper in 1 Cor. 11:23–26. On other possible connections, see F. F. Bruce, *Paul and Jesus* (1974; repr., Eugene, OR: Wipf & Stock, 2019), 69–80.

6. Amy Orr-Ewing, *Why Trust the Bible? Answers to Ten Tough Questions*, rev. ed. (London: Inter-Varsity, 2020), 13.

the brokenness, injustices, and systemic evils in our world. It also provides the solution through God's grace and the saving work of Jesus Christ. That is, the Bible's story of redemption is internally coherent.[7] The story of Scripture corresponds to the world we live in and makes sense of this world. Derivative of the authority of the Word is that the Bible and Christianity are reasonable.[8] This does not mean that the final authority is reason, as in rationalism; rather, it means that Scripture has internal coherence and comprehensive meaning. The biblical text was meant to be understood and applied.

In the current postmodern era, many people are like Pilate in the New Testament (John 18:38); they ask "What is truth?" but then they don't stay for the answer![9] Truth is questioned, and the notion of absolute truth is often rejected. As Richard Bauckham notes, there are many competing truth claims in our pluralistic Western societies; however, many people resolve this by claiming that truth is relative. They assert that individuals in this postmodern world are free to choose their own truth.[10] But as Pilate's question reminds us, issues of truth have been with humanity for a long time. The problem, though, is not that objective truth doesn't exist. Instead, it is our human ability to know truth that is in doubt. That is, our capacity to grasp knowledge and understand this world is limited. Humans are fallible, but God is infallible. Therefore, seeking truth requires us to adopt a posture of epistemic humility.[11] This means we should remain humble, because we don't know everything. It also means that truth can and does exist external to us. So while not being dogmatic or arrogant, we can still affirm that absolute truth exists, and we can still trust the Word, which provides this truth.[12]

---

7. Orr-Ewing, *Why Trust the Bible?*, 15.

8. An observation noted by the Christian literary critic C. S. Lewis (1898–1963), following Augustine (354–430) before him; see, e.g., C. S. Lewis, *Mere Christianity*, rev. ed. (New York: Macmillan, 1960). On Lewis and reason, see Alister E. McGrath, "An Enhanced Vision of Rationality: C. S. Lewis on the Reasonableness of Christian Faith," *Theology* 116, no. 6 (2013): 410–17, and McGrath, *The Intellectual World of C. S. Lewis* (Malden, MA: Wiley-Blackwell, 2014).

9. This observation is based on the famous words of Francis Bacon (1561–1626). See Richard Bauckham, *The Bible in the Contemporary World: Hermeneutical Ventures* (Grand Rapids: Eerdmans, 2015), 159.

10. Bauckham, *Bible in the Contemporary World*, 159.

11. For further discussion, see Tania M. Harris, *Hearing God's Voice: Towards a Theology of Contemporary Pentecostal Revelatory Experience* (Leiden: Brill, 2023).

12. There are many quality works affirming the trustworthiness of Scripture contra postmodernism; two such works, using speech-act theory and other tools, are Kevin J. Vanhoozer, *Is There a Meaning in This Text? The Bible, the Reader, and the Morality of Literary Knowledge* (Grand Rapids: Zondervan, 1998), and Nicholas Wolterstorff, *Divine Discourse: Philosophical Reflections on the Claim That God Speaks* (New York: Cambridge University Press, 1995). A note of thanks to Jerry Ireland, who pointed us to these works.

Second, the Bible is trustworthy because God is trustworthy. Jesus says, "I am the way and the truth and the life" (John 14:6). Similarly, the Spirit is truth and promises to guide us into truth (16:13). So the triune God is truth and reveals truth. This reminds us that Scripture itself is not divine. However, the origins of Scripture in the triune God give us confidence that the words of the biblical text are true. Again, Jesus says, "If you hold to my teaching, you are really my disciples. Then you will know the truth, and the truth will set you free" (8:31–32). The reliability of the Bible is grounded in God's reliable and self-less love, which brings real freedom. As Michael Bird writes, "Scriptural truthfulness is simply the outworking of God's faithfulness."[13] It is God who, affirming the words of Scripture as his own, provides the authority. The Holy Spirit confirms the words of Scripture as true. This is also witnessed in our own hearts. The Westminster Confession states, "Our full persuasion and assurance of the infallible truth and divine authority thereof, is from the inward work of the Holy Spirit bearing witness by and with the Word in our hearts."[14]

Third, authority is also held in the text itself. Notably, we do not have the original human authors with us, so we cannot clarify their thinking or perspectives. What we do have are the texts themselves, which bear witness to the original message. While the literary and historical context of a passage can establish parameters on what that passage could mean, it also sets parameters on what the text definitely could not mean. Thus, we make a distinction between interpretations (which are within the contextual parameters of the text) and just bad hermeneutics (which are outside those parameters).

Fourth, external data supports the historical reliability of the Bible. This includes archaeological data that verifies many of the events and people to which the Bible refers. In particular, there is overwhelming evidence for the person of Jesus Christ—his life, death, and resurrection. The Gospel records of Jesus are also well attested, thereby affirming the integrity of the texts handed down to us.[15]

Fifth, experience suggests that the Bible is authoritative and trustworthy. Whereas evangelicals tend to emphasize the cognitive nature of why the Bible is authoritative, Pentecostals and Charismatics emphasize that Scripture is experientially true, verified pragmatically by how it operates in the church, and thus trustworthy and reliable. As the believer sees the truth of the Bible played out in their own life, they adopt an affective approach to the question

13. Michael F. Bird, *Seven Things I Wish Christians Knew about the Bible* (Grand Rapids: Zondervan, 2021), 66.
14. Westminster Confession of Faith 1.5.
15. For further reading, see Orr-Ewing, *Why Trust the Bible?*

of why the text is authoritative.[16] This type of validation for the veracity of the Bible should not be belittled. Of course, we each have the capacity for self-deception and to uncritically interpret an experience as God-given rather than formed by our own will or even satanic inspiration. Because of this potential for self-deception, some people dismiss the role of experience as unimportant or invalid; however, it is a reputable means of verifying the legitimacy of a belief claim or practice.

Empirical evidence (that is, study based on experience) helps to validate the truth and authority of the Bible because it demonstrates the authenticity of the Bible by experience or observation. If the Bible says that it is useful for living, and this is our experience, then our experience reinforces the Bible's claims. Using a more mundane example, take the claim of a recipe—namely, that if you follow its instructions, you will produce a rich, moist chocolate cake. If you follow the recipe's instructions and indeed produce a delectable cake, then your experience has validated the truth claims of the recipe. So experience can function as a valid way of verifying the truth claims of the Bible, especially when used alongside the other points noted above. But notice that its claims are verified experientially only by faithfully following its instructions. Therefore, experience highlights the holistic nature of biblical truth; it is true in its worldview, affective impact, and application.

The fundamental idea underpinning the whole enterprise of biblical interpretation is the question, What has authority for our lives? Ultimately, the question becomes, What has authority for our spiritual walk, and in what ways? Within Christian theology, a wide range of understandings about authority exists. While all Christian traditions consider Scripture (the Old and New Testaments) to be authoritative, they differ in terms of how it interacts with other sources of authority—such as tradition, reason, experience, and the Holy Spirit. The resulting differences lie in which sources are emphasized, given primary or secondary weight, and taught foundationally. Protestants start with the Bible and stress that the dynamic interplay between Word and Spirit is necessary in theological development and the Christian life in general.

God's Word is living and powerful to transform human lives and achieve God's purposes for creation. As Hebrews 4:12 says, "For the word of God is alive and active. Sharper than any double-edged sword, it penetrates even

---

16. Scott Ellington, "Pentecostalism and the Authority of Scripture," *Journal of Pentecostal Theology* 9 (1996): 16–38; Paul W. Lewis, "Toward a Pentecostal Epistemology: The Role of Experience in Pentecostal Hermeneutics," *The Spirit and Church* 2 (2000): 95–125; and James K. A. Smith, "The Closing of the Book: Pentecostals, Evangelicals, and the Sacred Writings," *Journal of Pentecostal Theology* 11 (1997): 49–71. See most recently Craig S. Keener, *Spirit Hermeneutics: Reading Scripture in Light of Pentecost* (Grand Rapids: Eerdmans, 2016).

to dividing soul and spirit, joints and marrow; it judges the thoughts and attitudes of the heart." Scripture is authoritative in belief and practice. So the Bible is informative, applicable, and powerful. To this, we say amen—which essentially means "it is true!"

The Development of the Canon

The role of the development of the canon cannot be overemphasized.[17] The term "canon" comes from a Greek word meaning "measuring stick." It refers to a list of writings considered authoritative for the church. The formation of the canon was an extensive process that spanned many centuries. This process included the rabbinical means by which the Old Testament was set and the ecclesiastical, conciliar means that established the New Testament (and affirmed the Old Testament).

For the Old Testament (or what the Jewish people call the Hebrew Bible or the Jewish Scriptures), the canonization process took centuries to unfold, from the postexilic period to the beginning of the Christian era.[18] The resulting collection became known as the Tanakh, something of an acronym for its three principle parts: the Torah (or the Pentateuch, also called the Five Books of Moses), the Nevi'im (the Prophets), and the Ketuvim (the Writings). By the time of Ezra, the Torah was regarded as a sacred text.[19] Further, while the prophets had a special status throughout the Old Testament period, their texts, from Elijah onward, were eventually elevated as sacred alongside the Torah. As such, the Prophets became a collection, comprising the Former (or early) and Latter Prophets. The Former Prophets include the books of Samuel and Kings and others that tell the stories of early prophets, and the Latter Prophets consist of the written texts *of* the prophets (e.g., Isaiah, Malachi).[20]

---

17. There are many works on the canon, but two recent volumes and a popular older one are Craig A. Evans and Emanual Tov, eds., *Exploring the Origins of the Bible: Canon Formation in Historical, Literary, and Theological Perspective*, Acadia Studies in Bible and Theology (Grand Rapids: Baker Academic, 2008); Lee Martin McDonald, *The Biblical Canon: Its Origin, Transmission, and Authority* (Peabody, MA: Hendrickson, 2007); and, F. F. Bruce, *The Canon of Scripture* (Downers Grove, IL: InterVarsity, 1988). See also William W. Klein, Craig L. Blomberg, and Robert L. Hubbard Jr., *Introduction to Biblical Interpretation*, 3rd ed. (Grand Rapids: Zondervan Academic, 2017), 165–83.

18. In addition to the works on canon noted above, see also Paul R. House, "Canon of the Old Testament," in *Foundations for Biblical Interpretation*, ed. David S. Dockery, Kenneth A. Mathews, and Robert B. Sloan (Nashville: Broadman & Holman, 1994), 134–55.

19. This first part of the Tanakh includes Genesis, Exodus, Leviticus, Numbers, and Deuteronomy.

20. More specifically, the Former Prophets include Joshua, Judges, Samuel, and Kings, while the Latter Prophets include Isaiah, Jeremiah, Ezekiel, and the Book of the Twelve (they all fit

For the Jews, there came to be a third grouping of books called the Writings. This includes much of what is now called Wisdom literature, such as Proverbs and Ecclesiastes, as well as the worship book of ancient Israel, the Psalms.[21] So the first book of the Tanakh is Genesis, and the last book is Chronicles. Historically, the date given for the finalizing of the Old Testament canon is around AD 90–100, when the rabbis met about key concerns for the Jewish faith at Jamnia (or Jabneh) in Palestine. They were concerned that some texts "defiled the hands," which meant that these texts were holy (noting the difference between sacred and other texts). However, it is probably more accurate to say that canonization was a process of official acceptance over the centuries. Other evidence for the acceptance and development of the Christian Old Testament canon can be found in first-century AD authors like Philo (ca. 20 BC–AD 50) and Josephus (ca. 37–100), the New Testament, and the Dead Sea Scrolls found at Qumran, which date prior to AD 70. While there were sometimes additional works considered for inclusion in the Old Testament canon, the eventual Christian consensus was the thirty-nine books of the current Protestant Bible.[22]

An important resource for understanding the development of the Old Testament canon and Hellenistic Judaism, and which also had a strong impact on the early years of Christianity, was the Septuagint (abbreviated LXX). The Septuagint is a Greek translation of the Old Testament that began in the third century BC and was completed mostly in the second century BC. The Septuagint eventually came to include other books beyond the ones later accepted as canonical by the church.[23] These other books, referred to as the Apocrypha ("hidden") or as deuterocanonical ("secondary"), were mainly written in Greek (rather than Hebrew) and mostly originated in what we refer to as the intertestamental period. These fourteen books are considered secondary literature by Protestants and include writings such as Tobit, Judith, and the historical 1 and 2 Maccabees. While they have been seen as helpful or informative, they

---

on one scroll)—otherwise known as the Minor Prophets (called such because of their size)— which includes Hosea, Joel, Amos, Obadiah, Jonah, Micah, Nahum, Habakkuk, Zephaniah, Haggai, Zechariah, and Malachi.

21. More specifically, the Writings include Psalms, Proverbs, Job, Song of Songs (or the Song of Solomon), Ruth, Lamentations, Ecclesiastes, Esther, Daniel, Ezra, Nehemiah, and Chronicles.

22. It should be noted that the Jewish Scriptures list twenty-four books (the Minor Prophets form one book, and the dual texts in the Christian Bible, such as 1 and 2 Samuel, are one book each), and Josephus notes twenty-two books (since Judges and Ruth were one book and Jeremiah and Lamentations were one book as well).

23. For a good chart that compares what is in the Septuagint, the traditional Jewish Scriptures, the Protestant Old Testament, and the Roman Catholic Old Testament, see House, "Canon of the Old Testament," 137. Note that the Protestant Old Testament canon comprises what is shared in the other lists.

were not sacred Scripture for most Jews and early Christians. A second feature of the Septuagint is important: by translating the Old Testament from Hebrew to Greek (albeit in an order different from the compositional order of the Tanakh), it established a broader principle regarding the translation of Scripture. Both Judaism and Christianity, while accepting the sacredness of the biblical text in its original languages, viewed its translations as authoritative too. Thus, biblical texts could be translated into Greek, Syriac, (Old) Latin, and other languages within the first few centuries of the Christian era with full acceptance of their authority. To this end, Lamin Sanneh notes, "Translation is a dynamic process, and in Bible translation the Spirit is the guiding agent of that process—this is as it should be if faith has any meaning at all."[24]

The New Testament canon was already forming by the time the last of the New Testament books was composed. By the late first century and into the second century, several references to our New Testament works were made in non–New Testament writings of the early church, such as works by Clement of Rome (ca. 35–99), Ignatius of Antioch (ca. 35–107), Justin Martyr (ca. 100–165), and Tertullian (ca. 160–240), as well as in the Didache. Most notably, Irenaeus (ca. 130–202) cites as Scripture all books found in the later New Testament canon.[25]

However, recognizing these books as Scripture and formalizing the collections are two different issues. A major influence toward formalizing the collection was the work of Marcion (ca. 85–160) in the mid-second century. Marcion, despite being a theologian in Rome, was seen as divergent from the apostolic faith and later denounced as a heretic in AD 144. Marcion believed that the God of the Old Testament was not the God of the Christ (or of the New Testament) and, therefore, that the Old Testament Scriptures were of no importance. He also made a collection of acceptable New Testament texts that he adhered to as his own canon. This canon included some of the writings of Paul and a modified version of Luke. (He edited out what he did not believe was valid in that Gospel.) The leaders of the church at that time responded to this threat in several ways, especially by highlighting the rule of faith (the basic teachings passed down from Jesus and the apostles), apostolic succession (the direct lineage of bishops reaching back to the apostles), and subsequent doctrinal succession (the detailed teaching handed down by the apostles to their disciples, then by those believers to their disciples, and so

24. Lamin Sanneh, "The Significance of the Translation Principle," in *Global Theology in Evangelical Perspective: Exploring the Contextual Nature of Theology and Mission*, ed. Jeffrey P. Greenman and Gene L. Green (Downers Grove, IL: IVP Academic, 2012), 39.

25. See James Daniel Hernando, "Irenaeus and the Apostolic Fathers: An Inquiry into the Development of the New Testament Canon" (PhD diss., Drew University, 1990).

forth). In addition, these leaders affirmed the connection between the Old Testament God and the God of Jesus and Paul. This resulted in an intentional move to refine what would later become the New Testament canon. Most of the New Testament books were already accepted as Scripture by the second century—the four Gospels, the key writings of Paul, and a few others—yet the final collection was not fully accepted until the time of Athanasius (ca. 296–373) in the fourth century.[26]

The criteria by which the church discerned what was acceptable New Testament Scripture included five key elements. These were determined by church leadership and corporate consensus. First, the book in question needed to have a sense of divine inspiration. This means that these books had to have God's fingerprints on them. Church leaders could discern this qualitative difference from other writings. Second, the books needed to be apostolic—directly or indirectly tied to the apostles. For example, of the four Gospels (viewed as written by Matthew, Mark, Luke, and John by early tradition), Matthew and John were written by two of the twelve disciples, Mark was closely tied to Peter, and Luke was tied to Paul. Of course, the many books by Paul were apostolic, and the books of James and Jude were seen as written by the (half-)brothers of Jesus. The book that was a bit more problematic was the book of Hebrews. There is no explicit connection to an apostle; yet because some believed early on that it was written by Paul, it received acceptance.[27] Third, the texts had to be orthodox, in terms of Christian faith. "Orthodox" means to reflect the "right glory" of Christ. These works, then, needed to demonstrate accurately the glory of Christ (including theology), as noted in the rule of faith. Fourth, the books were catholic, or universal, in that the various branches of the church needed to accept them.[28] So believers in the Latin, Syriac, Greek, and other cultural-linguistic areas, despite their culturally distinctive sensibilities, needed to accept these texts as sacred. Some early Christian books, such as the Shepherd of Hermas and Didache, were popular in one area but did not receive catholic acceptance, so they were

---

26. See Athanasius's *Thirty-Ninth Easter Letter* (AD 367); see also Bruce, *Canon of Scripture*, 208–10, and Linda L. Belleville, "Canon of the New Testament," in Dockery, Mathews, and Sloan, *Foundations for Biblical Interpretation*, 374–95.

27. While many still believe that the book of Hebrews is apostolic in time frame and theology, most scholars no longer tie it to Paul. (Some have suggested it was written by Barnabas, others Aquila and Priscilla, and yet others Apollos.) Notably, the New Testament canon organizers put it after the shortest Pauline epistle and as the largest of the General Epistles.

28. By the sixth century, this diversity was cemented with five patriarchs of the church collective, referred to as the Pentarchy, which included the patriarchs of Rome, Constantinople, Antioch, Alexandria, and Jerusalem, as well as their respective sees (the area of their oversight or jurisdiction).

not included. While all branches of the church within the Roman Empire accepted the New Testament canon by the fourth century, it took two more centuries before the Syriac church (in Persia and places further east) moved from twenty-two books to the finalized twenty-seven books. (The last ones added were 2 Peter, 2 and 3 John, Jude, and Revelation.)

A final comment on the process of canonization needs to be made. While the canon was being set, those spearheading this process also ordered their texts in a specified fashion. As noted above, the Jewish Scriptures have traditionally maintained a certain order: Torah, Prophets, and Writings. The Christian canon of the Old Testament starts with the Torah but moves into the historical books, then to the Wisdom literature, then to the written Prophets—Major (including Daniel, which is in the Writings in Jewish Scripture) and Minor. The Old Testament canon then ends with Malachi, which has the prophecy noting the forerunner of the Messiah (Mal. 3:1). So the order of the Christian Old Testament canon is tied to certain messianic and historical considerations. As for the New Testament, the order is generally thematic and by size. The four Gospels are in the order of their traditional compositional sequence; according to early tradition, Matthew was written first—and is more closely associated with the Old Testament—then Mark, Luke, and John.[29] Then comes the early history of the primitive church, the book of the Acts of the Apostles, which was also written by Luke.[30] The Pauline Epistles are arranged basically in order of size, although related books are coupled together, such as 1 and 2 Corinthians and 1 and 2 Thessalonians. Then come the General Epistles (also called the Catholic Epistles), which are in order of size, and the last book of the New Testament is the Apocalypse or the book of Revelation, which is future oriented.

Theological Affirmations about the Bible

In conclusion, we want to highlight seven important theological affirmations about the Bible as we begin the task of biblical interpretation. These beliefs

29. Note that the prevailing consensus of modern scholarship is that Mark was written first and that Matthew and Luke came later, adding their own materials (called M and L, respectively) not only to Mark's work but also to a collection of stories about Jesus called Q (German for *Quelle*, or "source"). The closeness of these three Gospels is why they are called the Synoptic, or "one-vision," Gospels. John, however, wrote a decidedly different Gospel. (For more on the Gospels, see chap. 7.)

30. One common question in New Testament scholarship has been why the canonical organizers separated Luke and Acts, with the Gospel of John in between, since they were presumably parts 1 and 2 of a two-volume work.

about the Bible and its nature provide an important foundation for the hermeneutical enterprise.

First, the Bible is our sacred book—a theological book, which means that it has a theological agenda. However, as the process of canonization highlights, God has revealed his message progressively over time, from the Old Testament to the New Testament. This means that while reading the Bible, we need to note the diachronic nature of the Bible. That is, the theological revelation generally increases as we move through the canon. For instance, Abraham's understanding and knowledge of God are substantially less than Paul's. Accordingly, not only are we affirming God's self-revelation through history and the Bible, from Genesis through Revelation; we are also affirming the progressive nature of revelation and the importance of looking at each passage and time period through its own lens. In other words, earlier periods are not to be judged based on later ones.[31] This also means that clarity on theological issues usually is provided by later sections of the Bible, without devaluing the insights of earlier texts. Yet the Bible is also a book that expresses a unified theological message, while containing a vast diversity of genres, contexts, themes, and so on. There is unity in diversity.

Second, the Bible is God's revelation, and thus it is God centered (theocentric). However, as was clearly noted by the New Testament and the early church, the only way to interpret Scripture correctly is through the lens of Christ (see chap. 3). All the Old Testament prophecies and typologies (that is, images and themes) related to the Messiah point to Christ Jesus. Christ was the hope to which writers looked (see, e.g., Deut. 18:15–22; Ps. 22; Isa. 7:13–16; 53; Mic. 5:2), and so our interpretations as Christian readers include this lens.

The third affirmation regards the perspicuity of Scripture. That is, the Bible was and is meant to be understood, not only by the original audience but also in the present day. The Bible and early Christians were not Gnostic, nor did they follow some form of a mystery religion that emphasized secret knowledge; rather, the Bible was meant to be understood widely, and studying it within its cultural-sociohistorical[32] and literary contexts assists in its understanding, which is accessible to all who seek such knowledge.

Fourth, there are foundational concepts in the text that should be affirmed despite prevailing antagonism toward them today (notably, in the Western

31. Note, however, that at times dating biblical texts can be difficult since dates can vary widely among scholars, often due to philosophical and theological presuppositions rather than the textual evidence itself.

32. The cultural-sociohistorical context includes a variety of other considerations including rhetorical and political.

world). God and the supernatural are part and parcel of the biblical text. The metaphysical existence of God and other spiritual beings (e.g., angels, demons) and workings of miracles are real. It should also be noted that (1) the affirmation of miracles does not assume that all supernatural operations are necessarily divine in origin—they can be demonic[33]—and (2) not everything calling itself miraculous is real; some may be counterfeit, whether demonic or human in origin. However, the existence of the counterfeit can also point us to the evidence for the really real. For example, the Bible warns against false prophets and deceptive signs (Matt. 7:15–20; 24:24), speaking strongly against occult practices and false visions that lead God's people astray (Jer. 14:14). These practices do not negate the need for and evidence of genuine prophetic activity; however, this reinforces why epistemic humility is needed. Our human knowledge is limited, and we have the capacity for (self-)deception. Understanding supernatural experiences requires spiritual discernment practiced in community (1 John 4:1–6) to ensure Christ is glorified (see chap. 10).

Fifth, we affirm that the Spirit can guide our interpretation and illumine our minds, but the Spirit does not exclusively ensure sound interpretation. Our shortcomings or blind spots can also influence our interpretation. With this in mind, we are reminded of the role of prayer in the whole hermeneutical process. We need to constantly read, study, and pray with an attitude of humility. We need God's guidance and presence to aid us and to mitigate our own failings.

Sixth, wrong attitudes can sidetrack the whole enterprise (see the discussion of preunderstanding in chap. 5). Wrong attitudes in reading the Bible can include seeking our own agenda, using the Bible for selfish gain, or using the text as a weapon against others. It is easy to approach the Bible to reinforce our own presuppositions or ideas; instead, we are to critically evaluate our hearts and intentions as we study God's Word. As just noted, it is important to have the attitude of humility, recognizing our fallibility. Therefore, we need the hermeneutical community—brothers and sisters of faith, locally, globally, and historically (which includes the academy and the church)—to work through the text together in order to grow (see chap. 5).

Seventh, we affirm that the Bible as a whole should guide us in interpreting its parts. We should see the Bible as a whole canon without diminishing the differences and, thereby, let Scripture interpret Scripture. That is, we seek to understand individual passages in light of the whole of Scripture. Logistically,

---

33. Missiologist Paul Hiebert notes that Western theology has tended to neglect this point; see Paul G. Hiebert, "The Flaw of the Excluded Middle," *Missiology* 10, no. 1 (1982): 35–47.

this means that biblical texts of clear and plain meaning take priority theologically over opaque or difficult passages. Similarly, repeated themes are to be emphasized over concepts that are found in one text or book only.

The Bible is authoritative and trustworthy. This firm foundation strengthens our understanding of Scripture and ultimately leads us to confidently and competently interpret the Bible.

Selecting a Good Translation

As we approach the task of interpreting Scripture, it is essential that we start with a good translation. Unless you can read the original biblical languages (Hebrew, Aramaic, and Greek), you will need a good translation in your own language. When selecting a translation, the student must first keep in mind that there are various translation philosophies that influence translation work. Translation philosophies tend to flow along a continuum. On one end of the continuum, translations aim to be as close to the text in the original languages as possible (called formal equivalence), which means that the syntax and grammatical structures might be more awkward in English (or whichever target language is in view). A good example is the New American Standard Bible. On the other end of the continuum, translations focus more on readability in the target language, so instead of translating merely words and phrases, they emphasize the translation of larger concepts (called dynamic or functional equivalence). The Good News Bible is a fitting example.[34] However, many translations try to follow a mediating path between closeness to the original text and dynamic equivalence or readability—for instance, the New International Version. Not surprisingly, each translation approach has benefits and challenges.[35] So in selecting a Bible version, look for what fits your needs. Then, when doing Bible study, consult various translations, especially from differing translation philosophies, to aid you in getting a broader perspective of what the text can mean (whether due to translation decisions, textual variations, or

---

34. There are also "free translations," which are actually paraphrases. While very readable, they are not, strictly speaking, translations. Examples include the Living Bible and the Message.

35. Some good resources for the beginning student on the variety of Bible versions are J. Scott Duvall and J. Daniel Hays, *Grasping God's Word: A Hands-On Approach to Reading, Interpreting, and Applying the Bible*, 4th ed. (Grand Rapids: Zondervan, 2020), 3–21; Gordon D. Fee and Mark L. Strauss, *How to Choose a Translation for All Its Worth* (Grand Rapids: Zondervan, 2007); Gordon D. Fee and Douglas Stuart, *How to Read the Bible for All Its Worth*, 4th ed. (Grand Rapids: Zondervan Academic, 2014), 36–56; and Klein, Blomberg, and Hubbard, *Introduction to Biblical Interpretation*, 191–92.

translation philosophies themselves).[36] No matter what translation(s) you choose, the preface of a translation is usually a good resource to consult when you want to learn of the translators' philosophy and process of translation for that specific version.[37]

It is important to note that translation decisions are unavoidable. Many words do not have a one-for-one equivalence in other languages. As noted above, things like semantic range and contexts can heavily influence the translation decisions made. When we are translating a word, phrase, or concept from an original language, our rendition may cover part of the meaning but not the whole range of possible meanings of a word. An example in English includes the words "couple" and "pair." Both mean "two" and can in some cases refer to the same things (such as "look at that couple" or "look at that pair"—the two phrases have slightly different implications, but both mean "look at those two"). However, "a pair of pants" or "a pair of glasses" refers to one item, whereas "a couple of shirts" or "a couple of jeans" refers to two items. So it is important to be aware of the range of meanings a word may have, while also noting its context. Likewise, a word, phrase, or sentence can sometimes mean multiple things simultaneously, and to translate this in one way may miss the other meanings.[38] Thus, if students do not know the original languages, consulting multiple versions will help them catch these nuances, especially if they use translations with a variety of translation philosophies.

WHAT DO I DO NOW?

The Bible is holy and its purpose is to shape us as a holy community, as 2 Timothy 3:16 reminds us. As we reflect on this purpose, we begin with an awareness of what biblical inspiration means, which also acknowledges the authority, trustworthiness, and reliability of Scripture. These concepts are foundational for the task of biblical interpretation. It is also important to understand the process by which we have received the Old and New Testaments

36. A couple of helpful, short discussions on selecting your Bible and the varieties available in English are Duvall and Hays, *Grasping God's Word*, 14–21, esp. 18–20, and Klein, Blomberg, and Hubbard, *Introduction to Biblical Interpretation*, 192–97, esp. 196–97.

37. It should be noted, however, that many languages in the world may have only one or very few Bible translations available (with various degrees of quality), and in some cases, only the New Testament is available. In the worst-case scenario, no translation of any portion is available; nor are there study aids. (This will be discussed more in chap. 14.)

38. Several Bible versions (e.g., NIV, NASB) note significant translation alternatives in the margins of the text.

as Scripture. The Bible was meant to be understood and applied both to the original audience(s) and to us today. The Spirit can illumine our minds with divine truth and understanding, yet our own blind spots and sinful nature can distort or dull our openness to God's revelation, so we need the Spirit's help as we adopt a posture of humility.

Next, select a translation of the Bible that resonates well with you and can be regularly used for your personal study. Your own copy of the Bible is something to treasure and not to be taken for granted. The translation you have selected can be supplemented by reading other versions that have a different translation philosophy as you dive deeper into the study of God's Word.

PRAYER

Lord, thank you for your inspired Word.
    Let me sense your Spirit guiding me in and through your Word.
    May I be transformed by your Spirit into Christ's image.
    And let me not transform the Word into my own image.
    Amen.

TOPICS FOR REVIEW

1. Why is the Bible authoritative?
2. In what ways does the canonization process encourage our awareness of the Bible's trustworthiness?
3. What are the notable affirmations about the Bible in this chapter?
4. Which of the affirmations most resonated with you and your understanding of Scripture?

3

HEARING THE LORD THROUGH HIS WORD WITHIN CHURCH HISTORY

In this chapter, you should expect to learn the following:

► Jewish biblical interpretation as a backdrop to the New Testament
► Biblical interpretation in the New Testament and early church
► Biblical interpretation in the medieval church—West and East
► Biblical interpretation in the Reformation and post-Reformation eras
► Biblical interpretation in the modern period

Above all, you must understand that no prophecy of Scripture came about by the prophet's own interpretation of things. For prophecy never had its origin in the human will, but prophets, though human, spoke from God as they were carried along by the Holy Spirit.

—2 Pet. 1:20–21

This passage from 2 Peter highlights that the prophets of old, while human, spoke under divine direction by the Holy Spirit. Second Peter was written to believers being disturbed by false teachings, particularly the denial of Christ's return. Accordingly, Peter reminds them that the prophecies of

Figure 3.1. Stained glass window of a church in Bochum, Germany

Scripture validate this future hope. The biblical texts did not originate in human thought but were inspired by God through the Holy Spirit. What this also reminds us is that as God spoke to the prophets of old, God desires to speak with each of us today. Likewise, as the image of the stained glass window in figure 3.1 demonstrates, hearing the Lord is directly personal. God has been speaking to people and revealing himself throughout church history. Thus, as we consider the importance of biblical interpretation in our lives today, we are also mindful that it has been important throughout the history of the church. Individuals in every generation must come to grips with how to interpret Scripture and how to apply it in their own context. This chapter will summarize the history of biblical interpretation, from its Jewish roots to the twenty-first century.[1] This subject is important because our approach to reading the Bible today is informed by earlier interpreters, whether we realize it or not.

Jewish Biblical Interpretation

Underlying biblical interpretation in the early church is the usage of Jewish interpretation.[2] Within the Old Testament itself are early forms of interpretive activity. For example, 1 and 2 Kings were used in the writing of 1 and 2 Chronicles. Similarly, in Nehemiah 8:7–8 the Levites read from the Mosaic law, translating it into Aramaic for the people. This approach to reading, which combined translation with additional explanation, was common during the time of Jesus. Such a practice led to the Targums, which are free translations or interpretations from Hebrew into Aramaic.

The rabbinic interpretive tradition was central to the biblical interpretation and understanding of the early church. While the rabbinic approach includes a literal understanding of the biblical text, it can also include what is called *midrash*. Midrash fills the gaps of the text's plain sense and searches for a deeper spiritual meaning. The Torah was understood as divinely revealed and so contained eternal truths—both literal and hidden meanings (regardless of context). This meant that new meanings of a text could be uncovered, yet still rooted in tradition.

While rabbinic Judaism was especially influential with Aramaic-speaking Jews, Greek-speaking Jews were more closely tied to Hellenistic Judaism. The Greek translation of the Old Testament, the Septuagint, was produced

---

1. The summary given here is very short but structured loosely according to a longer summary found in William W. Klein, Craig L. Blomberg, and Robert L. Hubbard Jr., *Introduction to Biblical Interpretation*, 3rd ed. (Grand Rapids: Zondervan, 2017), 66–116. One-volume versions can be found in Robert M. Grant, *A Short History of the Interpretation of the Bible*, with David Tracy, rev. ed. (Philadelphia: Fortress, 1984), and Gerald Bray, *Biblical Interpretation: Past and Present* (Downers Grove, IL: InterVarsity, 1996). For extensive treatments, see Alan J. Hauser and Duane F. Watson, eds., *A History of Biblical Interpretation*, 3 vols. (Grand Rapids: Eerdmans, 2003–17), and Henning Graf Reventlow, *History of Biblical Interpretation*, trans. James O. Duke, 4 vols. (Atlanta: Society of Biblical Literature, 2009–10).

2. See Karlfried Froehlich, trans. and ed., *Biblical Interpretation in the Early Church*, Sources of Early Christian Thought (Philadelphia: Fortress, 1984), 1–8; Klein, Blomberg, and Hubbard, *Introduction to Biblical Interpretation*, 66–77; and Richard N. Longenecker, *Biblical Exegesis in the Apostolic Age*, 2nd ed. (Grand Rapids: Eerdmans, 1999), 6–35.

primarily in Ptolemaic Egypt over mostly the third and second centuries BC and used by most of the early church as their Old Testament of choice. An early biblical interpretive model was devised by a Hellenistic Jewish philosopher also in Egypt around the time of Christ—namely, Philo, who attempted to combine Greek philosophy with Jewish Scripture, especially the Mosaic law. Philo utilized the allegorical method of interpretation, which was influential for centuries to come, especially in Alexandrian biblical hermeneutics. Hellenistic Judaism then interpreted the text as having both literal and allegorical meanings. For Philo, the true meaning of a passage was found in the ideas hidden behind the text.[3] Notably, Philo taught that the text was not to be taken literally if it was seen as not worthy of God, if it was problematic, or if it clearly communicated an alternative allegorical message (such as with numbers).[4]

Another notable avenue of Jewish interpretation was espoused by the Qumran community (ca. second century BC–first century AD). Common within the Qumran community was the *pesher* method of interpretation. This made use of three different techniques that were each considered to be revelatory in nature. One of these techniques was textual emendation for the sake of fitting a given interpretation that included a deeper mystery or concealed eschatological interpretation. A second technique was identifying prophecy as being fulfilled in their time, mainly using a "this is that" approach. For example, the Qumran community saw themselves as fulfilling the prophecy of Isaiah 40:3 (or hoping to) by choosing to live on the edge of the Judean desert, ready to receive God's glory. Third, the Qumran community could also focus on a subset of terms or just a word in their interpretation. This approach can be likened to examining pearls on a string whereby each word or subset of a passage was examined with little regard for the context.

The New Testament and the Early Church

Fundamental to the New Testament authors' interpretive scheme was that Jesus is the fulfillment of the Old Testament.[5] This point cannot be over-

---

3. Klein, Blomberg, and Hubbard, *Introduction to Biblical Interpretation*, 71.
4. Klein, Blomberg, and Hubbard, *Introduction to Biblical Interpretation*, 71.
5. For more on biblical interpretation in the New Testament and by the early church—in addition to the sources cited above—see G. K. Beale, *Handbook on the New Testament Use of the Old Testament: Exegesis and Interpretation* (Grand Rapids: Baker Academic, 2012); John J. O'Keefe and R. R. Reno, *Sanctified Vision: An Introduction to Early Christian Interpretation of the Bible* (Baltimore: Johns Hopkins University Press, 2005); and Keith D. Stanglin, *The Letter and Spirit of Biblical Interpretation: From the Early Church to Modern Practice* (Grand Rapids: Baker Academic, 2018).

emphasized. All Old Testament prophecies about the Messiah and the future of Israel were read through the lens of Christ. The New Testament is pervaded by belief in the sacredness of Scripture. Predominantly, when Scripture is referred to, the Old Testament texts are in view. The Old Testament prophecies, including the psalms of David, are seen as authoritative, especially when they refer to the coming Messiah (or Christ in Greek). Thus, in the writings of Paul, Peter, and others, the Old Testament is viewed as the Scripture that demonstrates God's revelation to humanity, and notably for them, the only way to correctly understand the Old Testament is through the lens of Christ. This became the main lens through which the early church understood the Old Testament—through the interpretative grid of Christ.

Additionally, the New Testament is full of figural or typological interpretations. A "type," from the Greek *typos*, was usually a historical theme, event, or image in the Old Testament seen by the New Testament writers to prefigure aspects of Christ. We see the use of typology in the identification of Jesus as the "suffering servant" of Isaiah 53. This is similar to but different from allegory (as utilized by Philo and the Alexandrian school, noted above), which provides a deeper meaning of a theme or image, often in parallel with an earlier text, but with no organic or clear connection between the text and its plain meaning or historical context.[6] The New Testament writers also made use of the literal-contextual approach, which highlights the plain meaning of the text within its contexts.

Finally, another interpretive approach used by the New Testament writers included drawing out an application from a biblical principle for the contemporary situation. For example, Paul quotes the Old Testament in 1 Corinthians 9:9 and 1 Timothy 5:18—"Do not muzzle an ox while it is treading out the grain"—while apparently emphasizing a principle spoken by Jesus in Luke 10:7. In both passages, Paul uses the principle of this Old Testament verse (i.e., Deut. 25:4) as support for why ministers should be paid.

Soon after the time of the New Testament was the period of the apostolic fathers, which can be dated from the late first to the early second century. During this time, spiritual gifts, particularly prophecy, continued to exist. Following the New Testament writers, these church fathers commonly used figural interpretations, particularly typology and allegory. Further, at times they followed the rabbinic style of biblical interpretation, notably midrash.

---

6. It should be noted that there is a difference between the allegorical method of biblical interpretation, in which the result has no connection with the original text, and the allegorical method of proclamation, in which certain spiritual realities are put forward through stories to highlight and promote certain truths. For the latter, think of John Bunyan's *The Pilgrim's Progress* and C. S. Lewis's *The Lion, the Witch and the Wardrobe*.

Another key interpretive lens was called the rule of faith, which associated an interpretation with the oral traditions going back to the apostles and ultimately Jesus himself.

After the apostolic fathers, there came an era when two competing theological and hermeneutical schools, in Alexandria and Antioch, dominated the interpretive landscape (from roughly the mid-second to the fourth century). These two schools set the stage for two different interpretive schemes.

First was the noted Christian hub of Alexandria in Egypt, which would later become one of the seats for Christian patriarchs.[7] Historically, Alexandria was a center of great learning in the Hellenistic period (with a very famous library), and later it was the home of Philo. It also hosted a school of Christian thought, with the key headliners being Clement of Alexandria (late second to early third century) and Origen (early third century; he later moved to Caesarea to serve as bishop). Two of the primary interpretive approaches of this school were the literal method and, following Philo, the allegorical method. However, Origen added the "moral" meaning to the text, which emphasized principles for Christian living.

The contrasting school—not an actual school but rather a school of thought—was in Antioch. As in Alexandria, there were many famous teachers from Antioch, but the most notable were Diodore of Tarsus (died ca. 390), Theodore of Mopsuestia (ca. 350–428), and Nestorius (ca. 386–451).[8] The Antiochian school rejected the hermeneutical position of the Alexandrian school, especially the moral and allegorical meanings not clearly present in the plain meaning of the text. Their emphasis was on the historical and literary (including grammatical-rhetorical) contexts to find the one plain meaning of the text. The Antiochian school did allow for a spiritual meaning of the text (called *theōria*; see below), but always within the parameters of the text's plain meaning.

In the fourth to the fifth century, biblical interpretation was tied to tradition, which was maintained by apostolic succession, a line going back, from bishop to bishop via oral tradition, to the apostles. Likewise, the notable theologian Augustine had a strong impact on ecclesiastical patterns of biblical interpretation. He highlighted the importance of the authority of the church, including in biblical interpretation. Connected to this was the importance of the rule of faith, which guided the appropriate interpretation of Scripture.

7. As noted in chap. 2, by the sixth century the "rule of five" included the five major episcopal sees of the church, centered in Constantinople, Rome, Antioch, Alexandria, and Jerusalem.

8. These three were later condemned by the Catholic Church, but they were honored as teachers of the church by the Syriac church (and the Persian church). John Chrysostom (ca. 347–407) and Theodoret (ca. 393–460) were also noted students of this school.

These guides were intended to limit the superfluity of figural readings and to protect against the corruption of false teachers—concerns that help explain why church councils and the finalization of the canon were so important during this time. However, Augustine also highlighted the principle that in the interpretation of and theological reflection on biblical passages, the plainer meaning should be prioritized more than obscure texts or readings. Jerome (ca. 345–420) was instrumental in providing an updated translation of the Bible into Latin—namely, the Vulgate—which used the Hebrew text instead of the Greek Septuagint as the basis for the Old Testament. Along with Augustine, Jerome strongly influenced the subsequent church of the West to highlight the historical aspects of interpretation.

The Medieval Church

The Western Church (Sixth to Fifteenth Century)

As just noted, in the fourth and fifth centuries, biblical interpretation in the Western church emphasized both traditional approaches (particularly allegory) and tradition (the rule of faith). However, during the medieval period (notably after the eleventh century), the importance of Scholasticism was felt in biblical interpretation, philosophy, and theology. Scholasticism was a movement that sought to engage and reconcile doctrine and human reason. It attempted to harmonize philosophical metaphysics with Latin church dogma. Within the medieval Western church, biblical interpretation identified four distinct meanings of the text.[9] First was the literal meaning. Second was the allegorical meaning. Third was the moral meaning, which led to conduct. And fourth was the anagogical meaning, which was eschatological in nature and looked toward the afterlife. For the medieval biblical interpreter, all four of these senses were present in any biblical text. As might be observed, the first three were a continuation of the approach exemplified by Origen (discussed above), with the fourth sense added during the medieval period.[10]

The Eastern Church (Sixth to Fifteenth Century)

Contrasting with the Western church, the Eastern church adopted primarily Antiochian perspectives, which were later taught in derivative schools in Edessa,

---

9. For more on medieval interpretation, see Henri de Lubac, *Medieval Exegesis: The Four Senses of Scripture*, trans. Mark Sebanc and E. M. Macierowski, 3 vols. (Grand Rapids: Eerdmans, 1999–2009).

10. Klein, Blomberg, and Hubbard, *Introduction to Biblical Interpretation*, 85.

Syria, and Nisibis, Persia. The Eastern approach held a high view of Scripture based on a literal understanding of the text as a historical document; therefore, Eastern readings of Scripture—such as prophecies or psalms, for instance—focused on the historical context while still upholding a christological lens. Furthermore, a passage was to be understood in its literary context. This meant that biblical exegetes in the Eastern context started with the literal meaning based on grammatical-rhetorical and historical contexts. From this basis, additional approaches such as *theōria* (or "spiritual exegesis") were expounded; however, these other readings were still tied to the historical foundations (contra the ahistorical nature of allegorical approaches). *Theōria* could thus give understanding beyond the text, but it was always directly drawn out of the plain meaning of the text.[11] Yet while ecclesiastical leaders sometimes taught hermeneutics (especially in the schools of Edessa and Nisibis), authors more frequently "modeled" hermeneutics. Like the early church, they read Scripture christologically.[12] Finally, following the work of Ephrem the Syrian (ca. 306–73) and other Syriac ecclesial luminaries (e.g., Narsai [ca. 399–502] and Jacob of Serugh [ca. 451–521]), the proclamation part of the hermeneutical process tended to have a practical expression through the form of songs and poems to be more memorable, even when they were fundamentally homilies. In other words, the "sermons" in which the Bible was proclaimed were presented as songs or poems.

It can be clearly seen that these strands of the medieval church—West and East—focused on differing methods in biblical interpretation. Yet in both contexts, the literal or plain meaning of the biblical text was still important. Common to both was also the increasing importance of applying the Bible to Christian living.

Reformation and Post-Reformation Biblical Interpretation[13]

The Reformation (Sixteenth Century)

One of the most influential thinkers in Christian history is Martin Luther (1483–1546). His impact theologically and ecclesiastically cannot be over-

11. Two helpful discussions along these lines are Bradley Nassif, "'Spiritual Exegesis' in the School of Antioch," in *New Perspectives on Historical Theology: Essays in Memory of John Meyendorff*, ed. Bradley Nassif (Grand Rapids: Eerdmans, 1996), 343–77, and Frances Young, *Biblical Exegesis and the Formation of Christian Culture* (Cambridge: Cambridge University Press, 1997), 161–85.

12. David S. Dockery, *Biblical Interpretation Then and Now: Contemporary Hermeneutics in the Light of the Early Church* (Grand Rapids: Baker, 1992), 127.

13. See Hauser and Watson, *History of Biblical Interpretation*, 2:299–481, and Reventlow, *History of Biblical Interpretation*, 3:65–235.

estimated. Likewise, he was and still is influential in biblical interpretation, especially within Protestantism. There are a few key theological affirmations from Luther that demonstrate his lenses for the interpretation of Scripture. First, he is known for his support of the five *solas*, one being *sola Scriptura* (Scripture alone).[14] For Luther, Scripture alone is the foundation for Christian thought. This was clearly in opposition to what Luther thought was inappropriate authority granted to church tradition and the Roman Catholic hierarchy known as the magisterium. Tied to *sola Scriptura* was the concept that the Bible needs to be viewed as a whole (i.e., as the whole counsel of God) and that Scripture interprets Scripture. Further, while accepting typology, Luther completely rejected allegory, which he saw as speculative. Luther also noted that in biblical interpretation, we need to be aware of the Spirit's role. The Spirit illumines our minds and helps us understand Scripture and its theological and spiritual depths. Also contemporary with Luther were the so-called Enthusiasts, led by a successor of Luther, Andreas Karlstadt (1486–1541), who held much in common with the Reformers but also emphasized the experience and activity of the Holy Spirit.

Another important figure of the Reformation was John Calvin (1509–64). Similar to Luther, Calvin emphasized *sola Scriptura* and rejected allegory. Further, like Luther, Calvin noted the importance of the illumination of the Spirit for biblical interpretation. He further emphasized the self-authentication of the Spirit in biblical interpretation, meaning that Scripture is authenticated in one's spirit by the Holy Spirit. The Spirit works in interpreters (experientially) to verify the spiritual aspects found during the interpretive process.[15] Accordingly, Calvin highlighted the interplay between Word and Spirit.

The Post-Reformation Period (Mid-Seventeenth Century to 1800)

The renewal movement called Pietism, in primarily German-speaking Europe, had a strong influence in Europe and elsewhere. Pietism emphasized an intimate relationship with and a personal experience of God, which were undergirded by the belief that all can read and understand the Bible. It had a very clear interpretive emphasis—namely, the "common sense" study of the literal or plain meaning of the text. Related to a strong Lutheran perspective, it also held that the biblical text should have practical and devotional results

---

14. The other four solas being *solus Christus* (Christ alone), *sola fide* (faith alone), *sola gratia* (grace alone), and *soli Deo gloria* (glory to God alone).

15. For further discussion, see Simeon Zahl, *The Holy Spirit and Christian Experience* (Oxford: Oxford University Press, 2020).

in the lives of readers. Further, like Luther, Pietists saw the importance of typology in interpretation.

The contemporaneous renewal movement in the English-speaking world, led by John Wesley (1703–91) and Charles Wesley (1707–88), was commonly called Methodism, due to the spiritual methods this movement espoused for devotional reading. Like Pietism, Methodism focused on the plain (devotional) meaning of the text and the role of prayer and Bible study for personal growth. The practical outcome was the result of appropriate Bible study.

While Pietism and Methodism continued to grow, rationalism developed and pervaded Europe. This philosophical school of thought extolled reason as the final authority, such that anything seen as irrational or supernatural was disallowed. Accordingly, things like miracles were rejected out of hand, and thereby the biblical narratives that tell of miracles had to be reconfigured. Everything, including biblical interpretation, was viewed through the lens of reason.

Modern Biblical Interpretation

The Nineteenth Century (1799–1914 / World War I)

With the strong influence of rationalism and other philosophies came the development of historical-critical methodologies.[16] This development resulted in the adoption of the methods of the human sciences and the treatment of the Bible as any other document. One biblical critic of this period was Julius Wellhausen (1844–1918), who promoted the Documentary Hypothesis of the Pentateuch, which separates the Torah into four source documents (i.e., the Jahwist, Elohist, Deuteronomist, and Priestly sources), the earliest of which he dated to 850 BC and the latest he dated to 550 BC. (Later documentary theorists have adopted differing time frames.) Wellhausen proposed, through an intrabiblical analysis, that the Mosaic books were actually a compilation developed from these four ancient sources, finalized in the later periods of Israel's history (i.e., after the exile, around the time of Ezra-Nehemiah). Wellhausen's perspective was foundational to source criticism, which viewed the identification of sources as fundamental to getting "behind the text." The text itself became secondary to the world from which the text emerged. This critical approach to the Bible was replicated in other disciplines of history and the social sciences, such as archaeology, sociology, and anthropology.

16. For more about modern biblical interpretation, see Hauser and Watson, *History of Biblical Interpretation*, vol. 3, and Reventlow, *History of Biblical Interpretation*, vol. 4.

Since these studies were primarily conducted in the academy, they also became known as "higher criticism." It can be seen, then, that the critical methods of the nineteenth century took a very different approach to biblical interpretation—one that prioritized critical reconstruction and the world behind the text and, therefore, deemphasized the meaning of the text itself. Meanwhile, other groups in the nineteenth century, such as the Anabaptists and other restorationist movements (considered proto-Pentecostal), were advocating a return to primitive Christianity, with an emphasis on narratives such as Luke-Acts.[17]

The Twentieth Century (1914–2000)

World War I (1914–18) transformed the theological and philosophical landscape of Europe. One of the developing arenas of thought was the history of religions school, which started in the 1890s and grew during the first part of the twentieth century. It was another branch of higher criticism, and it compared the development of Judaism and Christianity with the development of other religions and cultures. This led to comparisons between the Bible (the Old Testament primarily) and other ancient sources. Likewise, Christianity was seen as a syncretistic amalgamation of ancient Israel and Hellenistic Judaism, mystery religions, and other contemporaneous Hellenistic movements. While utilizing comparative material from the ancient world can enhance our knowledge of the biblical world, this approach tended to be driven by philosophical concerns to nullify the uniqueness of the biblical text. Interestingly, the comparative approach has challenged, via extrabiblical archaeological findings, Wellhausen's proposal for the dating of the Pentateuch (noted above), suggesting that the sources of the Torah date to a much earlier time. Equally interesting, the comparative element of the cultural context has been received as helpful in biblical interpretation, even by those who usually reject such rationalistic methods. For example, key texts unearthed from the ancient city of Mari (in northern Syria) contain descriptions of prophets in the broader ancient Near East, and those descriptions have provided profitable insights for understanding prophecy in the Bible.

Another key development during this period was form criticism, which, in both the Old Testament and the New, analyzed various genres to glean insights about their forms and smaller units of text (called "pericopes"). This study has proven a helpful way to better understand individual texts, not least by identifying the common features of each genre and form.

---

17. Klein, Blomberg, and Hubbard, *Introduction to Biblical Interpretation*, 102.

The Post–World War I Period

Between the World Wars, the major theological and biblical-interpretive movement was called "neoorthodoxy." A major player was Karl Barth (1886–1968), whose notable initial work was his 1919 commentary on Romans. In this work and subsequent works, Barth highlighted the importance of a personal experience of Christ through the study of the Bible. Another major figure in neoorthodoxy was Rudolf Bultmann (1884–1976). He, like Barth, emphasized the experience of God through both the Word preached (or *kerygma*, from the Greek) and an existential hermeneutic, which engaged the biblical text in an ahistorical manner. However, Bultmann was most noted for his emphasis on demythologizing the Bible. Central to this approach was the concept that the Bible was written in a prescientific age; therefore, myths were created to explain miracles, the worldview, and the like. However, according to Bultmann, in a modern scientific understanding of the universe, there is a need to demythologize the Bible, which functionally seeks to strip away embedded myths. All in all, neoorthodox biblical interpreters, including Barth and Bultmann, highlighted a few points for biblical interpretation. First, God is subject, not object, so the goal of interpretation is an encounter with God and not information or theology per se. Underlying this is the theological belief that there is an infinite gulf between God and sinful humanity; thus, there is the need for myth, which helps humanity bridge the gap to the "wholly other." Further, the whole hermeneutical experience highlights that truth is paradoxical or dialectical.[18] Notably, then, the Bible is not the Word of God; it *contains* the Word of God as the reader meets God in an encounter.

The Post–World War II Period

After World War II (1939–45), another major movement, called the biblical theology movement, impacted the field of biblical interpretation. It emphasized going back to the Bible and its purported theology. Brevard Childs (1923–2007) was particularly associated with this movement. Childs also emphasized canonical criticism, which focuses on the received biblical canon (see chap. 2) rather than on the historical development of the text, whether based on sources, forms, or other documentary considerations. From these theological and canonical approaches came a focus on the Bible's theology and canonical unity, not just its history or its diversity as a collection of discrete sources and disparate documents. While recognizing the cultural and

---

18. Cf. Emil Brunner, *Truth as Encounter*, trans. Amandus W. Loos, David Cairns, and T. H. L. Parker, enlarged ed. (Philadelphia: Westminster, 1964).

religious contexts of the Bible, interpreters valued the Bible for the ways in which it differed from comparable ancient documents (contra the history of religions school). This approach also emphasized the idea of progressive revelation—how theological and thematic ideas central to the canon developed over time.

Another key post–World War II development was redaction criticism. Redaction criticism is the area of study that focuses on the final edition or redaction of the text (*Redaktion* in German) and the redactors' or editors' work on the text, most notably in the Gospel accounts. That is, the writers and editors of texts, such as the Gospels, wove together different stories and traditions into their accounts, written for a particular community at a particular time, and this approach looks at that process. It highlights those aspects that set apart the authors' or editors' perspectives from each other (Matthew vs. Mark vs. Luke, for instance). This also led to a renewed interest in the quest for the historical Jesus.

Following the neoorthodox movement, Bultmann's students Ernst Fuchs (1903–83) and Gerhard Ebeling (1912–2001) championed the "new hermeneutic," in which an interpreter encounters God through the text, in what is called a language event. From this perspective, the biblical text interprets the reader, so the text guides interpretation during the encounter. As an existential theory, this hermeneutic emphasizes the reader's experience and the current relevance of the text, but it also deemphasizes the historical meaning of the text. The influence of this emphasis on the reader continues today.

The shift toward language and literature during this period also led to the development of rhetorical studies in the 1970s and onward. This approach considered how rhetoric and the art of persuasion was used within the Bible, as well as how the Bible was used for rhetorical purposes. This sparked the interest of many feminist scholars throughout the 1980s and 1990s to today, exploring how the Bible has been used to reinforce patriarchal attitudes. Phyllis Trible was one of the first feminist scholars to use rhetorical criticism to unpack feminine imagery used for God. Similarly, the literary approach also blossomed into the study of narrative criticism in which the storytelling techniques of the biblical writers and other literary techniques began to be further explored for exegetical purposes.

Today (2000–Present)

As you may have observed already, approaches to biblical interpretation have continued to expand and develop. In today's context, the variety of approaches to hermeneutics has exploded. In particular, approaches that investigate the contexts and perspectives of the reader have flourished. Similarly, a hermeneutic of suspicion, which has developed from questions raised by postmodernism, has led to greater scrutiny of the role of the interpreter, particularly regarding issues of power. Many approaches today critique the presuppositions of past interpretations, highlighting how some readings are based on racist or sexist assumptions. The rise of approaches such as postcolonial and feminist interpretations has both challenged and enriched the academy today. Similarly, the voices of scholars in the Global South, which have previously been ignored, are becoming much more prominent. This, again, enriches the academy and the church, as we hear how the Bible is understood in foreign contexts and thereby are confronted with our own contexts and presuppositions. We will further explore the value of global voices and reading from different contexts in chapter 14.

In summary, we have explored many approaches to the interpretive task and seen how approaches have changed over time. Different types of interpretation have grown and diminished in popularity. These trends stress how much we are creatures of our culture. As noted in the previous chapter, this recognition should (hopefully) produce in us a sense of humility as we realize our epistemic fallibility—how much we are formed by our context and limited in our knowledge. Yet we can also see at least five consistent threads throughout this historical summary. The first thread is the emphasis on the historical context of the biblical text. In short, there has always been a strand of interpretation that focuses on the contextual meaning of the text in a plain or literal sense. The second thread is the identification of the form or genre of a biblical text. The type of writing in view, such as poetry or a letter, has always been significant for how a text is interpreted. This leads to the third thread: the use of a christological lens to read the Bible. Many texts, particularly in the Old Testament, have been viewed as signposts pointing to the significance of Christ in our world and in our lives. Fourth is the concern to read the Bible theologically, which was also the foundation for figural readings in the early church. Finally, the fifth thread is the concern to live out the Word of God in an ethical and practical way.

We will continue to emphasize these threads throughout this book. However, this summary encourages us to remember that we are part of a grand history of believers seeking to faithfully read the Word of God. We are participating in a glorious heritage, which extends all the way back to the early church. It is important to learn from the various hermeneutical methods used throughout church history.

WHAT DO I DO NOW?

While the study of previous approaches to interpreting the Bible is not a specific step in the PERSONAL method, it is an important consideration as part of our personal evaluation. We noted in the very first chapter that we are historically and culturally distant from the Bible. The study of the history of interpretation helps us to evaluate ourselves to see how we are products of our generation. Another reason we study history is that it helps us learn from the mistakes and challenges of the past. Such reflection provides important background knowledge for how and why we interpret the Bible today. It helps us see our blind spots and better appreciate our interpretive emphases today. An important blind spot in our history is an oversight of how our context shapes our readings. Therefore, first, the student can reflect on their own context: How are our assumptions and approaches to interpreting the Bible shaped by our context? Further, we can see how our historical, philosophical, and cultural values can inform our hermeneutics. This is a cautionary tale for us as well.

Second, the student can reflect on the importance of the consistent use of the three threads in Christian interpretation historically. How and why are the historical context, literary context, and the christological lens foundational to the hermeneutical task? These threads also reflect the very nature and purpose of Scripture as God's redemptive story. However, while there has always been a strand of interpretation that has emphasized the plain meaning of Scripture—we value this approach—it is also important to not become wholly reliant on our intellectual and scientific approaches to the Bible alone. We need to make room for the illumination of the Holy Spirit and the mystery of Scripture, which we will explore in the next two chapters.

PRAYER

Lord, we thank you for your Word.
Let us learn from those of the past,
to learn from their mistakes and to grow from their successes,
that we may be better followers of you.
Amen.

TOPICS FOR REVIEW

1. In what ways did the Alexandrian and Antiochian schools agree and disagree with each other?
2. Which postapostolic group reflected the apostles' concerns? Why?
3. Why are new interpretive lenses highlighted in one period but not in others?
4. In what ways does the study of interpretive history (a) clarify what is included in biblical interpretation, (b) help us discern the differences between various theological traditions, and (c) help us appreciate interpreters who have gone before us?

4

THE SPIRIT, THE WORD, AND INTERPRETATION

In this chapter, you should expect to learn the following:

- ▶ The interplay of the Spirit and the Word
- ▶ The basics of communication
- ▶ Key issues in biblical interpretation

But when he, the Spirit of truth, comes, he will guide you into all the truth. He will not speak on his own; he will speak only what he hears, and he will tell you what is yet to come.

—John 16:13

In the painting shown in figure 4.1, Rembrandt captures the figure of an angel whispering in the ear of Matthew. This represents the divine guidance provided by the Holy Spirit to the biblical writers. Similarly, we are also assured in John 16:13 that the Spirit will guide us "into all the truth." The Spirit is the guide, the arbiter of truth, who inspired the biblical writers. This verse is part of the teaching of Jesus to his disciples, warning them of the harassment they

Figure 4.1. *The Evangelist Matthew,* by Rembrandt van Rijn

will experience as his followers.[1] However, the verse teaches that the Spirit of Christ will not only remind them of Jesus's words (that is, help them remember) but also reveal the ongoing words of Christ to them (that is, revelation).[2] Of course, Scripture provides the words of Jesus, but this text emphasizes that Jesus, through the Holy Spirit, continues to speak to us today. We measure these new words of revelation by the Bible (see chap. 10). We can trust the Holy Spirit, as we humble ourselves, to lead us into truth.

This also leads us to ask, What makes the biblical text different from other texts? It is the involvement of God in the whole production of the text and in the hermeneutical process. As was noted in chapter 2, God is active in the inspiration of the biblical text. Chapter 3 highlighted that the process of biblical interpretation has had varied perspectives over the centuries, yet amazingly, the biblical text has constantly been viewed as sacred—and as the

1. Gerard Sloyan, *John,* Interpretation (Louisville: Westminster John Knox, 2009), 174–75.
2. Gary M. Burge, *John,* NIV Application Commentary (Grand Rapids: Zondervan, 2000), 636.

Triune God

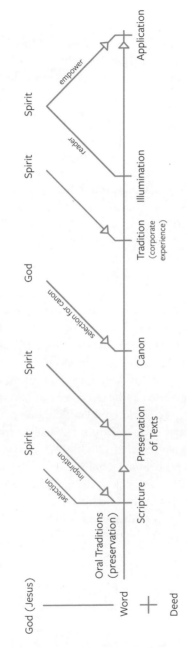

Figure 4.2. God's initiative, from his revelation throughout history to our application / Paul Lewis

final authority for faith and practice among Christians. We also noted that often, throughout the ages, believers have affirmed the Spirit's role not just in inspiring the production of the text but also in the process of illuminating our reading/hearing of the Scripture. We can trust the Holy Spirit, as we humble ourselves, to continue to breathe upon and illuminate the biblical text as we seek to understand it. In this chapter, we will explore this concept further.

The Spirit and the Word

A fundamental belief in the task of biblical interpretation is the ongoing role of God throughout the process (see fig. 4.2). The process begins with God. It starts with the revelation of God through his deeds. God is clearly seen in his actions, such as in the exodus, or in Jesus's actions, such as in his healings. Likewise, God's Word was expressed directly through dialogue (as with Abraham and Moses), through his prophets, or through Jesus. Thus, God is known through both Word and deed. His Word is clearly demonstrated and modeled through his deeds, and his deeds are clearly demonstrated through his Word proclaimed. God through Word and deed is remembered, and his words and deeds are remembered and taught through oral traditions, with the Spirit guiding the process of preserving these spoken traditions.[3]

Later, the Spirit would guide the writers in organizing the traditions (of Word and deed) into written texts through selection, compilation, and construction processes via inspiration (see chap. 2). Luke describes the process by which eyewitnesses were used in the resourcing of his Gospel (Luke 1:1–4). Similarly, John notes that the world could not contain all that Jesus did and said (John 21:25), and with his Gospel record as an eyewitness (21:24), John's account was written to inspire belief (20:30–31). Accordingly, the selection and organization of the biblical material is part of the Spirit's inspiration. We also need to add that in some cases, the material had later editorial corrections or updates (notably in the Old Testament). For example, there are numerous references to places or monuments in existence or called a certain title "to this day," especially in the Historical Books (e.g., Gen. 22:14; Josh. 4:9; Judg. 10:4; 1 Kings 9:13). Pneumatologically, these can be seen as the

---

3. A classic text along these lines is F. F. Bruce, *Paul and Jesus* (1974; repr., Eugene, OR: Wipf & Stock, 2019); also, James D. G. Dunn, *The Oral Gospel Tradition* (Grand Rapids: Eerdmans, 2013); Craig S. Keener, *Christobiography: Memory, History, and the Reliability of the Gospels* (Grand Rapids: Eerdmans, 2019). On this point, relating to Paul's use of "tradition," see Stephen Finlan, *The Apostle Paul and the Pauline Tradition* (Collegeville, MN: Liturgical Press, 2008); Stanley E. Porter, *Sacred Tradition in the New Testament: Tracing Old Testament Themes in the Gospels and Epistles* (Grand Rapids: Baker Academic, 2016).

Spirit working through the authoring and editing process to the finalization of the canon (see below).

While there are textual variants (notably copying errors) that have come down to us through the process of transmission, it is understood that in terms of both the current biblical text itself and the usage of language (i.e., religious language), God's salvific message can be gleaned and understood by any reader through the Spirit's activity.[4] This salvific awareness and understanding about God are clearly guided by the Spirit. This does not imply that all transmissions are completely accurate, but the pneumatological assurance is that despite the textual challenges, people can sufficiently understand God's provision of salvation and the text's language about God and his grace in order to be saved. This study of the various copies of a text, particularly to identify the earliest and most original copy, is called textual criticism.

The writing and development of the text leads next to the canonization process. In brief, the Spirit guided the leaders of the church to select texts to incorporate into our Bible, both Old Testament and New Testament.[5] This process was very involved over time, as seen in chapter 2.

Further, throughout church history, the Spirit has guided the church corporately. As Thomas C. Oden highlights, the Spirit's work can be seen in the theological consensus of all major branches of the church, including Roman Catholic, Eastern Orthodox, and Protestant churches.[6] This corporate journey, which can be called tradition, is actually corporate experience. It is not capital T "Tradition" in the sense that it is on equal level with or even supersedes Scripture, but tradition does show the Spirit's ongoing engagement with the church. The consensus of the whole church is a corrective for linguistic-cultural blind spots.[7]

This journey of the Spirit at work producing the biblical text leads to the contemporary reader—you and me. As we read the text, the same Spirit who inspired the biblical authors/editors is also at work to illumine our minds with fresh insights. ("Fresh insights" does not mean that there is something novel; rather, we are committed to the gospel of Jesus Christ. Yet our culture and times may ask different questions and have different concerns than in the past; thus, we address these with fresh insights.) The same Spirit who inspired the

4. While it is clear that the vast majority of textual variants do not make any major theological impact, some variants do have potential theological import.

5. See Thomas C. Oden, "Back to the Fathers," *Christianity Today*, September 24, 1990, 30.

6. Among his many works that note this consensus, see Thomas C. Oden, *After Modernity—What? Agenda for Theology* (Grand Rapids: Academie Books, 1990), 160–63, 175–81, and Oden, preface to *The Word of Life*, vol. 2 of *Systematic Theology* (San Francisco: Harper & Row, 1989).

7. Accordingly, the notion of a textus receptus as the only authoritative "received text" is dismissed, yet with the understanding that someone may read it and still find salvation.

authors inspires us readers today.[8] In fact, Clark Pinnock calls illumination a
"second inspiration" to highlight this connection between the Spirit's work
in the author and in the reader.[9] Furthermore, the same Spirit who illumines
the mind equally enables and empowers interpreters to apply these things in
their lives and in their proclamation for others. (You can see this two-action
dynamic in fig. 4.2.) Thus, application leads to a hermeneutic circle and, hopefully in a way of growth, to an upward hermeneutical spiral (see chap. 13).

The central theme is that God's initiative and presence can be seen throughout the whole process, from the initial revelation of the original writer to our
engagement with and application of Scripture. From God's personal declara-
tions in word and deed to illumination—including oral traditions, the inspiration of authors and editors, the preservation of sacred texts, and the selection
of books in the canonization process—the Spirit works through the church in
tradition and corporate experience and, ultimately, in us as readers (in community). The Spirit illumines the mind to understand and to implement (see
chap. 13). The Spirit empowers and enables the person to live a Spirit-filled
life that is Bible-based and Christocentric. The often-missing piece is that the
triune Godhead is active in all stages of this process. From the beginning to
end, God is the initiator and plays an active role. Furthermore, as highlighted
in the Protestant Reformation, there is a clear recognition of the interplay
between the Spirit and the Word (see chap. 3). The ongoing interaction of
Word and Spirit is necessary and foundational for biblical interpretation.
We look at the biblical text as it is, yet we are also fully aware of our need to
personally engage the text and, through the text, God. The Spirit provides
the dynamism, and the Word provides the parameters for our Christian life.[10]

The Basics of Communication

Central to issues of interpretation is communication. While communication
theory can take many forms and have a variety of elements, a basic model will
be summarized here. As originally put forth by David K. Berlo in his seminal

8. On illumination, see John W. Wyckoff, *Pneuma and Logos: The Role of the Spirit in
Biblical Hermeneutics* (Eugene, OR: Wipf & Stock, 2010).
9. Clark H. Pinnock, "The Work of the Holy Spirit in Hermeneutics," *Journal of Pentecostal
Theology* 2 (1993): 2–23, and Pinnock, "The Role of the Spirit in Interpretation," *Journal of
the Evangelical Theological Society* 36, no. 4 (1993): 491–97.
10. As noted above, this does not mean that all aspects of this process are always correct.
In the same way that I may miss the illumination of the Spirit due to my blind spots or due to
being part of the sinful world, we can also miss things corporately. However, God's purposes
will always move forward, and his salvation will always extend to the nations.

work, *The Process of Communication*,[11] the process is such that four central components need to be considered in an analysis of any communication; the components are commonly abbreviated as SMCR. First is the sender or source (S). Second is the message (M) intended to be communicated. Third is the channel (C) by which the intended message is sent. Fourth is the receiver or recipient (R). This model can help us understand communication as it relates to biblical interpretation. As noted in the discussion of inspiration above, the senders in view were both human and divine, so the first question is, How do these two interact in the communication of their message? (More on this below.) Also, we have two additional aspects regarding S: first, there is the original "sender" situation, such as a prophet or Jesus proclaiming their message orally; second, there is the author or editor of the written text given to the original audience and subsequently to us. Both the proclaimer and the author need to be considered.

The message (M) is also important. In a broad sense, M is the gospel message or the story of redemption, yet specifically M relates to the individual texts (e.g., the message of Paul in 1 Corinthians 1–4 or of Isaiah in Isaiah 7). The role of exegesis is to try to glean what the original message was to the original audience.

As described above, the channel (C) was initially through oral traditions— the original declaration or proclamation. Yet by the time a biblical message reaches us, it has long been written down in Hebrew or Aramaic (in the case of an Old Testament message) or Greek (in the case of a New Testament one). The Sermon on the Mount was originally an oral presentation in Aramaic, yet we have received this as a text written as a section in Greek in Matthew's Gospel. So we need to be mindful that the channel of communication often involved a process.

Another consideration is that the message was intended to be communicated to an audience (R). The biblical message was for an original audience both orally and via written text (e.g., the original receivers of the spoken prophetic oracles of Isaiah, or the original receivers of Paul's written text at the church in Corinth, who would have heard Paul's letter read in its entirety to the assembly). The message was also for the original audience of the final written text (e.g., Matthew's or Luke's audiences). Later generations (secondary readers) have similarly received this message through the preservation of

11. David K. Berlo, *The Process of Communication: An Introduction to Theory and Practice* (San Francisco: Rinehart, 1960). Of course, there are many other communication models available, including Aristotle's, Wilbur Schramm's, and Dean Barnlund's; a helpful one from a Christian-witness lens is Charles H. Kraft, *Communication Theory for Christian Witness*, rev. ed. (Maryknoll, NY: Orbis Books, 1991).

the texts in the Bible. This brings to mind that as part of a later, secondary audience, we need to make sure we understand the contexts of the original sender(s) and original recipient(s) in order to have a better grasp of the intended message (M).

Further, as anyone can understand who has experienced a variety of communication scenarios—especially cross-cultural or cross-linguistic situations—it is common for a sender's intended message to be misunderstood by the receiver—orally, in writing, or nonverbally. It is therefore important to engage seriously with the exegetical process to connect properly with the (human and divine) authors' intent, as well as the (oral and written) message intended for the original recipients and then for us as recipients in later generations.

Issues of Interpretation

Understanding how communication operates leads naturally into a discussion of interpretation itself, including key interpretive affirmations. We interpret biblical texts in their socio-historical-cultural and grammatical-literary-rhetorical contexts with the SMCR model in mind, as well as our biases and preunderstandings as part of a later audience. When we approach the biblical text as sacred text and follow certain affirmations about both Scripture and the interpreter (delineated in chap. 5), we start with prayer, appropriate attitudes and methods, and an openness to hear from God on the cognitive, affective, experiential, and aesthetic levels. On the cognitive level, we follow measured processes and techniques to interpret passages (as the PERSONAL method outlines).[12] On the affective level, we engage the biblical material to open up our affections to the imprint of God on our lives by the Spirit.[13] Experientially, the Spirit's activity is seen through the text and equally through our lives, so the scriptural truths are experienced and verified.[14] Aesthetically, we sense the beauty of God and his Word as listeners and doers. Further, dealing realistically

---

12. Most textbooks on biblical interpretation highlight the techniques and methods by which appropriate biblical interpretation can take place. This is one of the goals of this volume—to train the mind to follow proper methods in order to interpret Scripture well.

13. There are many works on this affective level; two notable ones are Robert O. Baker, "Pentecostal Bible Reading: Toward a Model of Reading for the Formation of the Affections," *Journal of Pentecostal Theology* 7 (1995): 34–38, and Lee Roy Martin, "Longing for God: Psalm 63 and Pentecostal Spirituality," *Journal of Pentecostal Theology* 22, no. 1 (2013): 54–76. Both are also found in Lee Roy Martin, ed., *Pentecostal Hermeneutics: A Reader* (Leiden: Brill, 2013).

14. On experiential hermeneutics, see Craig S. Keener, *Spirit Hermeneutics: Reading Scripture in Light of Pentecost* (Grand Rapids: Eerdmans, 2016). On verificational hermeneutics, see William Menzies, "The Methodology of Pentecostal Theology: An Essay on Hermeneutics," in *Essays on Apostolic Themes*, ed. Paul Ebert (Peabody, MA: Hendrickson, 1985), 1–14.

with biblical interpretation also means that some interpretation issues must be addressed.

First, as was noted in chapter 1, a variety of distances exists between any modern interpreter and the Bible. When we overlook the distance between our time and the times of the Bible, we can unwittingly substitute our own cultural context for a passage's original context. Thus, we misinterpret the text by divorcing it from its ancient context, and we create a faulty hermeneutic. Therefore, we need to keep these distances in mind. While we affirm the timeless nature of truth in God's Word, the inspired Word that comes down to us is linguistically, geographically, historically, and culturally situated.

Another issue is about the locus of meaning—in other words, Where does meaning come from? Historically, there have been three primary avenues by which this question is answered.[15] First are author-based theories. E. D. Hirsch is frequently cited in support of this position, though he was not actually writing about the Bible.[16] In this view, the proper meaning of a text is predicated on the authorial intent of a text. Hirsch and others highlight that a distinction should be made between *meaning*, as in the original meaning of the text, and *significance*, as in its relevance to us today (see chap. 13 below). So according to this view, a text can have one original meaning and yet have multiple significances, as interpreters apply texts to their own respective contexts. The second predominant set of theories is focused on finding the meaning within the text itself.[17] It should be noted concerning the biblical text that we have only the texts themselves to clarify the meaning of a passage, since all the original human authors have long been gone. The third main arena is reader-based theories. According to these theories, meaning is based on what the reader receives and appropriates.[18]

15. A general discussion of these answers can be found in Tremper Longman III, *Literary Approaches to Biblical Interpretation* (1987), in *Foundations of Contemporary Interpretation: Six Volumes in One*, ed. Moisés Silva (Grand Rapids: Zondervan, 1996), 107–23, and W. Randolph Tate, *Biblical Interpretation: An Integrative Approach*, 3rd ed. (Peabody, MA: Hendrickson, 2008), 1–7.

16. E. D. Hirsch Jr., *Validity in Interpretation* (New Haven: Yale University Press, 1967), and Hirsch, *The Aims of Interpretation* (Chicago: University of Chicago Press, 1976), cited in multiple biblical hermeneutics textbooks.

17. A text-oriented approach can be seen in structuralism, as in the work of the cultural anthropologist Claude Lévi-Strauss, *Structural Anthropology*, trans. Claire Jacobson, Brooke Grundfest Schoepf, and Monique Layton, 2 vols. (New York: Basic Books, 1963, 1976).

18. Two noted works in this area are Stanley Fish, *Is There a Text in This Class?* (Cambridge: Harvard University Press, 1980), and Wolfgang Iser, *The Act of Reading* (Baltimore: Johns Hopkins University Press, 1978); on the interplay between text and reader, see also Edgar V. McKnight, *The Bible and the Reader: An Introduction to Literary Criticism* (Philadelphia: Fortress, 1985), 128–30.

While there are multiple variations of these three theoretical foci, two additional emphases are significant. The first is from Hans-Georg Gadamer—namely, the concept of the two horizons. Every interpretation (in this case, of a biblical text) is the interaction between the horizon of the text (history, culture, etc.) and the horizon of the interpreter. Hermeneutics is the interplay of the two horizons.[19] As Jacqueline Grey notes, this "approach . . . does not contradict the legitimacy of the historical and cultural context of the text, but . . . *extends* it."[20] The second emphasis is the attempt to bring aspects of author-based, text-based, and reader-based theories into an integrated whole.[21] While all theories have important considerations, a biblical understanding of inspiration ensures that authorial intent and, by derivation, the text itself are formative for one's theory of meaning, yet we are also very much aware of the significance of the interpreter in the process.

Another issue is whether the text has one or multiple meanings. While from the above discussion it is clear that text- and reader-based theories are open to multiple meanings, the debate historically has been whether author-based theories can have multiple meanings.[22] This discussion can include the issue of New Testament quotations of the Old Testament that *seem* to diverge from the original meaning (e.g., the use of Hosea 11:1 in Matt. 2:15). Some scholars insist that there is only one meaning, even when the New Testament cites the Old Testament in an unexpected way,[23] yet others see the possibility of multiple meanings—for example, via puns or intentional double meanings.[24]

Related to the issue of multiple meanings is the concept of the plenary sense or *sensus plenior*, which means "fuller sense." This concept highlights the possibility that while the human author had a certain intent, the Spirit was capable, via inspiration, of embedding a fuller meaning in the text that was beyond that author's awareness. Even among evangelical scholars, there

---

19. This is a well-known turn of phrase based on Hans-Georg Gadamer, *Truth and Method*, trans. G. Barden and J. Cumming (New York: Seabury, 1975). On Gadamer, see also Anthony C. Thiselton, *The Two Horizons: New Testament Hermeneutics and Philosophical Description with Special Reference to Heidegger, Bultmann, Gadamer, and Wittgenstein* (Grand Rapids: Eerdmans, 1980).

20. Jacqueline Grey, *Three's a Crowd: Pentecostalism, Hermeneutics, and the Old Testament* (Eugene, OR: Pickwick, 2011), 156, reflecting on Brevard S. Childs, *Biblical Theology of the Old and New Testaments: Theological Reflection on the Christian Bible* (London: SCM, 1992), esp. 380. See also Keener, *Spirit Hermeneutics*, 146, 354n42.

21. See, e.g., Tate, *Biblical Interpretation*.

22. For an extended discussion, see Klein, Blomberg, and Hubbard, *Introduction to Biblical Interpretation*, 247–63.

23. Walter Kaiser is an example, as noted in Klein, Blomberg, and Hubbard, *Introduction to Biblical Interpretation*, 250.

24. Klein, Blomberg, and Hubbard, *Introduction to Biblical Interpretation*, 251–53.

is a range of perspectives on this issue. First, some believe that there is no such thing as a plenary sense and that authorial intent is all tied to the original human author's intentional meaning.[25] A second position allows for *sensus plenior* to be employed by the New Testament authors in their use of Old Testament passages but asserts that this sense is unique to the New Testament writers, who were inspired by the Spirit.[26] A third position likewise allows for *sensus plenior*, but it argues that the same Spirit has the potential to open up the fuller sense to us today.[27] While we certainly affirm that the Spirit can operate in any way he wants in terms of inspiration and divine guidance, whichever position one takes, there are possible theological ramifications that go with it.

Another relevant issue of interpretation is that while there is a clear interaction between the Holy Spirit and biblical interpretation, there are some significant cautions that need to be noted. First, as stated above, the Holy Spirit does aid in the illumination of the text; however, this illumination does not guarantee the correctness or accuracy of one's interpretation. This is because a reader's preunderstanding (see chap. 5) can strongly affect or even mislead one's interpretation. Similarly, we can underestimate the power of human sin to distort our thinking and the interpretive task.[28] It is all too easy to use the Bible for our own purposes and to reinforce our own lifestyle and attitudes with it. Scripture then becomes a reflection of our own desires and a tool to justify and reinforce our own ambitions and greed. When treating the Bible this way, we remove its power to prophetically challenge and correct our own assumptions (2 Tim. 3:16). We also affirm that while a nonbeliever can enjoy the fruits of biblical interpretation to some degree (especially when using appropriate contextual methods), it is through illumination by the Holy Spirit, within a hermeneutical community, that a more accurate, dynamic, and experiential interpretation is possible.

Another caution has to do with our ongoing journey following the Lord. It is possible that the Lord uses a turn of phrase or a specific verse in the Bible to catch our attention or to speak to our heart. These moments can be revelatory and revolutionary in our spiritual formation. We desire the Holy Spirit to speak to us through Scripture. Yet it is very important to distinguish this

---

25. Walter C. Kaiser Jr., "Legitimate Hermeneutics," in *Inerrancy*, ed. Norman L. Geisler (Grand Rapids: Zondervan, 1979), 117–47.

26. Douglas J. Moo, "The Problem of *Sensus Plenior*," in *Hermeneutics, Authority, and Canon*, ed. D. A. Carson and John D. Woodbridge (Grand Rapids: Baker, 1995), 175–211.

27. William Sanford LaSor, "The *Sensus Plenior* and Biblical Interpretation," in *Scripture, Tradition, and Interpretation*, ed. W. Ward Gasque and William Sanford LaSor (Grand Rapids: Eerdmans, 1978), 260–77.

28. Simeon Zahl, *The Holy Spirit and Christian Experience* (Oxford: Oxford University Press, 2020), 20.

direct communication from God from the meaning of the text itself. The two are not the same; to collapse the two is to lead to interpretive confusion (see chap. 10). This point does not diminish what God is speaking to you; it only suggests that what God is speaking to you need not be the actual message of the text. Regardless, we still need to test the perceived communication with the whole counsel of God—that is, the Bible as a whole should guide us in interpreting its parts.

In addition, there are several helpful criteria by which to validate our interpretation. First, does the genre of the text (see part 2) agree with its language? And related: Is the interpretation reasonable within the parameters (i.e., the social-cultural-historical and grammatical-literary-rhetorical contexts) of the text? Gordon Fee states, "A text cannot mean what it could never have meant for its original readers/hearers."[29] We might extend this statement to global church history as well: if an interpretation does not fit the original contexts, and if it is not found in church history or the global church, there is a very clear danger of importing ideas into the biblical text and inventing interpretations.

WHAT DO I DO NOW?

The revelatory role of the Holy Spirit is essential in the hermeneutical enterprise. In every step of the interpretive process, the Spirit is at work to guide the reader who humbly opens their heart and mind, ready to be challenged, encouraged, and inspired. The Holy Spirit can illuminate a text to speak to the reader and thereby deepen their understanding of God's Word.

First, we must recognize that the Spirit and the Word operate in an interplay that brings belief and life together, through the study of the Word and the dynamism of the Spirit. Second, the Berlo communication theory, signified by the initialism SMCR, is a helpful way to see the basics of communication, including when discussing Scripture—both in terms of the original audiences and in terms of modern audiences.

Further, as we approach biblical interpretation, we must address several issues. First, we recognize that we start from a different location (historically and culturally) than the biblical writers. Second, we ask these questions: Where does meaning come from? Does the text have more than one meaning? And is there a Spirit-induced fuller sense (*sensus plenior*)? The answers to these questions are important and impact our biblical interpretation. We are fully

29. Gordon D. Fee and Douglas Stuart, *How to Read the Bible for All Its Worth*, 4th ed. (Grand Rapids: Zondervan Academic, 2014), 34.

supportive of the illumination of the Holy Spirit as we engage with the biblical text; yet while we affirm and are open to the Spirit's role in illumination, we are also aware that we can get things wrong and should have a humble attitude accordingly.

PRAYER

Lord, we thank you for your Word and your Spirit.
  Let us be faithful students of your Word, meditating on it daily.
  Let us be sensitive to the guidance, illumination, and correction of your Holy Spirit.
  And let us be open to learn and grow with brothers and sisters together.
  Amen.

TOPICS FOR REVIEW

1. In what ways does the triune Godhead inform the whole process, from God declaring himself in word and deed to my application and teaching? What does this look like in my life?
2. What does the interplay of Word and Spirit look like?
3. Does the separation of meaning and significance help in your understanding of biblical interpretation?
4. What issues of interpretation do you see as present besides those listed?

5

BEAUTY, THE BIBLE, AND THE INTERPRETER

In this chapter, you should expect to learn the following:

- ▶ The art of biblical interpretation
- ▶ The significance of beauty and truth in biblical interpretation
- ▶ The role of appreciating beauty in the Bible
- ▶ Key issues related to the interpreter
- ▶ Foundational preunderstandings for the Christian as an interpreter

> One thing I ask from the LORD,
>   this only do I seek:
> that I may dwell in the house of the LORD
>   all the days of my life,
> to gaze on the beauty of the LORD
>   and to seek him in his temple.
>
> —Ps. 27:4

As the psalmist proclaims, nothing is more valuable than to "dwell in the house of the LORD" and to "gaze on the beauty of the LORD." This is a passionate prayer. It expresses an intense desire to encounter God. The temple in the Old Testament, located on Mount Zion, was the place people went to

Figure 5.1. *Bible Reading,* by Eduard Karl Gustav Lebrecht Pistorius

worship God and to seek him. No one is more beautiful than the Lord. God is not only the God of truth; he is also the God of beauty. He is beautiful, and his Word is beautiful. Even Moses prays in Exodus 33:18: "Show me your glory." Dwelling in God's presence and experiencing his splendor stirs our hearts, affections, and imaginations. Once we've been overwhelmed by the beauty of God, seeking him becomes our central goal in life.

Further, as the painting in figure 5.1 illustrates, there is a beauty, value, and enthralling quality in reading the Bible. While we cherish Scripture personally, the Bible is valuable in communal experience as well. We experience God's truth and beauty individually as we read his Word, yet we also experience such truth and beauty in community. We read together. Historically, in fact, "to read" meant "to read out loud"; thus, reading the Bible, for much of Christian history, was to read it out loud to oneself as well as to others. When we read Scripture, our minds and our affections are stirred. Scripture models and encourages us to passionately seek God. Thus, it is important not to neglect the "art of interpretation."

The Art of Interpretation

Biblical interpretation has been described as both an art and a science.[1] While much in the previous chapters has been looking at the science of biblical interpretation (i.e., methods, techniques, and tools), this chapter will focus more on the art of interpretation.

The science of interpretation can readily be seen in the process and procedures of hermeneutics, examining the text in its original context (there-then) and applying it to today (here-now). In a similar way, how a translator translates a sentence into another language represents the science of the endeavor. However, there is also an art to interpretation. Interpretation is an art because it requires the reader to catch the nuances, ebbs and flows, and heart of a translation. Catching these nuances and having a "feel" for the translation process is part of the art of interpretation. This reality reflects the fact that the Bible is not just a book of information; rather, it also appeals to our hearts, wills, affections, and imaginations. As noted in chapter 3, modern scholarship is generally focused on the science of interpretation and has left little room for approaches that engage our affections and imaginations.

We must learn from the historic church that our reading of the Bible also needs to address our hearts. This means that both the science and the art of biblical interpretation are central. We grow in both of these approaches through practice, including learning from our mistakes. Yet our growth in the science and the art of interpretation will look comparatively different. For the scientific component, practicing and refining exegetical techniques and methods are the key to growth. For the artistic component, though, developing an "eye" or "ear" for interpretation and translation comes through practice, including learning from others' feedback. For good biblical interpretation, both art and science are needed; thus, practice, practice, practice, and evaluate your work by engaging with historical readers (through commentaries) and the current global community of faith (e.g., through dialogue).

A universal goal of Christianity is to search for what is good, beautiful, and true. Truth is fundamental to the enterprise of theology and biblical interpretation. In the postmodern world, there has been an undermining of absolute truth and truth claims. Furthermore, we are aware that due to our distorted perspectives and our living in a sinful world, we will not always be right. In fact, throughout history, there has only been one completely cor-

---

1. See, e.g., Bernard Ramm, *Protestant Biblical Interpretation*, 3rd ed. (Grand Rapids: Baker, 1970), 10–11.

rect theologian: Jesus Christ.[2] The rest of us try the best we can, knowing our epistemic fallibility (that is, our knowledge is limited), so our theology is always a work in progress. While this reality requires us to be humble, it does not diminish the fact that absolute truth exists or that seeking absolute truth is still a goal worth pursuing. It also reminds us that truth is not exclusively found in evidence-based scientific method, which is often considered to have godlike authority in today's world. Truth can be revealed through other expressions, including beauty, art, philosophy, propositions and logic, phenomenology, wisdom, and morality.

While truth is an important aspect of following God and is a goal of biblical interpretation, an often-neglected aspect is beauty. As much as God is the source and measure of righteousness, holiness, and truth, he is also the standard of beauty.[3] God through his creativity demonstrates beauty (see Gen. 1–2; Ps. 8). The whole of creation manifests the majesty, glory, and beauty of the Lord. Accordingly, God directly and through his Word connects with humans cognitively, aesthetically, experientially, and likewise through their affections. This truth is reflected in Psalm 27:4, which addresses us and inspires us to seek God with our entire being. Our engagement with God includes our whole person. The beauty of God reminds us that all biblical interpretation and theological reflection must engage us and the Christian life holistically. Therefore, Christianity and biblical interpretation are not only about cognitive truth claims; following Christ includes our affections, our emotions, and our psychological and sociological selves. Thus, the art of biblical interpretation connects with our whole person to inform and develop a more robust hermeneutical outcome.

Appreciating the Beauty in the Bible

In a similar but different way, God's beauty can also be seen in his Word. The Bible's unity and diversity are one expression of its grandeur. That the Bible contains a variety of texts that were written over multiple centuries and yet share a common focus on God's redemptive plan to all of humanity is impressive. Such variety includes the Bible's chronological and literary diversity. There is a wide range of literary genres used in the biblical text (see

2. Jürgen Moltmann sent our thoughts down this direction in an interview he had with Michael Bauman; see Bauman, "Jürgen Moltmann," in *Roundtable: Conversations with European Theologians* (Grand Rapids: Baker, 1990), 41.

3. There are many works on this topic; see Junius Johnson, *The Father of Lights: A Theology of Beauty* (Grand Rapids: Baker Academic, 2020), and Jonathan King, *The Beauty of the Lord: Theology as Aesthetics* (Bellingham, WA: Lexham, 2018).

part 2), and yet God and his work in the world are always central (albeit in various ways).

Traditionally, biblical interpretation has focused on the Bible as a theological or spiritual sourcebook. While the Bible's theology and spirituality are important, it is also important to see the Bible as literature. While the doctrine of the inspiration of Scripture stresses that the Bible is qualitatively different from other literary works, viewing the Bible as literature allows us to see the beauty of the passages, books, and the canon as a whole.[4] The Bible contains arguably some of the greatest literature ever produced, such as Psalm 23 and Isaiah 53. It is hard not to be moved by the beauty of poetic passages, such as the Psalms, or challenged emotionally and socially by the Prophets. The emotions can be moved, the affections can be stirred up, and insights can be caught through the text's beauty and the illumination of the Holy Spirit. This beauty ensures that the biblical text, by the Holy Spirit, engages persons at multiple levels and not just cognitively. The biblical text not only testifies to the beauty of God, it also models beauty through literary means.

Seeing beauty in Scripture also leads us to recognize the mystery of the Word of God. Cheryl Bridges Johns reminds us that the Bible is "sacred, dangerous, and mysterious."[5] She suggests that approaching the Bible only through our cognitive lens has left us impoverished and disenchanted, because we have domesticated the Bible to make it fit our world. Instead, like Aslan in C. S. Lewis's literary tale *The Lion, the Witch and the Wardrobe*, who is described as an untamed lion, the Bible is not a tame book. Scripture invites us into a mysterious, supernatural world where the transcendent otherness of God overpowers us with his *mysterium tremendum* ("terrible mystery") of holiness and beauty. We can only respond as the prophet Isaiah does, in captivated awe and fearful quivering (Isa. 6). The Bible is an enchanted world in which the Holy Spirit pours water on the thirsty lands of our hearts and infuses our seeking with the presence of Christ (Ps. 27:4).

Issues Related to the Interpreter

Awareness of the impact of the Bible on our whole person leads us to consider once more the importance of the interpreter. While the role of the reader in

4. This observation is repeatedly made by the Christian literary critic C. S. Lewis. Two essays along this line, but with very different foci, are "Christianity and Literature" (1–11) and "Modern Theology and Biblical Criticism" (152–66), both in *Christian Reflections*, ed. Walter Hooper (Grand Rapids: Eerdmans, 1967).

5. Cheryl Bridges Johns, *Re-enchanting the Text: Discovering the Bible as Sacred, Dangerous, and Mysterious* (Grand Rapids: Baker Academic, 2023), 35.

the interpretive process was introduced in chapter 1, we turn once more to address the various issues related to the interpreter.

The first set of concerns has to do with the preunderstanding of the interpreter. Preunderstanding includes the understandings that are already set in the mind of the interpreter when he or she approaches the text. This concept recognizes that we all come to the Bible with preunderstandings, whether we are aware of them or not. We will always have forms of bias because of our presuppositions. Just reading this book means that you have an ability to read English, which creates a bias toward the English language and resources written in it. One advantage of learning another language is that it can reveal translational complexities and limitations of our expression. It is important to be aware of our own cultural-historical-linguistic situatedness. Such situatedness means that we can have cultural and linguistic blind spots and that we see things through a certain lens.

There are different types of preunderstanding. Duncan S. Ferguson, in his introduction to biblical hermeneutics, has created a taxonomy of four types of preunderstanding.[6] The first is *informational*, which has to do with the information that an interpreter already has and brings to the text, whether accurate or not. A second type is *attitudinal*, which highlights the attitudes about the text, including biases and predispositions that inform our engagement with the text. The third type is *ideological*, which emphasizes the philosophical structure we presuppose in our worldview, or understanding of reality. This type usually takes the form of shaping the text and its interpretation to fit our world as we know it. The fourth type is *methodological*, which stresses that there are acceptable and unacceptable methods by which the reader interprets the biblical text. As can be seen from these types of preunderstanding, everyone has various levels and ways of bringing their presuppositions to the text. However, it is crucial for us to consider and examine how pervasive these presuppositions are within the interpreter.

Let's dig a little deeper into issues of preunderstanding. First, it is perfectly appropriate and in fact expected to test our own preunderstanding. Such testing is important since some aspects of our preunderstanding may be erroneous, prejudicial in the negative sense, or limiting. So appropriate testing is necessary. However, this self-examination should always be conducted within a community of faith and with Scripture, as part of our ongoing self-development and growth. We are mindful that while we can examine our presuppositions, including the elements noted above in our own preunderstanding, we also

6. Duncan S. Ferguson, *Biblical Hermeneutics: An Introduction* (Atlanta: John Knox, 1986), 13–14. Also, see William W. Klein, Craig L. Blomberg, and Robert L. Hubbard Jr., *Introduction to Biblical Interpretation*, 3rd ed. (Grand Rapids: Zondervan Academic, 2017), 227–28.

realize that some of these elements are simply part of our identity and will always impact our biases. For instance, for Paul Lewis, part of his preunderstanding has been shaped by his development as a native English speaker; while he can analyze that fact and even modify related attitudes, he cannot change it. Similarly, Jacqui Grey is of European descent, and she cannot change that. However, we can certainly seek to learn other languages, understand other cultures, and consider other perspectives. Our inherent cultural biases can be recognized and altered—and with this, our preunderstanding in coming to the biblical text. Another example relates to our Christian belief system. While we can analyze what it means to be a Christian—including the core belief that Christ is the Son of God, who is wholly God and wholly man—due to our faith commitment, we consider Christ's nature as the Son of God a nonnegotiable in our Christian preunderstanding. However, evaluating and understanding what this concept means theologically and personally can change as we grow.

As an example of ideological preunderstanding, in more recent decades, both Marxist and Nietzschean lenses have been put forward as biblical interpretive models in certain circles. Marxist philosophical critiques tend to highlight economic and political power structures at play. Similarly, liberation-theology approaches seek to overthrow these structures, whether political, economic, or cultural. These approaches can be helpful in raising awareness of power issues and unjust structural systems; however, they are sometimes used to reinterpret the biblical text to fit the ideological interpretive lens of the reader.[7] In both cases, rather than challenging the presupposing commitments and worldview of the reader, a Marxist liberation perspective can then be seen as an essential ideological foundation in their understanding of the Bible.

Likewise, Friedrich Nietzsche (1844–1900) emphasized the philosophical assertion that we all have "will to power"—that is, we each have a desire for control and power over ourselves and our environment. Accordingly, we must overcome and overthrow oppressors, including any texts viewed as contrary to one's core beliefs, as supporting dominant powers, or as endorsing oppression. This might be worked out in readings that seek to overthrow oppression of race or gender.[8] Again, exposing unjust oppression can be a prophetic activity, but sometimes these approaches ironically weaponize the Bible for their own political agenda.

7. See, e.g., Larry Dean Pettegrew, "Liberation Theology and Hermeneutical Preunderstandings," *Bibliotheca Sacra* 148, no. 591 (July–Sept. 1991): 274–87. Similarly, for a postcolonial interpretation, see Peter Lau, "Back under Authority: Towards an Evangelical Postcolonial Hermeneutic," *Tyndale Bulletin* 63, no. 1 (2012): 131–44.

8. For a summary of these perspectives, see John D. Woodbridge and Frank A. James III, *Church History*, vol. 2, *From Pre-Reformation to the Present Day* (Grand Rapids: Zondervan, 2013), 732–44.

Another prominent philosophical movement over the last several decades, which focuses heavily on the interpreter, is postmodernism. Postmodernity has a variety of characteristics and a plethora of versions. Some prominent versions are deconstructionism (Jacques Derrida, François Lyotard, Michel Foucault), continental hermeneutics (Hans-Georg Gadamer, Paul Ricoeur), reader-response theory (Wolfgang Iser, Stanley Fish), American pragmatism (Richard Rorty, Richard Bernstein), heightened rationalism (Jürgen Habermas), pluralism and relativism (David Tracy), and pre-Enlightenment approaches (Thomas C. Oden, Robert Webber). While other prominent voices exist, these alone demonstrate the sheer variety within postmodern thought, and even within postmodernity, some of these perspectives oppose each other. However, what all of these approaches have in common is an emphasis on the role of the reader; they stress that biblical interpretation is informed by one's philosophical position(s) and commitments. If nothing else, we must be aware of our preunderstanding and how it impacts our interpretation and biases when reading Scripture. Yet as already noted, preunderstanding is not always negative. Our preunderstandings can include our repository of theological knowledge or experience of God that provides a positive foundation for understanding the Bible. In fact, the Bible encourages us to build a strong foundation for our faith, which we also bring as a preunderstanding to the task of interpretation.

Foundational Presuppositions for Christian Interpretation

So what presuppositional foundations should be sought by the Christian interpreter? First is a faith in Christ. There is well-known Latin phrase in the Christian tradition: *lex orandi, lex credendi* (the law of prayer is the law of belief). What you pray and live reveals what you believe. What you pray is what you believe. As we prayerfully open our Bibles in faith, we bring our faith and belief to our interpretation of the Bible. We then build on this faith each time we study the Bible, particularly as we read the text christologically. In the same way that the early church interpreted Scripture through the lens of Christ, so also should faith in Christ provide the foundation and the primary lens of interpretation for us as believers. This presupposition also explains why a believer and a nonbeliever can read the same passage in the Bible but come away with vastly different understandings.[9] Our presupposition of faith can positively inform our interpretation.

9. Craig S. Keener, *Spirit Hermeneutics: Reading Scripture in Light of Pentecost* (Grand Rapids: Eerdmans, 2016), 39–42, 317n13.

A second foundational principle is that the spiritual insights gleaned during biblical interpretation are the result of the Spirit's illumination. In a broad sense, as we read the Bible, it is the Spirit's illumination that brings us to a deeper understanding. The redemptive Spirit guides our understanding and growth. Perhaps another way to think about this is that the Bible reads us. As we read Scripture, the Holy Spirit works to penetrate our hearts. The Bible then becomes a prophetic voice that confronts us with our own anxieties and fears. Our ambitions are exposed. The Spirit works to transform our selfish desires. As at creation (Gen. 1), the Spirit broods over these barren places in our lives. Then God speaks his light and life into existence to fill those empty spaces. The Bible also functions like a mirror, exposing our ambitions and smallness, while revealing God's righteousness and holiness, his mercy and forgiveness. As we seek God's beauty (Ps. 27:4), our misplaced self-confidence becomes swapped for perfect confidence in God.

In a related way, another foundational preunderstanding is that we approach the Bible with an attitude of obedience. The interpretation of the Bible is not only a cognitive or academic exercise alone; it is also meant to move us from understanding to application. Understanding what the text meant to the original audience is not enough; it should move us to implement the text's teachings for growth. As Jesus notes in Matthew 28:18–20 (the Great Commission), by going, making disciples, baptizing, and teaching, we are called to teach others to obey everything he has commanded us. Note that we are not called to divulge information about what Jesus taught; we are called to teach obedience to everything Jesus taught. Obedience comes through application. As Craig Keener says, "Merely knowing information about a text is not the same as embracing the text's message in faithful obedience."[10]

Another foundational element is that our approach to the biblical text should operate in a robustly contextual way—by reading the texts with the original audience in mind and appropriating them for our time. Since we believe the Scriptures are meant to be understood, we also accept that a proper approach to the text is needed to ensure clarity and appropriate application. As noted in chapter 1, such an approach must pay attention to the text's historical and literary contexts (including its structure and grammar).

Finally, as readers, we are part of a hermeneutical community. The rampant individuality of contemporary Western culture isolates us from one another. Yet we are called to be a community—the body of Christ reliant on one another. This reliance includes the task of interpretation. We must interpret the Bible together and interact with the church locally, globally, and historically.

10. Keener, *Spirit Hermeneutics*, 11.

Such interactivity requires us all to be part of a hermeneutical community. In much the same way that the biblical text functions as a mirror, showing us the glory of God while also giving us a sober portrayal of ourselves, the community of faith also functions as a mirror as we both reflect God and spur each other on to greater ethical integrity.[11] Notably, this community exists within the local body of Christ, where we can grow together. Yet we are also enriched by other global voices that highlight the value of different cultural lenses. These global, cross-cultural interlocutors also aid us in overcoming our biases and ignorance of the experiences of others. Walking in the shoes of another can transform our reading of the Bible. Similarly, hermeneutical engagements with the past help us overcome our situated blind spots. Reading the works of earlier believers, such as John Wesley, Martin Luther, Augustine, and the Cappadocian fathers, can give insights into the text but can also correct our own biased interpretations. In the interpretative task, together we are better.

WHAT DO I DO NOW?

We start with the understanding that hermeneutics is both a science and an art. Similarly, hermeneutics seeks the truth and beauty of God and his Word. We should not neglect the affective and experiential side of biblical interpretation, only focusing on the cognitive side (methods and techniques). While we affirm that God is beautiful, the biblical text as literature is beautiful in its own right and should be treasured for this quality.

We all bring presuppositions and preunderstandings to the text. Accordingly, we should be aware of our own biases and seek to be molded by God as we seek his face (Ps. 27:4). Further, various ideologies are prevalent in the academy today (e.g., Marxism, Nietzschean thought, and postmodernity). We must be aware of our biases and not allow prominent trends in philosophy to eclipse the divine truths provided for us in God's Word.

Christian interpreters need foundational presuppositions. First is a faith in Christ. Second is an openness to divine illumination. Third is an attitude of obedience and a commitment to application. Fourth is that the hermeneutical process includes the contexts of a passage. And fifth is that we are to participate in a hermeneutical community, which entails active involvement locally (in a local church), globally (with global voices outside our own

11. H. Richard Niebuhr, *The Responsible Self: An Essay in Christian Moral Philosophy* (New York: Harper & Row, 1963), esp. chap. 2.

cultural-linguistic group), and historically (with key historic voices, including voices outside our own theological tradition).

As we now move into part 2 of the book, we will begin by exploring the Bible as a narrative. That is, Scripture provides an overall story of redemption. This story of the Bible moves from creation (in Genesis) to the new creation (in Revelation). It climaxes with the coming of Jesus, God in the flesh and agent of redemption. The narrative of the Bible provides a glorious vision for our lives—a vision of personal transformation into the image of Christ and the Spirit's empowerment to preach the good news. We are invited to join this marvelous story.

PRAYER

Lord, we thank you for your Word.
We are aware of the presuppositions that we carry as we come to
your Word.
Let us be seekers finding your truth and beauty in your Word,
and let us be agents of truth and beauty, seeking what is right
rather than being concerned about being right.
Help us to be faithful stewards of your Word.
Amen.

TOPICS FOR REVIEW

1. What does the phrase "the beauty of the Lord" mean? In what ways does it relate to the Bible?
2. In what ways are beauty and truth parallel, and in what ways are they different?
3. Have any of the issues related to the interpreter surprised you? Or do you consider any of them especially important? If so, which ones?
4. What additional elements of preunderstanding should Christian interpreters of the Bible consider?

Transformational Reading

6

OUR GRAND NARRATIVE

In this chapter, you should expect to learn the following:

- ▶ The power of stories
- ▶ The narrative shape of Scripture
- ▶ An overview of the storyline of the Bible
- ▶ How we continue the story of Scripture today through improvisation

They asked each other, "Were not our hearts burning within us while he talked with us on the road and opened the Scriptures to us?"

—Luke 24:32

In this story, recorded in Luke 24:13–35, two of the disciples are traveling from Jerusalem to the nearby village of Emmaus. They have just seen Jesus betrayed by their Jewish leaders and crucified on the cross by the Romans. It seems all hope is lost. As they walk along the road discussing these tragic events, they encounter a person they think is a stranger. As it happens, this stranger is the risen Jesus himself—though the disciples are somehow kept from recognizing him. Jesus asks them what they are discussing. Cleopas and his friend are clearly despondent (as noted by their downcast faces) but are astonished that this stranger has not heard about Jesus. This stranger is

Figure 6.1. Two disciples on their way to Emmaus.
Stained glass window in the Saint Gervais and Saint
Protais Church, Paris, France.

surely the only one in Jerusalem not to know of Jesus's prophetic ministry and
crucifixion. They pour out the story of Jesus like a verbal flood as they explain
the recent events. They tell him of their shattered hope for the liberation of
Israel. The disciples recall the amazing testimony of the women returned from
the empty tomb, who were insisting that Jesus is alive. Of course, the irony is
that Cleopas and his friend are telling all this to Jesus himself.

Jesus then admonishes them for their flawed comprehension of Scripture.
Many prophets of the Old Testament clearly pointed to the suffering of the
Messiah before his glorification. As they walk, Jesus explains from the Scrip-
tures concerning the Messiah (that is, himself). He begins with Moses (the
Torah) and moves through the Prophets to explicate his identity and mission.
As they approach the village, Jesus indicates he is journeying further, but the
disciples convince him to accept their hospitality. While they are seated at the
table together, it is only when Jesus takes the bread, gives thanks, and breaks

it—in a kind of reenactment of the Last Supper (Luke 22:19)—that the eyes of the disciples are finally opened to recognize Jesus.

The artwork in figure 6.1, depicting this scene on the road to Emmaus, effectively captures a few key ideas from the passage. First, it portrays the disciples as very ordinary folk (albeit what ordinary people looked like in seventeenth-century France). Cleopas and his unnamed friend are not well known to us among the disciples of Jesus. Yet Jesus comes alongside and walks with them. This emphasizes the accessibility of Jesus to all disciples, including the least in society.[1] Second, the artwork reminds us that Jesus walks with us even in our darkest moments. Third, it captures the moment of Jesus teaching Cleopas and his friend the stories of the Old Testament and how these stories point to him. Jesus himself is pointing above, perhaps to the Father. So with Luke's story in mind, let us consider the role of narrative more generally, as well as how the Bible provides a bigger picture of God's redemption of the world. We will then consider how each of us participates in this narrative of reconciliation.

How Stories Shape Our Lives

"Will you tell me your story?" This is a question we sometimes ask a new acquaintance or friend to get to know them better. By sharing our life story or testimony, we provide insights into our background, personality, and character. Stories are powerful. They shape our thinking and understanding of the world. They shape the way we think about ourselves. Our personal stories help us make sense of past experiences that have molded us into the person we are today—why we are as we are now. Our life narration creates a coherent sense of our identity, meaning, and purpose. Stories also help us see possibilities for the future—that is, where we are going.[2]

Telling our personal story also taps us into a larger tradition. Stories not only construct our personal identities but also shape our corporate identities as a community. Storytelling is common to every known human culture.[3] Most cultures teach lessons about values and morals through stories.[4] Think of some of the key national holidays you celebrate in your community and the

---

1. F. Scott Spencer, *Luke*, Two Horizons New Testament Commentary (Grand Rapids: Eerdmans, 2019), 495.

2. Dan P. McAdams and Kate C. McLean, "Narrative Identity," *Current Directions in Psychological Science* 22, no. 3 (June 2013): 233.

3. McAdams and McLean, "Narrative Identity," 233.

4. Craig S. Keener, *Gift and Giver: The Holy Spirit for Today* (Grand Rapids: Baker Academic, 2001), 211.

stories attached to them. Stories and commemorations capture certain events and values of importance for national identities. In the US, Independence Day (the Fourth of July) is celebrated annually to remember the historic establishment of the nation and thereby instill the values of freedom and free speech. Similarly, in Australia and New Zealand, ANZAC Day (celebrated on April 25) is an annual remembrance of a significant military event in World War I, but it also celebrates esteemed qualities such as courage and "mateship."[5] These national holidays recall and retell historic events each year, yet they also inform our values and shape part of our national psyche and identity. Each new member and new generation of the community joins these narratives and internalizes the ideals exemplified in them. The stories teach us what is important to our community and provide meaning for our national identity.

For the Christian community, the biblical narrative also plays a formative role. The story of Scripture provides our theological identity. Learning the narrative of Scripture is important for each member of the Christian community. It shapes us and informs our values. The narrative guides us in learning how to live as citizens of God's kingdom. As we internalize the narrative of the Bible, we join a rich heritage of God's people throughout history and around the world today who pursue lives that are faithful to and consistent with its message.

The Bible as a Narrative

The Bible provides an overall narrative that stretches from the creation of humanity in Genesis to the future when creation will be restored in Revelation. It is an epic story in which we learn about God, not through propositional truth or abstract theorizing but by a narrative of God's interactions with people.[6] So the center of this story is God. God acts and is known through history. That is, God has been revealed through concrete interaction and involvement with embodied human communities. The Bible focuses first on God's involvement with the community of ancient Israel and comes to a climax with the life, death, and resurrection of Jesus Christ. Yet while this interaction focuses on specific people groups, it also recognizes that God the Creator is sovereign over all people and the entire creation.[7]

---

5. ANZAC is short for Australian and New Zealand Army Corps.

6. David J. H. Beldman and Jonathan Swales, "Biblical Theology and Theological Interpretation," in *A Manifesto for Theological Interpretation*, ed. Craig G. Bartholomew and Heath A. Thomas (Grand Rapids: Baker Academic, 2016), 152.

7. Richard Bauckham, *The Bible in the Contemporary World: Hermeneutical Ventures* (Grand Rapids: Eerdmans, 2015), 2.

However, even a cursory reading of the Bible shows that it is not written like a novel with one single human author.[8] The Bible comprises a diversity of writing styles, authors, and texts. It is a self-contained library of many individual books that form the one book: the Bible. There are many different types of texts and voices within the canon of Scripture (as noted in chap. 2). There are also various nuances and tensions regarding numerous ethical topics, such as violence. So how can the Bible be called a "narrative"? The individual stories, poems, and letters of the Bible all contribute to form an overarching story of God's redemption of the world. While the many different stories and texts in the Bible have their own significance, when they are collected and woven together, they are like a stained glass window, such as the one beginning this chapter. A stained glass window is not a motley mess of glass but an artwork in which the many individual pieces of colored glass are soldered into a large, coherent picture. The picture revealed in the stained glass window of the Bible is the narrative of salvation. When read as a whole, the Bible has a narrative unity and canonical consistency.[9] The unified message of the Bible is the unfolding redemption and restoration of creation. Narrative provides the main framework for the message of the Bible.[10] This is essentially what Jesus teaches Cleopas and his friend on the road to Emmaus—how the message and promises of the Old Testament point to him. Although there are many different types of writings (or genres) in the Bible, they each contribute to the overall narrative. We will explore the various types of genres used in the Bible in the next few chapters. At this point, however, it is helpful to consider how these different types of texts within Scripture are woven into its larger narrative.

Perhaps the most straightforward texts to consider first are the actual story portions within Scripture. The Bible is filled with individual stories. Sometimes, these stories connect directly to the overall story of Scripture. Consider the exodus narrative of God redeeming ancient Israel. The exodus story has an obvious contribution to the epic drama of the Bible as it describes the deliverance of ancient Israel from slavery in Egypt and provides the template for Christ's redemption of the world. Other, smaller stories connect to the bigger story but are perhaps less obvious. The reports of Elijah and Elisha in 1–2 Kings, as these prophets confront the apostasy of the Israelite kings, contribute to the overall plotline as they give us insight into the history of the covenant community of the Old Testament, but their contribution is perhaps

8. Bauckham, *Bible in the Contemporary World*, 3.
9. Bauckham, *Bible in the Contemporary World*, 1.
10. Walter C. Kaiser Jr. and Moisés Silva, *Introduction to Biblical Hermeneutics: The Search for Meaning*, rev. ed. (Grand Rapids: Zondervan, 2007), 123.

less obvious than that of the story of the exodus. Yet there are some stories in the Bible that do not seem to have any connection to the larger picture. They seem to be random bits of glass. In fact, stories such as the abuse and murder of the Levite's concubine in Judges 19 seem to undermine the message of salvation. Why include such a deplorable story in the narrative of redemption? In this case, we are supposed to be *appalled* by this story. It shows the depravity of people—even God's people—when they follow their own morals and reject God's ways. It is part of the overall narrative as it points to Israel's immediate need for a king, but it also points to the bigger picture of all peoples' need of a Savior.

Quite often, the stories in the Bible also contain nonnarrative material, such as poems, proverbs, songs, and sayings.[11] Consider the story of Hannah in 1 Samuel 1–2. It begins with the heartbreaking account of Hannah's childlessness and shame. It tells how she goes into the tabernacle to pray for a child, promising to dedicate her unborn child to God. God answers her prayer, and at the dedication of Samuel, she prays a magnificent poetic song of praise (1 Sam. 2). Yet while it is a wonderful story on its own, Hannah's story is part of the larger story of ancient Israel. It is through Samuel (the last of the judges) that a king in Israel is appointed and David is anointed. Eventually, Jesus Christ, a descendant of David, is born. Mary's poetic song at the annunciation (Luke 1:46–55) mirrors Hannah's psalm of praise. So Hannah's poetic song, embedded in the narrative of 1 Samuel, contributes to the overall story of God's salvation plan fulfilled in Jesus Christ.

While most of the prophetic writings of the Old Testament primarily utilize poetry, they also contribute to the overall narrative of the Bible. The prophets are historically located in the story of ancient Israel. This narrative setting provides the backdrop for their message to the covenant community. The same is also true of other nonnarrative genres, such as the psalms of the Old Testament and the letters of the New Testament. These diverse texts, voices, and perspectives in the Bible contribute to its larger, unified message of salvation. However, according to postmodernity, we should be suspicious of metanarratives that represent what Richard Bauckham calls "comprehensive systems of explanation."[12] Such metanarratives are critiqued because of how they have been used historically to oppress certain people groups or ideas. This is a valid critique; some metanarratives have been used manipulatively to serve the interests of those in power and suppress other voices through a selective retelling of history.

11. Bauckham, *Bible in the Contemporary World*, 1.
12. Bauckham, *Bible in the Contemporary World*, 9.

This is not the case with the biblical narrative. While the Bible contains a unified message, this coherence emerges from a diversity of voices. Of course, the voices and perspectives within the Bible are limited. Yet even perspectives that might normally be suppressed are radically given voice in the biblical text, such as the song of Hannah, which might normally be excluded in a patriarchal society like that of ancient Israel. This does not mean the Bible has not been used by later interpreters to serve other, sometimes unjust, purposes. Indeed, it has, as the study of reception history, or the history of effect (*Wirkungsgeschichte*), of the Bible shows. Yet overall, we can confidently assert that the coherent narrative of the Bible is a message of redemption, freedom, and grace. So what is the general storyline of Scripture?

The Grand Narrative of the Bible

Can you identify the storyline of the Bible's grand narrative? What events might you include if you were to share the "testimony" of the Bible? How would you choose what events to include? There are some events we might include because the Bible itself emphasizes their importance through repetition. We are told many times about how God rescued Israel from Egypt in the exodus (which we will discuss below). That we have four Gospel accounts of the life and ministry of Jesus ensures that the message about him will not be underestimated. Throughout the Bible, there are certain places where a summary of key historic events (up to the time of writing or editing) is shared. Interestingly, they each retell the story slightly differently and sometimes highlight different key events. This is because they are providing summaries for different audiences and purposes. That is, they adapt the story of Scripture for their context.

There are two summaries within the Bible that are particularly noteworthy: Nehemiah 9:5–37 and Acts 13:17–41.[13] The book of Nehemiah is set in the postexilic period, recalling the challenges of rebuilding Jerusalem following the exile in Babylon. The summary of the Old Testament story in Nehemiah 9 is part of a confession of the sins, past and present, of the postexilic community. The speech begins by praising Yahweh as Creator.[14] It then highlights the calling of Abram, the exodus from Egypt and the giving of the law, the conquest of the land, the rejection of the prophets, and the

13. Other summaries identified in the biblical text include (but are not limited to) Deut. 6:20–24; 1 Chron. 16:12–22; Pss. 78; 136; Acts 7:2–53.
14. Yahweh is the covenant name for God revealed to Moses at the burning bush, meaning "I AM WHO I AM" (Exod. 3:14). "LORD" is the most common rendering of this divine name in English translations of the Old Testament.

exile. The passage emphasizes the importance of the law for the covenant community and the great grace of God despite their faithlessness. Similarly, in Acts 13:17–41, Paul is preaching in the synagogue of Pisidian Antioch. He highlights most of the same key events as Nehemiah but also refers to the Davidic lineage of Jesus. Paul explains how the promises of the Old Testament are fulfilled in the life, death, and resurrection of Jesus Christ. He emphasizes to his Jewish hearers the forgiveness of sins found in the Savior, Jesus Christ.

From this cursory exploration, we can see that there are key events repeatedly highlighted within Scripture that form the backbone of its narrative. The story of Scripture begins with the book of Genesis, describing God's deliberate work of creating the world and humanity. Although humanity is designed to bear God's image and serve as stewards of God's good world, they reject God's rulership and choose independence. This act breaks the harmony of creation. How will God restore this world? The Bible then centers on one family, that of Abram and Sarah, who migrate from Mesopotamia (around 2000 BC) to the area that will become home to ancient Israel. Abram enters a covenant relationship with God, and his name is changed to Abraham. His descendants later move to Egypt in a time of severe famine. After a while, the Egyptians fear the expanding numbers of Abraham's descendants, so Israel becomes enslaved in Egypt. The Israelites cry out to God in this time of crisis. God hears their groaning and acts because of his covenant with Abraham, Isaac, and Jacob. God sends a deliverer, Moses, and miraculously liberates the people through him so they can worship God. (The exact date of the exodus event is disputed, but it was probably around 1500–1300 BC.) At Sinai, they enter a covenant with God as a federation of tribes. At this time, they are given the law to instruct them in how to relate to God and one another. As well as instructions for worship (i.e., the sacrificial system), the Israelites are given directives for the construction of the place of worship (i.e., the tabernacle). Following the wilderness wanderings, the next generation enters the promised land under the leadership of Joshua.

Unable to conquer the whole territory, the tribal groups of ancient Israel coexist in the land with other nations. The Israelite people are initially led by judges, but then they appoint a king. The first stable king, David (approximately 1000 BC), sets up a capital in Jerusalem, unifies the tribes into a confederacy, and begins plans to build a temple. God makes a covenant with David to establish a royal dynasty. The temple is built by David's son Solomon. However, the federation soon fractures, and the kingdom divides into North and South. Then a cycle of apostasy (turning from God), decline, and renewal follows. The prophets are active during this time to remind the people of their covenant commitments.

So, as small fish in the big pond of ancient Near Eastern politics, the two kingdoms become embroiled in the geopolitical conflicts of their time. Eventually, due to their persistent and protracted rejection of God, the two kingdoms fall. First, the Northern Kingdom is captured by Assyria (in 722 BC), and later the Southern Kingdom is captured by Babylon and taken into exile (in 587 BC). Interestingly, while the Southern Kingdom (Judah) is in captivity, the Babylonians are overthrown by the Persians. The Persian king Cyrus allows the Jews to return to their homeland (in 539 BC) to rebuild the temple (completed in 515 BC). While many Judeans (now called Jews) stay scattered among the nations in the Diaspora, some like Nehemiah return to the land. The land of Judea remains under foreign control by the Persians, then the Greeks, and then the Romans. The Jews long for a messiah to deliver them from foreign rule and restore the kingdom of David.

In the fullness of time, the Gospels record that Jesus the Christ (or Messiah), a descendent of David, is born. This child is God in the flesh. Jesus lives and ministers in the Roman province of Judea, preaching the good news of the kingdom of God. As the disciples on the road to Emmaus will testify, Jesus Christ is betrayed, crucified, and buried. However, Jesus rises from the dead and appears to many disciples. This is the climax of the story of Scripture; as Paul will emphasize in his speech in Pisidian Antioch (Acts 13:17–41), forgiveness and reconciliation are found through Jesus Christ. Before his ascension, Jesus promises to send the Holy Spirit to empower the believers to preach the gospel. At Pentecost (Acts 2), the Spirit is poured out on the believers, birthing the church. The book of Acts describes how the disciples spread the gospel across the Roman Empire, despite increasing persecution. In particular, the missionary endeavors of Paul and his coworkers result in many churches being established. Paul and others also write numerous letters of instruction to the early church communities. However, the New Testament canon finishes by looking forward to the renewal of all creation. As described in the book of Revelation, all who confess Jesus Christ will experience eternal life and fellowship with God.

Each new generation of believers enters and joins this same story. The narrative of Scripture shapes our identity as followers of Christ. This "redemptive history" (*Heilsgeschichte*) provides meaning and purpose for our lives. However, even within this overall story, there are two key events that highlight this grand narrative. These two events—the exodus event and the Jesus event—are the center and core of the story of Scripture.

The Core of the Story

At the heart of the story of Scripture are two events that Christians see as intimately connected. The exodus is the central event of the Old Testament, as it defines redemption and salvation—through the miraculous rescue of God's people from slavery in Egypt (Exod. 3–13), the crossing of the Red Sea (Exod. 14–15), God's provisions in the wilderness (Exod. 16–18), the establishment of their covenant as a nation (Exod. 19), and the giving of the law (or torah) as part of that covenant to live together in worship of God (Exod. 20–31). This unique story has shaped the Old Testament expectations of God acting in history. As God acted once to save the covenant people at the exodus, so God could do it again in a new way.

Stories that are important to a community are often repeated. It is how stories become engrained in our memory and psyche. As we hear them told again and again, they become part of us. To learn this way is to learn "by heart," as though it becomes part of our bloodstream. Repetition is also a common storytelling technique *within* a narrative. Repetition highlights what is important, so we should take heed of repetitions and recurring themes in the Bible. This is true of the exodus event within Scripture. The Old Testament community is to remember and perform the exodus story each year at the Passover festival. The exodus is also a central motif used by the prophets, such as Isaiah, to speak of God's future actions. While the Judean community is captive in the Babylonian exile, the prophet announces throughout Isaiah 40–55 that God will deliver them in a kind of second exodus. The exodus event will be repeated, but in a new way (43:18–19). For example, in Isaiah 43:1b–2a the community is told:

> Do not fear, for I have redeemed you;
>   I have summoned you by name; you are mine.
> When you pass through the waters,
>   I will be with you;
> and when you pass through the rivers,
>   they will not sweep over you.[15]

As the grand narrative continues into the New Testament, the exodus event is transformed once more and finds its fulfillment in the person and work of Jesus Christ (Matt. 5:17; Luke 24:46–47). It is Christ, not the exodus story or Moses, that stands at the center of this epic.

On the road to Emmaus (Luke 24), Jesus begins with Moses to explain the significance of his own life, death, and resurrection to the disciples. The

---

15. See also Isa. 40:3–5; 43:14–21; 48:20–21; 49:8–12; 51:9–11; 52:7–12.

exodus event is the interpretive key to understanding Jesus: Jesus has performed miracles, including feeding people in the wilderness (Mark 6:30–44); at the cross, he has rescued us from slavery to sin and established a new covenant based on a community of faith (Mark 14:24); and through his resurrection, he has given us a new way to live together and to worship God in Spirit and in truth (John 4:23; 13:34). The Jesus event is the climax of the biblical story.

So what do we do with this story? We are called to live in a way that is faithful to this story in our own culture and context. Herein lies the problem. Our culture and contexts today are very different from those of the world of the Bible. We cannot just pull out bits from here and there and try to apply them to our situation. That is not what being faithful to the Bible requires. Instead, we must live out the story of Scripture within our contemporary contexts. We will explore this further in chapters 13 and 15.

WHAT DO I DO NOW?

The Bible is a gift to us and a guide for us today. While it tells the story of God's people in the past, it is not just a history book. It is given as a light to show us the way for our lives today. It is given to guide us in our actions, thoughts, and emotions. We must study it faithfully and apply its teachings to our lives. As Jesus says, "If you love me, keep my commands" (John 14:15; similarly, James 1:22; 1 John 2:3–6). So we must seek to listen to the Bible with openness and expectancy, to understand how to love Christ and love others in obedience to his commands as found in his Word.

The Holy Spirit works in our lives as we read the Bible and seek to live it out in the here-now. As we apply the Bible, we slowly become more Christlike and more deeply immersed in the life of God. Ephesians 5:1–2 says, "Follow God's example, therefore, as dearly loved children and walk in the way of love, just as Christ loved us and gave himself up for us as a fragrant offering and sacrifice to God." One way we can become like Jesus is to imitate him. We live out his story of sacrificial love in our own stories, appropriate to our context today. As we read of Jesus in the Gospel accounts, we see his love for God and people. Jesus is friends with outcasts. He not only teaches but demonstrates love of enemies. He washes the mucky feet of his disciples. In the story of Scripture, Christ shows us what it means to love others and to give ourselves up for them. We honor Christ by following his example, worked out in all the peculiarities of our own messy world.

PRAYER

We thank you, Lord, for the gift of the Bible.
  May it be a light to guide us in the dark
  and an anchor in the storms of life.
  Teach us to live faithfully according to your Word, we pray,
  even in our own messy lives,
  so that we might be beacons that guide the lost to you.
  Amen.

TOPICS FOR REVIEW

1. What are some of the key events of the Bible that you would include if you were asked to share its grand narrative? Why did you choose those events?

2. Consider two very different texts, such as the books of Ruth and Song of Songs. How might these two texts contribute to the Bible's overall narrative of redemption?

3. How might we apply God's narrative to our messy lives?

7

READING STORIES

In this chapter, you should expect to learn the following:

▶ How to identify different genres or types of writing in the Bible
▶ The key features of narrative
▶ Different types of narrative texts found in the Bible
▶ How to apply biblical narrative to our context today

So all the elders of Israel gathered together and came to Samuel at Ramah. They said to him, "You are old, and your sons do not follow your ways; now appoint a king to lead us, such as all the other nations have."

—1 Sam. 8:4–5

The book of 1 Samuel opens with the birth of Samuel, a miraculous provision to the barren Hannah. Samuel is called as a prophet to lead the disunified tribal confederacy into a renewal of covenant obedience to God (1 Sam. 1–6). The confederacy's story continues well for a while. However, when Samuel has grown old, he appoints his sons as leaders over Israel. The problem is that these sons are corrupt. So the elders of Israel come to Samuel to demand that Samuel instead appoint a king to lead them. This may not seem like an unreasonable request. After all, the elders have rightly rejected

93

Figure 7.1. Illustration from the Morgan Picture Bible (ca. 1250)

the leadership of Samuel's corrupt sons, and there is an anticipation that Israel will eventually have a human king to rule them (reflected in Deut. 17:14–20). Yet when we read 1 Samuel 8 closely, we see that the elders do not request but *demand* a king. Rather than continue the current theocracy (in which God is King) or appoint another judge like Samuel, they want a human king.

The book of 1 Samuel recalls the early history of the monarchy in ancient Israel, particularly noting the rise of Saul and then David as kings. However, the narrative recalls these events from a theological perspective. It is part of the larger story of Israel's history, explaining how and why the people eventually end up in exile. The community rejects God and their covenant relationship. Most disappointingly, the kings are often instrumental in leading the people away from God.

The demand for a king, as narrated in 1 Samuel 8, is reflected in the artwork of the medieval illuminated manuscript shown in figure 7.1. There, the elderly Samuel is confronted by four representatives from Israel who insist, "Now appoint a king to lead us, such as all the other nations have" (1 Sam. 8:5). The narrator tells us that this displeases Samuel, so he turns to God in prayer. During that prayer, God speaks to Samuel. God affirms that it is not Samuel whom the people are rejecting but God. Nevertheless, Samuel is to listen to the people. The meeting of Samuel and the elders in the medieval manuscript above depicts Samuel pointing his finger at them, most likely in warning. He cautions them against their demand. In the story of 1 Samuel 8:1–21, the people desire the prestige of a human king so they can be like the other nations. Samuel advises them of the consequences of this desire. The repetition of the words "take" and "serve" points to the type of king that was ubiquitous in the ancient Near East; a king would perpetually take from them, and they would perpetually serve him.

Why might this demand be displeasing to both God and Samuel? Bill Arnold deftly summarizes the Israelites' demand as "sinful in its motives, selfish in its timing, and cowardly in its spirit."[1] First, their motives are sinful as they reject their identity as God's people. They no longer want to be the covenant people—that is, set apart by virtue of their relationship with God. Instead, they want to be like the other nations, to conform with those around them. They are dazzled by the potential for influence, prestige, and security in their region. Yet this rejection of God by the people has been habitual since the exodus. Second, they demand that this change happen immediately. They are not willing to wait for God's timing (as Deut. 17:14–20 suggests will happen), but instead, like petulant children, they demand it *now*. Third, as Arnold highlights, their demand is cowardly. The people want a monarchy (a human king) rather than a theocracy (God as King). To serve a human king who will fight their battles for them seems easier than trusting God to deliver and protect them.

Yet as the narrative unfolds, Samuel gives them what they desire by anointing and appointing Saul as king (1 Sam. 9–11), as depicted in the second painting of the illuminated manuscript. Saul is described as tall, handsome, and from a wealthy family. In this sense, he seems a natural choice as a leader. Saul has some early military victories; however, he craves power and status (see 1 Sam. 15), which eventually leads to his disobedience and God's rejection of him as king. This section of 1 Samuel is sobering. It reminds us today of the corruption of power and the human obsession with status. As Mary J. Evans observes, "The book of Samuel examines and reflects on the nature, accession, use, and abuse of power."[2] Christ also would be tempted by power and status but would choose the path of humility and obedience (Matt. 4:8–9). He demonstrates that the way of the triune God is not status seeking but selfless giving (Phil. 2:5–11).

1. Bill T. Arnold, *1 and 2 Samuel*, NIV Application Commentary (Grand Rapids: Zondervan Academic, 2003), 153–54.
2. Mary J. Evans, *1 and 2 Samuel*, Understanding the Bible Commentary Series (Grand Rapids: Baker Books, 2012), 9.

Genre

The Bible contains a variety of styles of writing. It includes story, history, poetry, proverb, prophecy, and letter, as well as many other different types of texts. While these various types of writing all contribute to the bigger picture of the overall scriptural narrative, each section of the Bible is important. Each section must be read for its own significance and according to its own purpose. Central to this task is identifying the type of writing or genre of a text. The term "genre" (which developed from the French language) is related to the word "general," referring to the general features that characterize similar types of writings.[3] For example, different types of movies include action, horror, comedy, drama, musical, and documentary. These categories of movies can be identified by the characteristics they share. Action movies are generally fast paced and include a lot of fight scenes, stunts, and car chases—usually ending in a hero (or superhero) defeating a villain. The genre of a movie or a piece of literature establishes its expectations, style, and content.

Usually, a writer uses a particular genre for a certain purpose. The genre and language selected by the writer are the channel of their message, which has an intention or goal.[4] Of course, we cannot get inside the mind of a writer, past or present, to know exactly what their intention was in writing. This task is made even harder due to the historical and cultural differences between biblical writers and us today—assuming we even know the exact identity of the writers of the biblical text. However, we can determine—via their communication, which includes their choice of genre—something of their purpose for writing. As Adele Berlin writes, "We must look not only for *what* the text says, but also *how* it says it."[5] Therefore, we must be attentive to the genre of a text, as the genre tells us something of its objective and how we should understand the message being communicated. The genre determines the reading strategy.[6] Michael Gorman suggests we ask two key questions: (1) What kind of writing is the passage? (2) What general principles for this kind of writing should we employ?[7]

---

3. Tremper Longman III, *Making Sense of the Old Testament: Three Crucial Questions* (Grand Rapids: Baker, 1998), 40.

4. Jeannine K. Brown, *Scripture as Communication: Introducing Biblical Hermeneutics*, 2nd ed. (Grand Rapids: Baker Academic, 2021), 140.

5. Adele Berlin, *Poetics and Interpretation of Biblical Narrative* (Winona Lake, IN: Eisenbrauns, 1994), 20.

6. Tremper Longman III and Raymond B. Dillard, *An Introduction to the Old Testament*, 2nd ed. (Grand Rapids: Zondervan, 2006), 31.

7. Michael J. Gorman, *Elements of Biblical Exegesis: A Basic Guide for Students and Ministers*, 3rd ed. (Grand Rapids: Baker Academic, 2020), 92.

Over the next few chapters, we will explore some of the key genres of literature found in the Bible and discuss their chief characteristics. We will also consider some of the general principles to be employed in the interpretation of the specific genres. In this chapter, we will focus on the genre of narrative, which also includes the subgenres of myth, history, Gospel, and parable. Narrative is, in fact, the most common genre in the Bible. In the following chapters, we will look at Old Testament law, poetry, and prophecy before finally turning to the genre of the New Testament letters. First, let us define the genre of story.

What Makes a Story?

In general, stories or narratives (we will continue to use these terms interchangeably) share common characteristics. A story has a sequence of events that moves toward an ending. This movement is driven by plot, which usually involves characters and a setting in which the events occur. The stories of the Bible are set in a time and place. The setting of the Old Testament focuses on Israel and neighboring countries in the ancient Near East, but the New Testament moves to locations within the Roman Empire. Often the beginning of each discrete story establishes the setting and characters. While we may be given some descriptive detail about a character in terms of their appearance or personality, mostly we get to know a character through their actions and speech. Often, we feel a closeness to a character as we journey with them through their challenges and resolutions.[8] We sometimes even imagine the characters being like us or looking like us, as did the illustrator of the illuminated manuscript in figure 7.1, which depicts the characters in the dress and style of medieval France. The characters of a story are involved in actions and events. The events of the story (or the plot) usually unfold due to a conflict or complication. The events included in the story are selective, mostly following a logical or chronological sequence. As J. Scott Duvall and J. Daniel Hays write, "Plot is the organizing structure that ties narrative together."[9] The events are not recalled at random but are selected due to their importance and arranged accordingly.[10] The plot moves a story from conflict to resolution. Yet occasionally this expectation is overthrown and

8. J. Scott Duvall and J. Daniel Hays, *Grasping God's Word: A Hands-On Approach to Reading, Interpreting, and Applying the Bible*, 4th ed. (Grand Rapids: Zondervan, 2020), 357.
9. Duvall and Hays, *Grasping God's Word*, 362.
10. Walter C. Kaiser Jr. and Moisés Silva, *Introduction to Biblical Hermeneutics: The Search for Meaning*, rev. ed. (Grand Rapids: Zondervan, 2007), 124.

no resolution is given, which may leave the reader feeling somewhat disappointed or frustrated.

At this point, it is helpful to clarify a common misconception. Many people associate "story" with fiction. While a story can be fictitiously created based on the imagination of an author, this is not always the case. At its heart, a story is the report of a sequence of events. The report of events may present historical actualities, such as a historical report. History mostly comes in narrative form. In contrast, some narratives may tell a moral tale that has no historical veracity but expresses a valuable principle. For example, parables are usually fictitious, yet they provide insight into the world. In these two cases, both reports of events (history *and* parable) may present "truth," but only one is based on historical events. However, while there are similarities in the genre of story regardless of whether the events are historically verifiable or not, we do not read all stories the same way, as we will explore below. Yet the genre of narrative is used throughout the Bible. In fact, it is estimated that somewhere between one third and a half of the whole Bible is narrative in form.[11] So there must be something about this type of writing that is useful for communicating about faith in God!

Storytelling is an art. That is, there are certain techniques and devices the author can use to tell their story. This is true even in the retelling of historical events. The study of the literary techniques used in a story is called *narrative criticism*. Paying close attention to the *how* of the story helps us discern the *why* of the story. There are many narrative techniques used in the Bible, but we will focus on three key literary devices.

The first technique involves the point of view of the narrator. The events of a story are told or narrated from a perspective. Sometimes, the narrator is a known character in the story (such as Luke), but most often the narrator is an unknown third person. The narrator plays a vital role in the storytelling as they provide both the perspective and the information revealed within the story. For example, the narrator of 1 Samuel 8 provides vital background knowledge about Samuel and his sons to explain the rationale for the Israelites' demand for a king. That is, Samuel is old, and his sons do not follow in his ways (1 Sam. 8:1–3). The narrator usually does not make explicit statements or moral judgments about the situation in a story but allows the reader to discern how the events and characters should be interpreted in light of the information provided and other relevant teachings in Scripture. In this case, the reader is given God's perspective on Israel's demand for a king, such that we can understand this demand as a rejection of God (1 Sam. 8:7).

11. Kaiser and Silva, *Introduction to Biblical Hermeneutics*, 123.

A second technique commonly used in narratives is the inclusion of dialogue or speech. Speeches are often used in narratives to slow down the pace of the story and thereby emphasize a point being made. Consider the speech of Samuel in the story of Israel demanding a king (1 Sam. 8:11–18). Samuel's speech is quite lengthy and detailed because it makes an important point about the consequences of Israel's petulant demand for a human king. It is a turning point in the narrative, where the institution of the monarchy is discussed and established. As noted above, the repetition of the word "take" warns the Israelites of the reality of serving a human king. As Samuel speaks, the pace of the story slows. The people are comprehensively warned of the nature of the institution they are demanding. Yet the Israelites do not listen to Samuel's warning and are determined to have a king (8:19–20). The people's speech is also recorded, with a decisive "No!" (8:19). This exchange of dialogue between the elders and Samuel tells us much about each of the characters. Samuel is circumspect, while the people are rash.

A third common literary technique employed in narratives is the use of irony. This is when there is an unexpected twist to the story.[12] We expect one outcome, but an unforeseen shift produces a different result. Usually, an element of humor or sometimes sarcasm appears in the revealing. The book of Esther is filled with irony. One of the ironies is that the name of God is never mentioned in the book, yet God seems to be present everywhere (albeit never acknowledged) in the unexpected coincidences and sudden reversals that pervade the story. The expected outcome is for Esther's postexilic community to be victims of genocide, but through the extraordinary twists of the story, they are delivered. Similarly, an irony in the story of 1 Samuel 8 is that Samuel, who has witnessed the demise of Eli's lineage because Eli did not discipline his sons (1 Sam. 2–6), follows the same pattern. We would expect that Samuel would be different from Eli, but Samuel's sons also misuse their power, and so Samuel's lineage (like Eli's) is rejected (8:5). Samuel does not learn the lesson of his predecessor, as would be expected.

What all these features and literary techniques have in common is that they are used to craft a narrative that has the power to engage the reader and draw them into its story world. As noted in the previous chapter, narratives powerfully shape and mold us. The narratives in the Bible reveal God working out his purposes through history. They show God at work in the world and God's people living out their faith. The stories also shape us as we learn and hopefully absorb godly character and Christlike virtues. They provide examples for us to follow and from which we can learn. We can also learn what not to

12. Duvall and Hays, *Grasping God's Word*, 296.

do through the experiences of others, such as Eli and Samuel, who do not address their childrens' character issues, with the result that power is abused and the community is corrupted. Yet not all stories function in the same way.

Types of Stories

While there are some common features of narratives, there are also specific types of stories (or subgenres) used in the Bible. These include history, Gospel, parable, and myth.

History

History is generally written in the form of a narrative, as it presents a sequence of connected events that move forward in time.[13] We sometimes think of history as the quest to objectively uncover what really happened in the past. While much history can and does present an accurate and factual reporting of events, we do recognize that it is usually told from a particular perspective. In the case of the Bible, the historical texts provide an accurate retelling of events from a theological perspective. The people and events recorded are selected by the biblical authors for the purpose of teaching a theological message. The historical settings and events provided in the different historical books do refer to events and persons based on various written, oral, and material sources; however, these narratives are not trying to present a modern, objective account of events but intend to inspire faith and trust in God. For this reason, some scholars refer to the historical narratives of the Old Testament as "theological history"[14] or "prophetic history writing."[15] This becomes clear when we consider the types of events and information the historical writings of the Bible record. Consider the retelling of the events in 1 Samuel 8. The account is grounded in real events and people, but it is also clearly providing God's perspective on those events. It records both Samuel's dialogue with God and God's instructions to give Israel a king according to their demands (1 Sam. 8:21–22). In this way, faith and history are closely connected.[16] This link between faith and history is seen even more in the New Testament. We

13. Edward W. Klink III and Darian R. Lockett, *Understanding Biblical Theology: A Comparison of Theory and Practice* (Grand Rapids: Zondervan, 2012), 16.

14. Duvall and Hays, *Grasping God's Word*, 356–57.

15. Kaiser and Silva, *Introduction to Biblical Hermeneutics*, 137.

16. For further discussion of the historical books of the Old Testament, see the classic text by Iain Provan, V. Philips Long, and Tremper Longman III, *A Biblical History of Israel*, 2nd ed. (Louisville: Westminster John Knox, 2015).

will discuss the subgenre of the Gospels (see below), but it suffices to note here that the historical veracity of the life, death, and resurrection of Jesus Christ is crucial to the gospel message.[17] As Paul notes in 1 Corinthians 15:14, "If Christ has not been raised, our preaching is useless and so is your faith." In fact, the use of eyewitness accounts about Jesus Christ is at the heart of the Gospel writings.

Gospel

The subgenre of Gospel is an eyewitness, biographical account of Jesus Christ. The New Testament begins with the four canonical books of Matthew, Mark, Luke, and John. They were written in narrative form to share the gospel (the "good news") of the life, death, and resurrection of Jesus. However, they are different from modern biographies in that they do not provide detailed material on the whole life of Jesus but rather highly selective material to underscore key events and teachings for theological purposes.[18] Richard Bauckham describes the Gospels as "testimony," as they provide trusted historical and theological insight into the reality of the events they record.[19] Similarly, Craig Keener likens the subgenre of Gospel to ancient biographies.[20] Each Gospel writer had a slightly different purpose and audience (sometimes referred to as the implied reader), so he arranged the material differently according to his purpose. So the Gospels are the same but different. Yet because the first three Gospel accounts are so similar in shape and perspective, they are often referred to as the Synoptic Gospels. Most scholars think that Mark was the first Gospel written and that Luke and Matthew borrow some of Mark's material (along with other sources) for their own purposes.

Parable

Parables do not retell historical events but are more like moral tales. We find parables embedded in the Gospels and other narratives of the Bible. Parables are short stories in which some of the elements of the story represent a greater meaning. Consider Jesus's parable of the lost son in Luke 15:11–32. The father in the story represents God, who runs to forgive and embrace his lost son (who

17. Kaiser and Silva, *Introduction to Biblical Hermeneutics*, 110.
18. Duvall and Hays, *Grasping God's Word*, 281.
19. Richard Bauckham, *Jesus and the Eyewitnesses: The Gospels as Eyewitness Testimony*, 2nd ed. (Grand Rapids: Eerdmans, 2017), 5.
20. Craig S. Keener, *Christobiography: Memory, History, and the Reliability of the Gospels* (Grand Rapids: Eerdmans, 2019), 43.

represents the sinners and tax collectors of Jesus's audience, as well as us) even after the son has rebelled. The father restores the son (sinners) back into the family, despite the objection of the older brother (the self-righteous religious leaders challenging Jesus).

Myth

The final subgenre we will explore is "myth." Like a parable, the purpose of a myth is not to retell historical events, though myths often contain historical material.[21] Instead, its purpose is to provide a model story of origins. That is in fact the technical meaning of "myth." The term does not refer to a fairy tale but rather to a story of beginnings. Myths are often grand and cosmic in scale. They involve supernatural events or characters that participate directly in human history. Genesis 1–11 contains many myths or stories of origins that were formative for the identity of Israel and later for the church. Myths also sometimes serve as a polemic or a defense against competing stories of origins told by other communities of the ancient Near East. For example, the epic of Enuma Elish is a myth told by the Babylonians about creation. In this origin story, the gods are capricious and create humans to be slaves. In comparison, the account of human origins in Genesis 1 describes God as supreme, gracious, and creating humans with dignity to mirror God's image. What a difference!

Because some of these subgenres are often embedded in a broader narrative, they should not be interpreted in isolation. Each embedded subgenre (say, a parable or a myth) must be interpreted within the contexts of the book at hand as well as the grand narrative of the Bible (outlined in the previous chapter). For example, the parable of the lost son makes sense when read in light of the overall story of Jesus's conflict with the religious leaders. The parable, then, can be seen as a response to the objection of the Pharisees that Jesus associates with tax collectors and sinners (Luke 15:1–2). Similarly, the demand of the Israelites for a king makes the most sense when read in light of the broader narrative of 1–2 Samuel and the failure of the royal institution as demonstrated in the books of 1–2 Kings.

So now that we have explored some of the features of the genre of narrative and considered some of its key subgenres, let's discuss how to interpret stories for our context today.

---

21. William W. Klein, Craig L. Blomberg, and Robert L. Hubbard Jr., *Introduction to Biblical Interpretation*, 3rd ed. (Grand Rapids: Zondervan, 2017), 427. Klein and company refer to this genre as "cosmic epic."

WHAT DO I DO NOW?

It is imperative when applying stories to our own situation today that we remember that they were written for a different community in a time and place very foreign to ours. That may seem ridiculously obvious, but it can easily be forgotten in our enthusiasm to make the Bible relevant to our world. As John Goldingay notes, the meanings of the biblical stories are not timeless but are time related. That is, the meaning of a story is connected to its historical and cultural contexts. But the timeliness of the stories for their own time is also what makes the biblical stories seem timeless in the sense of speaking to our community today.[22] Are you confused? Let me explain using three key questions.

The first question we can ask of a story, such as 1 Samuel 8, is, What did it mean for the people in its original historical context?[23] To answer this question, we must consider the history and culture of the people for whom the story was written—that is, its timeliness. Sometimes, identifying the precise time and place of the author or audience is difficult, so we may need to estimate. For example, the story of 1 Samuel 8 describes a situation at the start of the Israelite monarchy. However, it is part of the wider narrative of 1–2 Samuel. Most scholars think that the books of 1–2 Samuel were written in their final form around the time of the exile, using various historical sources and annals from the monarchic period. As noted above, 1–2 Samuel explains why the monarchy failed and the community ended in exile. So while the exact date of 1 Samuel 8's composition might be difficult to determine, we can generalize that this chapter was written in its final form for the Old Testament community around the time of the exile. However, we must also consider why the author used the specific genre they selected and utilized the literary techniques that we can identify in the passage. What was the message they were trying to communicate to the original community?

The second question we ask concerns our position as Christian readers of Scripture. Galatians 4:4 reminds us, "But when the set time had fully come, God sent his Son, born of a woman, born under the law." At the center of God's story is the coming of Jesus Christ. Christian readers, then, consider the Christ event as the key to understanding Old Testament texts, such as

22. John Goldingay, "Hearing God Speak from the First Testament," in *The Voice of God in the Text of Scripture: Explorations in Constructive Dogmatics*, ed. Oliver D. Crisp and Fred Sanders (Grand Rapids: Zondervan, 2016), 64.

23. For further discussion of the three questions outlined in this chapter, see Jacqueline N. Grey, *Them, Us, and Me: How the Old Testament Speaks to People Today* (Eugene, OR: Wipf & Stock, 2008).

1 Samuel 8. Therefore, it is important for us to consider the significance of a passage in the light of Jesus Christ and to read the text christologically. It may be that an Old Testament passage, such as 1 Samuel 8, foreshadows the coming of the Messiah, when the Son of God would be revealed as King. This might not reflect the intention of the human author, but as Christian readers, we look back and see this significance of Christ for us now. Or it may be that a passage from the Old Testament is simply part of the broader narrative that leads to the coming of Jesus Christ. We do not have to force a correspondence between a passage and Christ; quite often, there is an organic connection or analogy to Christ. Of course, in the case of the New Testament, there are direct statements about Jesus. The stories and texts we read may also have some implications for us today as followers of Christ to consider. So it is worth asking this second question: What does the passage mean for the Christian community as we consider "Christ-now"? What message does the text communicate about Christ, and how might it apply to the Christian community?

Third, the experiences described in the Bible are often typical of humanity, despite their time-related nature, and this makes them timeless. We might consider what we can we learn from these experiences. Throughout history, God has used stories and texts from the Bible to speak to people in their own situations. We do not want to miss an opportunity for God to speak to us through a passage of Scripture. The Holy Spirit may reveal to us a personal application or challenge us to change an attitude. So the third question we should ask when reading a passage of the Bible is, What does this passage mean to me in the here-now as a Christian reader? That is, what is the significance of this text for the here-now? We will explore in later chapters the importance of daily reading and personal application. But for now, we can ask this question in the hope and expectation that God will speak today through Scripture, just as God has spoken to believers in the past.

PRAYER

As we read the Scriptures, may they inspire in us faith and trust in you, our God.

We ask for you to speak to us through these stories from the faith community.

May the stories from your Word powerfully mold and shape us to live out our faith in love and obedience to you.

Amen.

TOPICS FOR REVIEW

1. What is your favorite story from the Bible? What appeals to you about this story?
2. Read 1 Samuel 8. How might this story point to Christ?
3. What do you think you can apply from 1 Samuel 8 to your own life? In what way(s) might this passage be applicable to your own life?

8

THE LAW AND THE SPIRIT

In this chapter, you should expect to learn the following:

- ▶ Covenants as the foundation for God's relationship with Israel
- ▶ The purpose of the Old Testament law
- ▶ The connection between the law and the Spirit in the New Testament
- ▶ How to interpret Old Testament law for our context today

When Moses approached the camp and saw the calf and the dancing, his anger burned and he threw the tablets out of his hands, breaking them to pieces at the foot of the mountain.

—Exod. 32:19

Following their deliverance from Egypt, the book of Exodus depicts the Israelites traveling into the wilderness to sojourn at the mountain of Sinai (Exod. 19). God prepares the nation to make a covenant with them. On the third day, the people wait at the foot of the mountain while Moses climbs to the mountaintop, meeting with God on their behalf. The presence of God is depicted through the symbols of fire, smoke, and a thick cloud. New Testament readers should note these same symbols present on the day of Pentecost in Acts 2. But here at Mount Sinai, Moses is given the law (the

The Yorck Project / Wikimedia Commons / Public Domain

Figure 8.1. *Moses Breaking the Tablets of the Law,* by Rembrandt van Rijn

Ten Commandments), inscribed on stone tablets. However, because Moses is delayed on top of Mount Sinai for forty days and nights, the people become restless (Exod. 32). The people convince Moses's brother Aaron to make a golden calf as an idol for them to worship. Idolatry (the worship of anything or anyone other than God) would be a continual snare for the Israelites throughout their history. So later, when Moses comes down the mountain and sees the people worshiping these idols, he is furious. He smashes the stone tablets containing the law and confronts the people with their sin. The painting by Rembrandt in figure 8.1 portrays Moses, shining with the glory of God, holding his arms raised, ready to throw down the tablets. Many of the people who have participated in the idolatry are judged harshly for this rejection of their newly made covenant (which is ratified in Exod. 24). It is a difficult lesson for the people to learn, that the sin of idolatry results in judgment. Yet God shows his grace by renewing the covenant with the people and making new tablets inscribed with a copy of the law (Exod. 34).

The connection between law and grace is vital, even in the Old Testament. The law is given to outline how the people should live in relation to God and each other. The sacrificial system, which is part of the law of the Old Testament, provides a way for the Israelites to be made right with God should they violate the covenant, as they do in the golden calf incident. The sacrificial system includes the rituals required to restore relationship with God. However, it is important to note that while the sacrificial system allows this possibility of restoration, it is only a mechanism to provide the right conditions for reconciliation to occur. As David Moffitt writes, "Reconciliation rests with God, not with completing the right rituals."[1] It is God who saves us, by his grace—even those in the Old Testament; it is not because we have performed the right actions or prayed the correct prayers. Salvation and reconciliation are a gift from God. At its heart, the Old Testament law is about ensuring right relationship between Israel and their covenant God. In this chapter, we will explore God's covenant with Israel, which is the basis for the giving of the law. We will explore the genre, content, and purpose of the Old Testament law before considering its relevancy for New Testament believers today.

God's Covenant with Israel

The Hebrew term *torah*, styled "Torah" when used as the name of the first five books of the Old Testament, is mostly translated as "law." However, *torah* can also mean "guide" or "instruction." This is helpful because when we look closely at the Pentateuch, it is presented as an overall narrative in which the covenant relationship between God and Israel is described. Even the sections that contain many detailed laws and instructions are presented in a broader narrative framework. This perhaps gives us a new perspective on what the Torah is primarily about—it is God's guidance, which includes direction through both law and story format. These narratives outline the formative events and provide the foundational guidance for the Old Testament covenant community.

Part of the covenant relationship between God and Israel involves covenantal expectations or stipulations. The word "covenant" refers to a formalized, legally binding agreement between two parties. It is similar to a marriage covenant today, in which two parties pledge their commitment to one another in a legally binding ceremony. A relationship of some sort already exists between the two marriage partners, but a covenant makes the relationship both legal and binding. A marriage covenant is usually formalized with a wedding ceremony, in which the commitment of the couple is publicly expressed. Dur-

---

1. David M. Moffitt, *Rethinking the Atonement: New Perspectives on Jesus's Death, Resurrection, and Ascension* (Grand Rapids: Baker Academic, 2022), 2.

ing the wedding ceremony, the two parties outline their expectations and pledge their commitment to those expectations, such as remaining faithful and loyal to one another. For this reason, the narrative of the Torah includes significant legal commands and instructions; these represent the stipulations of the two unequal parties in the formalization of their covenant.

There were numerous types of covenants practiced in the ancient Near East. However, perhaps the most well-known was the vassal-suzerain covenant. This was a political treaty made when a greater king conquered a lesser king. The stronger, victorious king was known as the "suzerain," and the defeated king as the "vassal." Because the suzerain was gracious and did not destroy the defeated king (that is, the suzerain saved the vassal), the relationship was not equal. The vassal was to serve and obey the suzerain. The vassal was to be loyal to the suzerain and to follow the laws set by the greater king. While God's covenant with Israel is unique, the study of ancient political treaties gives us insight into the concept of covenant in the Bible.

At the heart of the Old Testament (noting that "testament" is another word for "covenant") is God's selection of Israel, the formalization of their relationship with a covenant, and the ongoing maintenance of that relationship. There are several covenants in the Old Testament between God and individuals or groups, including God's covenants with Abraham (marked by circumcision), the exodus community (known as the Mosaic covenant), and David (known as the Davidic covenant). Each of these covenants builds on or assumes the previous one. However, the covenant that is mostly emphasized in the Old Testament is the Mosaic covenant. At the exodus, God chooses (or elects) Israel. God saves them by rescuing them from Egypt. In this sense, God is like the suzerain of the ancient covenant practices (Exod. 19:3–6). God acts out of grace and love for Israel (Deut. 7:6–8).

As was common in the ancient Near East, a vassal-suzerain covenant (or treaty) was formalized in a ritual ceremony. This event usually followed a customary structure. The book of Deuteronomy adopts the structure of the vassal-suzerain treaty. The name "Deuteronomy" can be translated as "repeated law." The first law of the Mosaic covenant is given and ratified at Sinai following Israel's rescue from Egypt (particularly in Exod. 19–24). Deuteronomy is like a reaffirmation of the covenant, given approximately forty years later to prepare the people to enter the promised land (perhaps like a wedding renewal ceremony). The first step in the vassal-suzerain treaty was to formally recognize the two parties (as in Deut. 1:1–5). The suzerain would then outline the history of his relationship with the vassal, usually emphasizing his kindness in preserving them (as in 1:6–3:29). This would lead to the giving of the law (as in 4:1–26:19; see also Exod. 20:2–17). Essentially, the law consisted of a list of requirements for the vassal to obey. However, in the Mosaic covenant, the law not only outlines the expectations for Israel's community life but reflects the nature and values of God, the covenant maker. It is crucial to remind ourselves that the relationship came before the law. Covenant was foremost a *relationship* before a set of rules; the laws were intended to maintain the relationship. Yet the law of the covenant was to be obeyed, and so there were consequences if it was violated. There were blessings for being obedient and curses for disobeying (Deut. 28). Finally, like many legal documents, the treaty was confirmed in the presence of witnesses (as in 30:19–20), and provision was made for its safekeeping and regular review to remind the parties of their agreement (see 31:9–13). So let us take a closer look at the purpose of the Old Testament law.

The Purpose of the Old Testament Law

The foundation for the Mosaic covenant is provided in Exodus 19–20. God calls the Israelites his "treasured possession" and "a kingdom of priests and a holy nation" (19:5–6; see also 1 Pet. 2:9). This gives us insight into the purpose of the Old Testament law. First, as a *holy nation*, the Israelites are to reflect God, their suzerain. The essential characteristic of God is holiness. In Isaiah 6:3, heavenly beings cry out, "Holy, holy, holy is the LORD Almighty." The character and holiness of God pervades the law. The law is given so that the people of God can reflect this holiness in their everyday lives and worship. The law concretely expresses how they are to relate to one another. By obeying the instructions and stipulations of the law, they are to be holy as God is holy (Lev. 19:2). Yet like most legal requirements, the law is not optional; obedience is required. Therefore, law as a genre tends to use imperatives and direct orders, such as "Remember the Sabbath day by keeping it holy" (Exod. 20:8). Obedience is not optional. Sometimes, the laws are presented inversely as a prohibition or negative command—for example, "You shall not murder" (Exod. 20:13).

Second, as a *treasured possession* or beloved people, the Israelites are to treat one another as beloved.[2] Exodus 20:2–17 outlines the Decalogue (what Christians call the Ten Commandments), which is sometimes referred to as moral law (see also Deut. 5:6–21). Respect, dignity, justice, and care for others are guiding principles evident in the Ten Commandments. These ethical principles are then worked out in specific contexts through the civil law (or case

2. Carmen Joy Imes, *Bearing God's Name: Why Sinai Still Matters* (Downers Grove, IL: IVP Academic, 2019), 31.

law). The civil law refers to laws pertaining to social and civic life: laws about food, housing, clothing, interpersonal conflict, and cooperation. These laws are often presented in the form of casuistic law; that is, they present a condition ("if . . .") and then a penalty for infringement ("then . . ."). [3] For example, case laws such as Exodus 21:28–30 apply the principle of protecting human life (20:13). That is, if a bull accidentally gores a person to death, then it is to be destroyed so it will not kill again. But if a bull is known to be dangerous and the owners, being warned, have not kept it contained—and if it gores a person to death—then the owners are responsible and are to be punished as guilty of murder. [4] The civil law, then, is specific to the agricultural society of ancient Israel, not universal in application. So the civil law is the conditional application of an unconditional law. In this way, the law emphasizes the flourishing of all people in the community, working for the common good.

Another type of law found in the Old Testament is ceremonial law. This kind of law is also an outworking of the Ten Commandments; Israel is to have no other God but Yahweh (Exod. 20:3). The ceremonial laws are those pertaining to Israel's worship: the sacrificial system, the priests, and the place of worship. Some examples of ceremonial laws include Leviticus 1–7 (instructions about the sacrifices and offerings) and Leviticus 21 (instructions about priestly purity). [5] These laws are intended to help Israel worship in a way that reflects the holiness of God. As noted above, the sacrificial laws also provide the mechanisms and right conditions for the broken community to restore their relationship with God. In addition to the worship activities prescribed by the law, there are also various festivals and annual feasts the people are to observe. Arguably, the most important feast in the Israelite/Jewish calendar is the Passover (Exod. 12). This is an annual festival that celebrates Israel's deliverance from Egypt and retells this historic event to each new generation.

Finally, as a *kingdom of priests*, the Israelites are to be a light to the nations. By following the instructions of the Mosaic covenant, the Israelites are to leave behind the old way of life in Egypt and enter a new way of living and thinking. They are not to replace Pharaoh's oppressive system of slavery and greed with another "pharaoh" from their own kin. Instead, their covenant establishes a new life of freedom and a new way of operating based on the Mosaic law. In fact, the nations are meant to marvel when they behold the law. Deuteronomy 4:6 says, "Observe [the Lord's decrees and laws] carefully,

---

3. William W. Klein, Craig L. Blomberg, and Robert L. Hubbard Jr., *Introduction to Biblical Interpretation*, 3rd ed. (Grand Rapids: Zondervan, 2017), 434.

4. Tremper Longman III, *Making Sense of the Old Testament: Three Crucial Questions* (Grand Rapids: Baker, 1998), 116.

5. Klein, Blomberg, and Hubbard, *Introduction to Biblical Interpretation*, 442.

for this will show your wisdom and understanding to the nations, who will hear about all these decrees and say, 'Surely this great nation is a wise and understanding people.'" So the Mosaic law also has a missional purpose, provided the people obey it. Such a condition ultimately becomes a problem for Israel. They are unwilling to keep the law, and they willfully reject their covenant with God. The Israelites fail to keep the covenant time and again. Consistently, they fall into idolatry and adopt the prohibited practices of neighboring nations. So the leaders and power holders often prefer to emulate Pharaoh's oppressive rulership for their selfish gain, rather than to trust in God and model a way of life that upholds the common good.[6] While the prophets try to persuade the people to return to God, the people's persistent rejection ultimately results in the tragedy and curse of exile. While it is easy to point the finger at the Israelites and think we would do better, their example shows us that we mere humans, as a whole, continue to willfully follow our own path in resistance to God. The law demonstrates that all sinful humans are law breakers and need a Savior.

The apostle Paul reminds us that while the law is helpful, it is limited. It is helpful as it identifies sin but limited because it cannot save us from the slavery of sin (Rom. 7). Even the Old Testament prophets recognize the limitation of the law. The law does not transform people's hearts. Both Jeremiah and Ezekiel, writing around the time of the exile, look forward to a new covenant. This covenant, they say, will not be written on tablets of stone, like the ones Moses smashed in Exodus 32. Instead, this new covenant will be written on human hearts. Jeremiah points to a time when, God promises, "I will put my law in their minds and write it on their hearts. I will be their God, and they will be my people" (Jer. 31:33). Similarly, God through Ezekiel foretells what he will do in that day: "I will give you a new heart and put a new spirit in you; I will remove from you your heart of stone and give you a heart of flesh. And I will put my Spirit in you and move you to follow my decrees and be careful to keep my laws" (Ezek. 36:26–27). That is, the Israelites are proof that sinful humanity cannot keep covenant. The exile marks the breaking of the covenant, like separation marks the end of a broken marriage. But God is faithful to his people. Exile is not the end. Instead of divorce, there is restoration of relationship. God promises a new covenant that will not be about keeping the external requirements of the law but will relate to an internal reality marked by heartfelt obedience.

6. Jacqueline N. Grey and Edward J. Helmore, "Do What Is Right and Good: The Theological Foundations for the Common Good in the Old Testament Prophets," in *The Politics of the Spirit: Pentecostal Reflections on Public Responsibility and the Common Good*, ed. Daniela C. Augustine and Chris E. W. Green (Lanham, MD: Seymour, 2022), 93.

Jesus Christ Has Fulfilled the Old Testament Law

Galatians 3:13 says, "Christ redeemed us from the curse of the law by becoming a curse for us." The New Testament is clear that Jesus not only has fulfilled the law (Matt. 5:17) but is the culmination of the law (Rom. 10:4). Scripture tells us that Christ fully embraced our sinful human condition, yet he himself was without sin (Heb. 2:17; 4:15). Jesus Christ has established a new covenant (or testament) and reconciled us to God through his death on the cross and his resurrection from the dead. We celebrate and remember Christ's new covenant when we participate in the Lord's Table. Luke tells us that the Last Supper of Jesus, before he went to the cross, was held during the feast of Passover. Jesus takes the bread and breaks it, saying, "This is my body given for you" (Luke 22:19). He also takes the cup of wine, saying, "This cup is the new covenant in my blood, which is poured out for you" (22:20). In doing this, Jesus inaugurates the new covenant. Christ, the Son of God, came to rescue humanity in a new exodus. If the exodus event, celebrated at Passover, gave liberation and redemption to a nation group, then the Christ event gives liberation and redemption to the whole world.

Therefore, because Christ gave himself as a sin offering, he met the requirements of the law for us. Believers in Christ are now freed from the law and sealed with the Spirit of Christ living in us (Rom. 8). We are no longer slaves, but through the Spirit we have been adopted into God's family and are now children of God. Christians are no longer required to keep the law in order to be made right with God. Christ completed the ceremonial law (that is, the sacrificial system) at his death and resurrection—once and for all (Heb. 10:1–18).[7] Additionally, the civil laws, such as the dietary requirements, have also been made void as Christ has declared all foods clean (Mark 7:19; Acts 10). Because this new covenant is no longer based on a geopolitical location but now includes believers throughout the world, the civil law no longer applies.

The Law and the Spirit

Yet while Christ has made clear that he came to fulfill the law, he has not abolished the law altogether (Matt. 5:17). That is, the moral law, including the Ten Commandments, is still upheld by Jesus and the writers of the New Testament (5:21–48). In fact, Christ intensifies the commandments (such as the law prohibiting murder) by challenging our motivations, seeing it as a matter of the heart as well as the hand. We might not murder our brother

---

7. Klein, Blomberg, and Hubbard, *Introduction to Biblical Interpretation*, 445.

or sister, but if we harbor anger and resentment in our hearts toward them, then we have sinned, even if we have not physically touched them (5:21–26). Instead, we are to be people of reconciliation and love. Therefore, the Ten Commandments are valued not as a means for salvation but as a means of helping us understand more fully the principles by which we can demonstrate love toward God and neighbor. So we are not saved by keeping the law, but the laws are still "useful for teaching, rebuking, correcting and training in righteousness" (2 Tim. 3:16). As Gordon Fee notes, there is no need for someone who is living by the Spirit to be told, "Do not murder," because to do so would be inconsistent with their lifestyle of love. When the life and fruit of the Spirit are evident among us, the law is not needed, or in this sense, it is irrelevant, because it is already etched on our hearts so that we obey.[8]

Yet while we are no longer required to keep the law to be made right with God, we would be wise to heed the ethical principles the moral law upholds, particularly in light of the teaching of Jesus Christ, such as the Beatitudes (Matt. 5:3–12; Luke 6:20–23). Yet our modern context is often very different from Bible times. Therefore, the way we apply and live out the principles of the law has changed. The application of the Ten Commandments has changed for Christians. We now live under the "law" of love in the New Testament (that is, the new covenant in Christ). Believers are no longer defined as belonging to a distinct nation or kingdom. Our identity as the people of God is no longer based on ethnicity or living in a social-geographic location. We are the people of God scattered throughout the nations of the world. We are living in a different point in redemptive history than the original audiences of the Old Testament did. Therefore, the New Testament writers rightly emphasize our new life in Christ and the formation of godly character in our lives (2 Cor. 5:14–17).

As Jeremiah and Ezekiel have foretold, in our new covenant in Christ, God has given us the Holy Spirit to help us live faithfully. The Spirit of Christ is given to all believers as a permanent, abiding presence. This point is demonstrated by the early church, as told in the book of Acts. When the Holy Spirit is poured out on the day of Pentecost, the accompanying description includes, as at Sinai, the symbols of wind and fire (Acts 2:1–4)—signs of God's presence. Fifty days after Passover and the resurrection of Christ, the Spirit is poured out on the church to mark a new jubilee, as announced by Jesus during his ministry (Luke 4:18–19; cf. Lev. 25:8–17). The narrative of Acts 2 draws on connections between the account of Sinai, the giving of the law, and the giving of the Holy Spirit at Pentecost. At Pentecost, the missional purpose

8. Gordon D. Fee, *Paul, the Spirit, and the People of God* (Grand Rapids: Baker, 1996), 123.

of the law is given greater fulfillment as the New Testament community is empowered for witness, which also overflows in their holy love and practical treasuring of one another through costly acts of service (Acts 2:42–47).

WHAT DO I DO NOW?

One of the key roles of the Spirit of God is to sanctify us—that is, to make us pure and holy, like the God we serve. This is essentially what the law was trying to address. We are not saved because we are holy, but once we are saved, the Holy Spirit works in our lives to make us holy. First Peter 1:13–16 encourages us: "Therefore, with minds that are alert and fully sober, set your hope on the grace to be brought to you when Jesus Christ is revealed at his coming. As obedient children, do not conform to the evil desires you had when you lived in ignorance. But just as he who called you is holy, so be holy in all you do; for it is written: 'Be holy, because I am holy.'" Sanctification is a process and an important aspect of Spirit-filled living. It is a lifelong pursuit to become Christlike. Colossians 3:10 also reminds us that we have put on a new self, "which is being renewed in knowledge in the image of its Creator." This image is then described in Colossians 3:12–14: "Therefore, as God's chosen people, holy and dearly loved, clothe yourselves with compassion, kindness, humility, gentleness and patience. Bear with each other and forgive one another if any of you has a grievance against someone. Forgive as the Lord forgave you. And over all these virtues put on love, which binds them all together in perfect unity." Sometimes, we can think that Spirit-filled living is all about the demonstration of the gifts of the Holy Spirit (1 Cor. 12); however, such living is also about the demonstration of godly love (1 Cor. 13) and the cultivation of the fruit of the Spirit (Gal. 5:22–23). The Holy Spirit wants to not only empower us but also purify us.

Yet how do we live this out? For many years, I (Jacqui) lived in Turkey. Many new believers would ask me there, "What are the rules of being a Christian?" I had to explain that being a Christian is not about following a list of rules, as in other religions. Instead, we are to be guided by the Holy Spirit. Paul tells us to "walk by the Spirit" (Gal. 5:16), referring to our whole way of life.[9] This is harder than following a set of rules or guidelines. To walk in the Spirit is dynamic. Of course, Scripture provides some of the boundaries and ethics for our decision-making. However, the Spirit of love works in our

9. Fee, *Paul, the Spirit, and the People of God*, 107.

hearts and lives to guide us, so that we can know and do the will of God. The Spirit transforms us, so our hearts and minds are renewed to reflect the character of God. Therefore, we are to rely on the Holy Spirit to guide us in our relationships, life decisions, and vocations. We are to be situated in a community of faith that will help us and walk with us along this journey. The Spirit-filled life is a Spirit-led life.

PRAYER

O Lord God, we lift our voices in praise.
  May your will be done in our lives today.
  Thank you, Holy Spirit, for guiding us into truth and freedom, by the grace of Jesus Christ. May we be faithful in our witness as an alternative community in the world for the sake of the world.
  Amen.

TOPICS FOR REVIEW

1. Consider the law from Leviticus 19:9–10: "When you reap the harvest of your land, do not reap to the very edges of your field or gather the gleanings of your harvest. Do not go over your vineyard a second time or pick up the grapes that have fallen. Leave them for the poor and the foreigner. I am the LORD your God." How should we read and interpret this passage today?

2. In what ways can we "improvise" (see chaps. 6 and 13) the law of the Old Testament?

3. Have you ever experienced the Holy Spirit guiding you in your decision-making or when contemplating a moral issue? If so, describe.

9

POETRY AND EMOTION

In this chapter, you should expect to learn the following:

► The importance and value of poetry
► Key literary devices used in biblical poetry
► Different types of poetic texts found in the Bible
► How to apply biblical poetry to our context today

> My God, my God, why have you forsaken me?
>
> —Ps. 22:1

Psalm 22 begins with a cry of raw emotion. It is a lament of suffering and despair. We do not know the exact circumstance of the poet, yet it is clearly a situation of deep pain, anguish, and loneliness. This psalm is traditionally connected to David, yet it presents emotion and experience common to humanity. David complains that God (who, we can infer, is personally known to him because he is "my God") is silent and unresponsive. He feels abandoned by God. Yet most notably, it is God to whom David turns in his distress. As the psalm continues, the poet is rejected and verbally mocked by opponents within his community (22:7). David complains that not only

Figure 9.1. *Christ on the Cross* (detail), from the Isenheim
Altarpiece of Matthias Grünewald

is God silent (22:2–5) but God has also failed to act on his behalf (22:6–11),
exposing him to ridicule by opponents.[1]

To express the emotions of this situation, the poet uses various images to
capture his feeling and mood. Imagery uses word pictures to powerfully express a situation or idea through comparison and analogy. For example, David
says, "But I am a worm" (22:6). That is, he feels reduced to an insignificant,
dirt-eating creature. In comparison, his opponents are described as bulls of
Bashan surrounding him, and their verbal bullying (pun intended) is likened
to the mouths of ravenous lions (22:12–13). Unlike the worm, these creatures are fearsome and powerful. This psalm also reminds us how emotional
distress and trauma can affect our material body, manifesting themselves
in physical symptoms and pain (22:14–17). The poet describes how all his
bones are out of joint (22:14)—pain and anguish are felt in our bodies. We
are whole people, so our spiritual and emotional health impacts our physical
well-being, and vice versa. Through poetry, the Bible addresses us as whole
people.

However, the lament of Psalm 22 does not end in despair. There is a turning
point in verse 22, where the poet's prayer to God is answered. The poem shifts
from lament to praise. The artwork in figure 9.1 captures a moment of light
infiltrating darkness and shining hope onto a question mark. This conveys

1. Gerald H. Wilson, *Psalms*, NIV Application Commentary (Grand Rapids: Zondervan,
2002), 1:414.

that God has intervened, resulting in the poet's thanksgiving. The poet shares a testimony of praise among the congregation (22:22, 25). Confidence in God and in his own self is restored. The poet has moved from helplessness and pain at the beginning of the psalm to praise and worship of God at the end. The psalm models a response to suffering as it does not deny the problem. Instead, it looks to God for answers and waits for God's intervention. The poet invites all those facing times of suffering to share in this same journey from despair to faith.

The opening words of this psalm are also spoken by Jesus during his suffering on the cross (Matt. 27:46; Mark 15:34).[2] By crying out the first few words of the psalm, Jesus both experiences the psalm and identifies with people of faith throughout the ages who have used this psalm to verbalize their own pain and affliction (Heb. 5:7). Like the poet, Jesus is mocked and ridiculed by his opponents throughout his crucifixion. His hands and feet are pierced. While this piercing would probably have been metaphoric for the poet of Psalm 22, it is a reality for Jesus Christ (Ps. 22:16; Luke 24:39–40). Even the soldiers gamble for his clothes (Ps. 22:17–18; Matt. 27:27–37; Mark 15:16–24). As James Mays writes of Jesus, "He gives all his followers who are afflicted permission and encouragement to pray for help. He shows that faith includes holding the worst of life up to God."[3]

However, Psalm 22 also has greater meaning for us, the church, as we reflect on its theological significance as part of the grand narrative of Scripture. Jesus Christ, the Son of God, became a sin offering for us on the cross. The Father allowed the Son to die on the cross for our salvation. Yet while the Father abandoned the Son to his death, he did not abandon the Son relationally. The Son was vindicated by God and resurrected from the grave. As in Psalm 22:22, there is a reversal of situation in the Easter story as Christ is resurrected and glorified.[4]

Psalm 22 is also treasured by the church community as a comfort and hope during times of suffering. This psalm can still speak to each person today. It can lift our attention from the immediacy of personal despair and reorient our focus toward faith in God. It reminds us that faithful believers are not exempt from hardship and suffering. In fact, many Christians in our world today are persecuted due to their faith. Yet this psalm provides hope—not just for the present but also in the time to come. The repetition of the future helping verb "will" in 22:25–31 emphasizes that our hope in God's deliverance

---

2. Note that Mark uses an Aramaic translation of these words.

3. James L. Mays, *Psalms*, Interpretation (Louisville: Westminster John Knox, 1994), 106.

4. See Thomas H. McCall, *Forsaken: The Trinity and the Cross, and Why It Matters* (Downers Grove, IL: IVP Academic, 2012), chap. 1.

and universal rule is not just for now but for all of time.[5] Our present suffering is temporal. God's sovereign reign will be made known as all nations bow before the Lord and future generations proclaim his righteousness (22:27–31; cf. Phil. 2:9–10). It is to this future and purpose that Psalm 22 orients our hope.

In this chapter, we will explore the importance of poetry by considering how this type of writing appeals to our emotions and imaginations. Over one third of the Bible is written in poetic form. There are books that consist almost entirely of poetry (such as Psalms, Proverbs, and Job) and other books that include poetry in a significant way (such as the Prophets, including Isaiah and Jeremiah). You may notice that most of these examples are from the Old Testament. While there is more poetry in the Old Testament, there are a few instances in the New Testament as well, such as Mary's Magnificat (Luke 1:46–55) and various Christian songs quoted, like the "Christ hymn" of Philippians 2:6–11. However, because narrative texts sometimes use poetic language, the boundaries of genre can blur. Yet there are some common features that the genre of poetry shares, and we will explore them throughout this chapter.

Why Is There Poetry in the Bible?

We may think that poetry belongs to the generations of William Shakespeare (1564–1616) and Walt Whitman (1819–92) or, perhaps, that it is read only by literary elitists and therefore no longer relevant today. However, if we are attentive, we can identify various expressions of poetry used in our world every day. Consider the lyrics of your favorite song, the hypnotic beat of rap music, the catchy advertisement jingles that get stuck in your head, the kitschy greeting card. These are all popular forms of poetic communication. Yet we can sometimes find poetry difficult to read. Poetry often uses images and comparative language to make its point. If only it just said it straight! Actually, this sentiment relates to a debate raging since the days of Aristotle (384–322 BC): Is poetry just flowery language, or does it have a deeper purpose?

Poetic language has a distinct way of appealing to our emotions and creativity. Poetry artistically paints vivid pictures through words that capture our imagination and vision. It is allusive and suggestive rather than precise. Poets can tickle our ears with their wit and cut to our hearts with their candid truth. They can invite us into new realms of ingenious thinking. The beauty, mystery, and pathos of a poem can stir our own feelings and passions. Lee

5. Wilson, *Psalms*, 1:425.

Roy Martin argues that the function of poetry in the Bible, particularly the Psalms, "is to evoke (and provoke) the passions and to form the affections."[6] That is, the purpose of biblical poetry is not just to trigger emotions in us so that we feel happy or sad but to direct the passions and desires of our heart toward love for God and what God loves. We are not robots or even merely rationalistic beings. We are holistic people who love, desire, imagine, and hope. Poetry especially speaks to this part of us. This suggests that the Bible is not only a book of information but also a book of transformation. Poetry plays a special role in the process of transformation by stirring our passions.

Features of Biblical Poetry

A quick flip through the pages of the Bible might highlight the sections that are written in poetic form. Poems often appear visually different from narratives, which generally extend sentences and paragraphs from margin to margin. By contrast, poetry tends to be written with truncated lines that are usually presented in parallel and then arranged into stanzas.[7] A poem says a lot with very few words. This is a key feature of poetry; it uses an economy of language, often described as *terseness* or *conciseness*. The use of parallel lines—that is, two side-by-side lines that are connected by thought, called *parallelism*—is particularly prevalent in Hebrew poetry. Essentially, the second line repeats the idea of the first through intensification or contrast. Consider Psalm 22:2:

> My God, I cry out by day, but you do not answer,
>   by night, but I find no rest.

These two lines are in parallel. The first line addresses God directly, accusing God of not answering even as the poet daily cries out to him. The second line intensifies the thought. Not only does the poet feel that God does not answer, but the absence of a response also leads him to distress and exhaustion so that he cannot find peace or rest. We also see the parallel between day and night, emphasizing that the sense of abandonment by God is comprehensive. While the second line does not directly address God, the address is inferred through a poetic technique called *ellipsis*. This technique occurs when a line of poetry intentionally omits words that either are superfluous

6. Lee Roy Martin, *The Spirit of the Psalms: Rhetorical Analysis, Affectivity, and Pentecostal Spirituality* (Cleveland, TN: CPT, 2018), 44.
7. Walter C. Kaiser Jr. and Moisés Silva, *Introduction to Biblical Hermeneutics: The Search for Meaning*, rev. ed. (Grand Rapids: Zondervan, 2007), 142.

or can be inferred from the context. We can conclude from the context that the second line addresses God without repeating that address unnecessarily. Such a technique forces us to read carefully and to fill in the gaps.

Parallelism and ellipsis are two of many poetic devices used in biblical poetry. There are many other rhetorical and literary techniques used in poetry that often distinguish it from narrative. Other techniques include *wordplay* (the witty use of words), *hyperbole* (deliberate exaggeration),[8] and *acrostics* (an arrangement in which each line begins with a letter of the alphabet, running "from *a* to *z*"). One of the challenges for the modern reader is that many of these techniques are used in the Hebrew text and do not translate easily into English. Yet even through translation, we can still see the artistry of the poet and be moved by the pathos of their words. Because of these various techniques—catchy wordplays and mnemonic devices—poetry is often easy to remember. Consider how easy it is for us today to remember song lyrics or advertisement jingles. This is another reason the biblical writers used poetry—namely, that their words could be remembered and easily transmitted to others.

However, perhaps the most significant feature of poetry is the use of *imagery*. While figurative language can occur across most genres, including narrative, it is a special feature of poetry. As noted above, images are word pictures. They create a picture of something unknown by comparing it to something known. When the comparison is made explicit using "like" or "as," it is called a simile (such as, "I am poured out *like* water" in Ps. 22:14). When the comparison is implicit, it is called a metaphor (such as, "But I am a worm" in 22:6). For example, the strength and ferociousness of the poet's enemies in Psalm 22 are portrayed through metaphor using the images of bulls and lions (22:12–13). The adversaries are not literal animals, but they share certain features in common with bulls and lions. These animals are fearsome and cause the poet to tremble in terror. Through comparison, the poet expresses in a creative way the feeling of anxiety and helplessness when confronted by opponents.[9] By imagining the word picture, the reader experiences something of the feeling and pathos the poet is expressing. The comparison works for us readers because we know something about the known *vehicle* of the image (lions and bulls), which helps us understand the unknown *tenor* (the human opponents). The image (vehicle) reveals truths through comparison. However, it also conceals, as the image does not fully reveal all the characteristics of the tenor. For example, Psalm 22:3 describes

8. Kaiser and Silva, *Introduction to Biblical Hermeneutics*, 146.

9. Artur Weiser, *The Psalms: A Commentary*, trans. Herbert Hartwell, Old Testament Library (Philadelphia: Westminster, 1998), 286.

God as "enthroned" and "holy." That is, God is pictured like a human king (enthroned), yet God transcends the human realm to be set apart in his perfection (holy). We can understand the unknown (God) by comparing him to a human king, which was a familiar and established figure in the ancient world.

The biblical poets of ancient times used images and metaphors familiar to the life of their audience, but unfortunately, some of these figures of speech may not be as familiar to us. Part of our task in interpretation is to seek to understand what an image meant in the original culture. To liken God to a king is to highlight God's sovereignty, power, and majesty for most of us. However, we might compare God to a king in a modern context, which is usually a person of limited power in a constitutional monarchy, unlike God. There are also other cultural limitations to imagery. While some positive characteristics of God are revealed through the image of a king, there might be some characteristics of an ancient king that do not apply to God, such as being power hungry or warmongering. So imagery both reveals and conceals. In a sense, this ambiguity both leads us to examine the imagery carefully and protects the mystery of God from the mundane.

Consider how we talk about God. Much of the Bible's talk about God uses imagery. This suggests that poetic language is not merely decorative speech or flowery description. Instead, poetry is not optional but essential for God talk. Imagery is vital for us as we seek to understand and transform our thinking about God. As Carolyn Sharp writes, "Metaphors are not mere stylistic devices. Our imaginations are shaped by metaphor in profound ways. Metaphors teach us how to think about the world and ourselves: they are powerful signals about values and concepts by means of which cultural systems defend certain understandings of truth, power, and relationship."[10] While God is pictured in Psalm 22 as a king, God is also pictured elsewhere in the Bible as a father (Ps. 103:13), mother (Isa. 49:15), rock (Ps. 18:2), potter (Isa. 64:8), and shepherd (Ps. 23:1). There are many word pictures for God, because there is no single image or metaphor that can capture the fullness of God's character and mystery. As God himself says in Isaiah 40:25, "'To whom will you compare me? Or who is my equal?' says the Holy One." This text highlights the paradox that while God cannot ultimately be compared to anyone or anything, we must compare God to figures and objects we know in order to understand him. Yet in doing so, we may find that these images and metaphors for God transform our understanding of him as they reveal the many facets of his

---

10. Carolyn J. Sharp, *Old Testament Prophets for Today* (Louisville: Westminster John Knox, 2009), 7.

character, such as his maternal love or his compassion for the poor. These images can penetrate our hearts and stir up new possibilities in our thinking.

Types of Poetic Texts in the Bible

While "poetry" refers to an overall genre, there are numerous types or subgenres of poetry that serve different purposes in Scripture. The subgenres summarized in this section are psalms, Wisdom literature, proverbs, and love poetry.

Psalms

The psalms of the Bible, in essence, are prayers and songs to or about God in poetic form. Unlike the messages of the prophets, who communicate a word *from* God to the people, the book of Psalms generally flows in the other direction. Psalms are Israel's (and our) communication *to* God. Walter Brueggemann offers a helpful framework for understanding psalms. He categorizes them as psalms of orientation, disorientation, and reorientation. Psalms of *orientation* are characterized by confidence, contentment, and a lack of tension. Life is good, and everything is in order. This type of psalm includes Psalms 23, 127, 128, and 131. However, life is not always easy and calm. Sometimes, we encounter challenges and problems. It is in these moments that we cry out to God (as in Ps. 22). Psalms reflecting this kind of circumstance are characterized by *disorientation*. They often include lament (personal or communal) and petition to God to change the dire situation at hand. Although they often complain or lament the circumstance, there is generally a movement within the psalm from grief to hope. Psalms of disorientation include Psalms 39, 42, 56, 74, and 109. Finally, when the challenge is resolved, we give thanks to God. Psalms of *reorientation* are characterized by thanksgiving (including Pss. 138, 146, and 150). They are different from psalms of orientation in that they are temporal and immediate—giving immediate thanks for God's deliverance or answer to prayer.

Wisdom Writings

There are three primary books of the Old Testament identified as wisdom writings: Proverbs, Ecclesiastes, and Job. In addition, some psalms are classified as wisdom texts (such as Pss. 1 and 37), and the Roman Catholic tradition includes the apocryphal books of Ecclesiasticus (Sirach) and the Wisdom of Solomon among the Wisdom literature as well. These types of writings are somewhat diverse but have in common their interest in wisdom. Wisdom is generally understood as applied knowledge. That is, it requires us not only to observe and understand the world in which we live but to apply our insights practically to the real world. Wisdom includes observations about creation and how the world works, encompassing both the natural and the social worlds in which we exist. The goal is *shalom*: a peaceful life in which we live in harmony and in generosity with others.

The first nine chapters of the book of Proverbs present a series of poetic speeches (or instructions) by Wisdom, a personification of the concept as a woman. She is contrasted with another woman, Folly. Woman Wisdom invites us to learn from her to ensure a flourishing, ordered life based on the fear of the Lord (Prov. 9:10). However, the expected order of the world sometimes fails. We see this particularly in the dramatic book of Job. The character of Job unexpectedly experiences great suffering. The book presents a poetic debate (sometimes called a disputation speech)[11] between Job and his friends, who consider Job's suffering to be self-inflicted. Because one of the basic principles of conventional wisdom is retributive justice—that is, we reap what we sow— Job's friends think he must have sinned to be experiencing such suffering. Instead, Job asserts his innocence (see Job 31). In the end, God intervenes in a surprising way, and Job is vindicated. The book highlights the limitations of traditional wisdom. This limitation is also reflected in the poetic book of Ecclesiastes. In this book, the poet-preacher takes on the persona of a king (in the heritage of David and Solomon) to survey how one finds satisfaction and meaning in life. He tests out various alternatives for satisfaction, including hedonism, social status, and conventional wisdom, but to no avail. In the end, we all die. So, he concludes, wisdom is to enjoy the life that God has assigned to each of us.[12]

Proverbs

There are numerous proverbs found in Scripture, especially in the book of Proverbs (no surprises there!).[13] Proverbs are short, pithy sayings that generally reflect everyday situations and the reality of life. Like psalms, they mostly present two lines in parallel. They offer principles for navigating life successfully.[14] The trick is to read the context of a situation accurately to identify which

11. William W. Klein, Craig L. Blomberg, and Robert L. Hubbard Jr., *Introduction to Biblical Interpretation*, 3rd ed. (Grand Rapids: Zondervan, 2017), 500–501.
12. For further reading, see George Athas, *Ecclesiastes, Song of Songs*, Story of God Bible Commentary (Grand Rapids: Zondervan, 2020).
13. Other examples of types of proverbs include Matt. 7:2 and Mark 10:31.
14. Tremper Longman III, *How to Read Proverbs* (Downers Grove, IL: InterVarsity, 2002), 16.

proverb applies. That is, to know when a proverb applies and when it doesn't. For example, Proverbs 26:4–5 observes the following:

> Do not answer a fool according to his folly,
>   or you yourself will be just like him.
> Answer a fool according to his folly,
>   or he will be wise in his own eyes.

These two proverbs may seem contradictory at first, but they likely refer to different situations. In the first proverb, the foolish (or immature) person is obstinate and unteachable. As Bruce Waltke notes, the wise person must respond in a fitting way; that is, it is unfitting to respond with the same insolence of the fool. To engage them with correction will result in a futile argument, and you will be lowered to the level of a fool. However, in the second proverb, the foolish person is different because they are teachable. Their erroneous thinking is due to ignorance, so correction will educate them. Waltke goes on to observe that while the wise person must not lower themselves to the level of the fool (v. 4) they "must expose the fool's folly for what it is (v. 5)."[15] The wise person can "read" the context and determine what type of fool is in view—obstinate or teachable—and respond appropriately. We sometimes call this emotional intelligence.[16] So proverbs provide general principles and observations on life, but they are contextual: to know when and how to apply them requires discernment.

Love Poetry

It may come as a surprise to learn that the Bible also contains romantic love poetry. The Song of Songs celebrates human physical love in a collection of poems that are essentially love songs. There are also other love songs in the Bible, such as the royal wedding song of Psalm 45. Traditionally, the love poetry of Song of Songs was mainly interpreted allegorically, referring to the love between God and humanity or that between Christ and the church. More recently, however, scholars have noted the similarities between the Song of Songs and other love poetry from the ancient Near East, particularly Egyptian love poetry. The imagery and themes of physical desire, yearning, and sexual fulfillment permeate these poems.

Yet the mystery of sexual desire and union can be a helpful way for us to think about God. According to Sarah Coakley, our sexuality, passion, and

15. Bruce K. Waltke, *The Dance between God and Humanity: Reading the Bible Today as the People of God* (Grand Rapids: Eerdmans, 2013), 194.
16. Longman, *How to Read Proverbs*, 15.

desire are ultimately about orientation toward God.[17] The unity and one-ness we seek, which the world often idolizes in sex, can be found only in the triune God, who is three but also one. Desiring God and being found in him result in wholeness and wholeheartedness in our relationships, including our relationships with our spouses, families, friends, and communities. It puts other physical and sexual passions in their proper place.

So what, then, do we do with all these different poetic texts? How do we interpret them in a way that is true to their original setting but also meaning-ful for us today?

WHAT DO I DO NOW?

Continuing the approach outlined in the previous chapters, we should seek to understand the poetry and imagery of the Bible by considering the original context and the audience for whom these texts were written. The first question we ask while reading a poem is this: What did the poem mean to the original audience there-then? Again, the images used in poetry are not timeless but time related. One memorable psalm tells us that "the LORD is my shepherd" (Ps. 23:1). It is crucial that we consider the function of a shepherd in ancient Israel before we jump to conclusions about what this image means today. Just as we asked when reading narrative, we should also consider when reading poetry: Why did the author use this genre and adopt the literary techniques identified in the passage? What was the message they were trying to com-municate to the original community through this poetry?

It is also important to consider a second question—that is, What does the poetic text mean to us? That is, how might it point to Christ, and how should we understand it as Christian readers? Numerous poetic texts are significant for the church beyond their historical setting, functioning as signposts pointing to Christ. As noted above, Psalm 22 is very important for Christian readers, as it both points to Christ and is also treasured by the Christian community. Finally, we ask a third question: What does the poetic text mean to me? What might God be speaking to me personally through this passage?

You might like to reflect on Psalm 22 or another poem, asking these three questions. Perhaps God wants to speak to you concerning your own current situation.

17. Sarah Coakley, *God, Sexuality, and the Self: An Essay "On the Trinity"* (Cambridge: Cambridge University Press, 2013), 10.

PRAYER

O Lord, may our hearts be filled and our imagination and vision be captured by your invitation to discover you anew.

As the many facets of your character are revealed to us, we pray our lives will be transformed. May we truly taste and see that you are good.

Amen.

TOPICS FOR REVIEW

1. Do you have a favorite psalm? If so, what speaks to you about this psalm? Would those same feelings be evoked if the writer of the psalm used a different genre?

2. Which word picture of God (e.g., shepherd, rock) do you most relate to? How does that picture give you insight into the character and nature of God?

3. Have you ever applied a proverb to a situation in your life? Even if not, how might you apply Proverbs 16:9 to your life?

10

PROPHETIC POWER

In this chapter, you should expect to learn the following:

▶ The role of prophets in the Bible
▶ Key features of biblical prophecy
▶ An overview of the message of the Old Testament prophets
▶ The fulfillment of Old Testament prophecy in the New Testament
▶ How to discern prophecy in our context today

Then I heard the voice of the Lord saying, "Whom shall I send? And who will go for us?"

And I said, "Here am I. Send me!"

—Isa. 6:8

In Isaiah 6, the prophet shares his testimony (or personal narrative) of a vision of God in which he is called to prophetic ministry. This vision occurs at the death of the human king Uzziah (around 738 BC), which was a time of political disruption for Judah. But in this moment, Isaiah sees God, the heavenly King, enthroned on high. God is so gigantic that only the edge of his robe fills the temple. This reminds us that despite the problems in our world today, God the sovereign Creator is perpetually on the throne. Isaiah describes the royal attendants, called seraphim (or "fiery creatures"), circling God's

Figure 10.1. Glass window portraying the prophet Isaiah in the Cathedral of Brussels, Belgium

throne. The seraphim cry to one another of the holiness of God, that God's glory fills the earth (6:3). It is a picture of the awesome majesty of the thrice-holy God. Here, holiness points to both moral perfection and awe-inspiring beauty. However, Isaiah realizes he has a problem: he is an unholy creature in the presence of the holy God. Isaiah describes himself as a man of "unclean lips," from a community of unclean lips (6:5). That is, he recognizes his own failings and the inadequacies of his community that are exposed by the holiness of God. Yet Isaiah is not left in despair. As pictured in the artwork shown in figure 10.1, one of the seraphim takes a burning coal from the altar and touches Isaiah's lips. His lips, which represent his whole person, are purified. His lips are also the mechanism by which he volunteers to be a spokesperson of the divine council to address his own unpurified people. He will use his lips to speak God's message to the Judean community (6:8).

For several of the prophets, the Old Testament includes a description of their calling to the vocation of spokesperson. In each case, God takes the initiative to call the prophet to be his messenger. Isaiah's experience of being in the throne room of the heavenly King is very important as a confirmation of his calling. His privileged attendance in God's heavenly court gives authority to his ministry and validates his message as authentic. This is the basis on which Isaiah can speak on behalf of God; he is authorized to speak because he has been in the very presence of God and sent by God to his community. We are also provided with the call narratives of several other prophets (including Jer. 1:4–10; Ezek. 1:1–3:9; and Amos 7:12–15). Some prophets, like Jeremiah and Micaiah ben Imlah, also contrast their authentic message with those of imposter prophets due to their experience of being in God's heavenly council (see Jer. 23:22; 1 Kings 22:19).

For Isaiah, his vision and revelation of God have a profound impact on his whole ministry and message. Throughout the rest of the book that bears his name, the prophet essentially has one key message: God is holy, so his people should also be holy (see also Lev. 11:44). The responsibility of the faith community (and our responsibility today as believers) is to live out the holiness of God in our world (1 Pet. 1:16). To be holy means to be set apart. As people of faith, we are meant to be different from nonbelievers. That difference does not necessitate us physically separating ourselves from the wider community; instead, it requires us, like Isaiah, to live in our world as people transformed by the living God.

However, the hearts of Isaiah's community are hardened toward God. Like many of the other prophets of the Old Testament, Isaiah faces both opposition and disbelief. Isaiah is told that he will speak but the people will not listen (6:9–10). The community has become like the idols they worship; they can neither see nor hear. Yet the prophet will preach until God's punishment of exile comes into effect. However, judgment will not be the end of Judah. God promises that a small group of survivors, those faithful to the covenant, will be preserved amid the catastrophe of exile (6:11–13).

This passage from Isaiah highlights many important questions regarding how we interpret the message of the prophets. These topics include how prophets were chosen and validated; why the Old Testament prophets so often raised the ethical issues of social justice and power; the role of the Holy Spirit in graciously empowering prophets, both then and now, as gifts for the church; and the importance of discernment for the church today. Such questions are also particularly relevant for the contemporary church as we seek to faithfully interpret the prophetic literature of the Bible and hear God's voice in and for our own contexts. First, let's begin with describing the role of the prophet as presented in the Bible.

What Is a Prophet?

A prophet is, in essence, a person who speaks on behalf of God. Through the prophet, the "invisible God becomes audible."[1] In the Old Testament,

1. Abraham J. Heschel, *The Prophets* (New York: HarperCollins, 2001), 27.

prophets are uniquely called and chosen by God. The idea of being God's spokesperson or mouthpiece is represented by the partnership of Moses and Aaron (Exod. 4:14–16). Because Moses is reluctant to be a public speaker, he will give the words to Aaron to then speak on his behalf. Moses will be "like God" to Aaron, who is to be the "mouth" of Moses. In this way, Aaron provides a prophetic analogy. This also points to why the prophets mostly speak with a messenger style, using terms such as "the Lord says"—because they are God's mouthpiece. Isaiah's call to ministry emphasizes the speaking role of the prophet through the purification of his mouth (Isa. 6:7). The prophets of the Old Testament speak a word from God to assist their contemporary generation to hear God's will and ways for their situation. We will discuss the role of prophets in the New Testament later in this chapter.

Yet how are the people of the Old Testament to know if a prophet is a true spokesperson for God and not a fake? Instruction is provided in Deuteronomy 18:15–22 to help the Israelite community discern between true and false prophets. It says that God will put his words into the mouth of his prophet, which the prophet will communicate to the community (18:18). The prophet is to speak faithfully only the message that God gives them to speak. For the biblical prophets, this was usually an oral proclamation that was later faithfully written down and edited. In this way, the prophet functions like a mediator between God and the people by speaking God's will, perspective, and commands. As Carolyn Sharp writes, "The prophets position themselves in the liminal space between sacred and profane, living a 'threshold' life of faith and inviting us into that life."[2] Deuteronomy also requires the people to listen and obey the message of the prophet (18:19). It sounds simple enough, but these instructions in Deuteronomy are given in the context of the ancient Near Eastern world.

The nations neighboring Israel practiced divination, so they also had prophets who spoke on behalf of their deities (Deut. 18:14, 20). The prohibited practices of divination (18:9–14) represent all kinds of human devices and initiatives to manipulate those gods. However, these forbidden practices also highlight that the prophet was a generally recognized figure in the ancient world. Consider how Paul or Jonah could cross geographic and political boundaries and still be somewhat recognized as a prophet.[3] This is because the role and function of the prophet was well known in the broader culture. Usually, the prophets of the ancient world were attached to the royal court or

---

2. Carolyn J. Sharp, *Old Testament Prophets for Today* (Louisville: Westminster John Knox, 2009), 15.

3. Ben Witherington III, *Jesus the Seer: The Progress of Prophecy* (Peabody, MA: Hendrickson, 1999), 8.

temple to provide advice and insight for the leaders of these institutions. So if Deuteronomy 18 also refers to these false prophets who wrongly presume to speak on behalf of God (or speak in the name of another god), how is the covenant community to tell the difference between a false prophet and a true prophet of God?

To discern between competing claims to speak for God, a test of sorts is provided in Deuteronomy 18: "If what a prophet proclaims in the name of the LORD does not take place or come true, that is a message the LORD has not spoken" (18:22). That is, the true prophetic word corresponds to historical reality in God's narrative of redemption. However, as later realized, not everything that a true prophet says comes to pass; sometimes, it does so only after their lifetime. For example, the prophet Jonah warns the Ninevites of judgment because of their wicked ways, but the judgment spoken by the prophet does not come to pass, because the people repent, much to Jonah's disgust (Jon. 3:6–4:3). Many other prophets, such as Isaiah and Hosea, warn that exile will come because of covenant violations by the community. Their message is rejected and ignored by multiple generations before finally coming to pass after their deaths.[4] Therefore, the test of future fulfillment proves somewhat limited in its scope when applied to later prophets of the Old Testament.

However, Deuteronomy 18:22 also notes about an illegitimate prophet: "That prophet has spoken presumptuously, so do not be alarmed." In other words, the message of a false prophet is conceited and inconsistent with God's character as revealed in Scripture. Earlier in Deuteronomy, we are told that the prophet (and the people) must be "blameless before the LORD [their] God" (18:13; see also Jer. 29:20–23) and that God will raise up future prophets like Moses (Deut. 18:15). Moses was renowned for his humility and wholehearted commitment to God. He epitomized the integrity and loyalty to God required of a prophet. So the test of character also provides additional criteria for determining the legitimacy of a prophet. The character of the messenger must match the message they speak and the God they represent. With this in mind, let's consider the message of the prophets and how to interpret the prophetic literature.

The Message of the Prophets in the Old Testament

The prophetic books of the Old Testament compose one of the largest sections of the Bible. This includes the larger books of the three Major Prophets (Isaiah, Jeremiah, and Ezekiel), Daniel, and the twelve Minor Prophets (so-called

---

4. Sharp, *Old Testament Prophets for Today*, 13.

because they are shorter). There are also many other prophets described in the Pentateuch and the Historical Books of the Old Testament (including Samuel and Elijah). However, our focus will be on the written texts of the prophets and the genre of prophetic literature. These prophets spoke in various historical contexts and in various forms. While prophetic literature incorporates some narrative or reports of visions (like Isa. 6) and enacted prophecy (for example, the prophet in Ezekiel 3:3 eats a scroll to signify God's word in his mouth and digested in his body), most of the prophetic books utilize the poetic form. As discussed in the previous chapters, it is important that we identify the literary type (or genre) of the text to aid us in interpreting the passage effectively. Interestingly, Rickie D. Moore suggests that the prophets often utilized the medium of poetic speech for their messages because it is "deliberately elusive and so captures well the mysterious nature of their encounter with Yahweh as it outworked in their messages."[5] The prophets felt intensely God's heart for his people.[6] This reminds us that the prophets were not puppets or robots but humans. Isaiah was a person, not just lips or a voice box. Therefore, the message of the prophets reflects their human personality, context, and concerns. Their concerns were for the prophetic message to be heard and thereby to stir the hearts of the people—to move them toward faith, hope, and love for God. The poetry of the prophets was written in a way to ensure their message was remembered and repeated by the recipients.

Yet while the communication style and historical circumstances of the various Old Testament prophets may differ, they all share a concern for the community to remain faithful to their covenant with God. Because the prophets were personally committed to live in integrity according to the covenant, they expected followers of God to also live by these standards. Gordon D. Fee and Douglas Stuart refer to the Old Testament prophets as "covenant enforcement mediators."[7] This is also why so often the prophets preached a message of judgment against the ancient Israelite community. It was because the people had rejected God and their covenant obligations, especially the ethical standards of the law. However, if the people would keep the covenant and obey the law (which provided guidelines on how to live faithfully and with integrity before God and each other), then they would be blessed and live peaceably in the land. These outcomes were the stipulations of their covenant agreement, explicitly outlined in Deuteronomy 28 (also Lev. 26; Deut. 4).

---

5. Rickie D. Moore, "The Prophetic Calling: An Old Testament Profile and Its Relevance for Today," *Journal of the European Pentecostal Theological Association* 24 (2004): 23.

6. Heschel, *Prophets*, 5–7.

7. Gordon D. Fee and Douglas Stuart, *How to Read the Bible for All Its Worth*, 4th ed. (Grand Rapids: Zondervan, 2014), 187.

The message of the prophets then oscillates between hope and judgment in accordance with the obedience and disobedience of the people. The prophets did not really preach a new message but inspired faithfulness to God and obedience of God's instructions in each new context. This emphasizes that prophecy should be understood first in its original historical-political context. God spoke a message to his people that was timely for their time. Yet the message of the prophets speaks beyond their own historical situation as well. While situations may change, God is the same. Their message can challenge us today to worship God in every area of our lives and practice love for our neighbor. The prophets can stir us to rise above the mediocrity of religiosity and tokenistic worship. Their message disrupts our comfortable lives. It causes us to see the world and our role in it differently, through God's perspective. Abraham Heschel describes prophecy as "a divine understanding of a human situation."[8] This hopefully encourages us today to seek God's perspective for our lives and purpose. It requires us be attentive to the message of the prophets and be courageous to confront important issues in our lives and communities.

Two issues are often raised by the prophets of the Old Testament. They address issues of the abuse of power by their leaders and express concerns to protect the vulnerable in their society. First, once the institution of kingship is established in Israel, the prophets often address the king and the leaders of the covenant community. As noted above, Isaiah is called to ministry in the year of King Uzziah's death, noting the close connection of his ministry to the Judean king. However, because the allegiance of the prophet is to the divine King, Yahweh, they are usually called to address the inadequacies of the human king. If the king and governing leaders are engaged in corruption or behavior contrary to the covenant, the prophets confront and condemn them. This means the prophets are often unpopular with unethical leaders. King Ahab calls the prophet Elijah a "troubler of Israel" (1 Kings 18:17) because Elijah pronounces judgment on Ahab due to his idolatrous practices and faithlessness. So the prophets boldly speak the truth to people in positions of power, even in the face of persecution and imprisonment. Second, the prophets often speak up for the poor and powerless. Those who are victims of injustice have no voice in such corrupt contexts. Therefore, prophets like Isaiah challenge the perpetrators of injustice to repent and instead to show care and compassion to the vulnerable and needy in their community, as befitting God's character and covenant (see Exod. 22:22–24; Isa. 1:16–17). As Carolyn Sharp writes, "Every community needs prophetic voices to call us

8. Heschel, *Prophets*, xxvii.

back to God, to hold us accountable for our misuses of power, and to urge us to compassion for those in need."[9]

An interesting prophetic development that occurs within Scripture is the emergence of apocalyptic literature. The term comes from the Greek word for "revelation" (*apokalypsis*). This is the primary feature of apocalyptic literature: it reveals God's hidden plans. Often, these texts were written in times of overt persecution, so the author "reveals" these plans through symbols and numbers. Due to the suffering of the faithful that comes with persecution, the writers encourage believers to persevere, looking forward to the radical intervention of God into human history to usher in a new era.[10] The book of Daniel in the Old Testament and the book of Revelation in the New Testament are examples of apocalyptic literature. This leads us to consider prophecy in the New Testament and its connection to the Old Testament.

Prophecy in the New Testament

There are three primary ways that prophecy continues from the Old Testament into the New Testament. First, we see how the New Testament writers used the words of the Old Testament as prophetic predictions, particularly as signposts to Jesus Christ. Some passages of the Old Testament (representing various parts of the Hebrew Bible, not just the prophetic literature) are understood by the New Testament writers as predicting the Messiah. They see these passages as forecasts or signposts in the redemptive plan of God that runs throughout the Bible. These are not random predictions; rather, they point to greater significance or correspondence beyond their original context in light of the person and work of Jesus Christ. This emphasizes the role of the divine author; that is, this greater meaning was intended by the Holy Spirit even if it was not likely intended or understood by the inspired human author (1 Pet. 1:10–12).

Second, we see that the New Testament affirms the ongoing use of prophetic and revelatory experience, albeit transformed by the coming of the Holy Spirit on the day of Pentecost. Throughout the book of Acts, God continues to speak to the early church through the prophetic word. However, rather than such messengers being unique and special like those in the Old Testament, since Pentecost, all God's people are called to the prophetic vocation. This includes all people in the church today as we all seek to hear God's voice for our communities and our own lives.

---

9. Sharp, *Old Testament Prophets for Today*, 18.

10. William W. Klein, Craig L. Blomberg, and Robert L. Hubbard Jr., *Introduction to Biblical Interpretation*, 3rd ed. (Grand Rapids: Zondervan, 2017), 427.

Third, we see Scripture used by the early church to provide prophetic guidance in their decision-making and in their understanding of God's perspective on their situations. Similarly, Scripture continues to be used today to guide and direct our paths. The challenge is to correctly discern the use of Scripture as a word from God. Let's unpack these ideas in greater detail.

For the Christian church, Old Testament texts can have significance beyond their original contexts as they point to Jesus Christ. For example, in Matthew 1:20–21 an angel appears before Joseph to tell him that Mary will give birth to a son. This son is to be named Jesus, who has been conceived of the Holy Spirit. Matthew then says, "All this took place to fulfill what the Lord had said through the prophet: 'The virgin will conceive and give birth to a son, and they will call him Immanuel' (which means 'God with us')" (1:22–23). This is a direct reference to the words of Isaiah when he spoke to King Ahaz in a time of political crisis, encouraging the king that God would be with him. However, the New Testament writer looks back at the words of Isaiah and sees a correlation with the birth of Christ. Just as the child Immanuel ("God with us") functioned as a sign to the Judean king, so Christ has come as a sign that is another—and greater—fulfillment of this earlier prophecy in Isaiah. While the child born in Isaiah's time was historically and politically significant himself, the Messiah born to the virgin Mary is significant for all humanity, as this means that God is literally with us (God incarnate), the Savior of the world. The fulfillment formula used in the New Testament points to the possibility of multiple layers of meaning in a text, beyond what it would have meant to the original hearers alone.

The New Testament also affirms the ongoing existence and activity of prophets (spokespersons for God), but with a twist. While the Gospel accounts refer to some prophetic people (such as Simeon and Anna in Luke 2:22–38), we see that with the coming of the Holy Spirit on the day of Pentecost, there is a new era established in which all God's people are called to be prophets. That is, in the new covenant, all believers can hear from God directly as part of the body of Christ. In his sermon, Peter quotes from the prophet Joel to explain the new work of God at Pentecost:

> In the last days, God says,
>   I will pour out my Spirit on all people.
> Your sons and daughters will prophesy,
>   your young men will see visions,
>   your old men will dream dreams.
> Even on my servants, both men and women,
>   I will pour out my Spirit in those days,
>   and they will prophesy. (Acts 2:17–18; see Joel 2:28–29)

Following this outpouring of the Spirit, the book of Acts refers to various disciples speaking prophetic messages or being identified as prophets. Such references include Agabus warning the local community of an impending famine (11:27–28) and Philip's daughters having the gift of prophecy (21:9). However, because the covenant community in the New Testament is not a sociopolitical group but a collection of believers spread throughout the nations of the world, prophecy in this post-Pentecost context does operate differently from Old Testament prophecy. As William Kay notes, we do not see prophets in the New Testament storming into Caesar's palace to announce a judgment. Neither do we see false prophecy punished in the same way as in the Old Testament.[11] Instead, prophecy generally functions in the New Testament for the encouragement of the church (1 Cor. 14:3–4). It is a gift of the Spirit, given to build up the body of Christ. It is also identified as a function in the church, in that some persons may be recognized as prophets (Eph. 4:11). Yet we do see some similarities between prophecy in the Old and New Testaments: it still requires the inspiration of the Holy Spirit, and it still demands that the community of faith judge it carefully.[12] This latter point requires us to discern together what the Spirit is saying to the church today.

Finally, just as Peter quoted from the book of Joel to interpret and understand this new era of the outpowering of the Spirit, so some believers also utilize Scripture to speak prophetically to new situations today in the life of an individual or local community. Biblical scholar John Goldingay shares a story of how God used a passage of Scripture to confirm his future direction, even though that passage had nothing to do with his situation:

> Eighteen years ago I had given in my notice from my job at another seminary in England and I was contemplating an invitation to come to Fuller. My first wife was wheelchair-bound, and there were various ways in which such a move might therefore be hazardous. During this period, in the regular chapel service at that seminary, one morning God told a student, "Tell John 'Judges 18:6.'" The passage reads, "Go in peace. Your journey has the LORD's approval"; or in another translation, "Go in peace. The mission you are on is under the eye of the LORD."[13]

God spoke through this passage, in what some may call a prophetic encouragement (though Goldingay does not use this term), to give it a new

---

11. William K. Kay, "Perspectives on Prophecy," in *Strangers to Fire: When Tradition Trumps Scripture*, ed. Robert W. Graves (Tulsa: Empowered Life, 2014), 447.

12. Kay, "Perspectives on Prophecy," 447.

13. John Goldingay, "Hearing God Speak from the First Testament," in *The Voice of God in the Text of Scripture: Explorations in Constructive Dogmatics*, ed. Oliver D. Crisp and Fred Sanders (Grand Rapids: Zondervan, 2016), 67.

significance for a personal situation. The Holy Spirit can breathe new life into a text to allow it to speak afresh to us today. While in the aforementioned situation the Scripture spoken to Goldingay provided a welcome affirmation, that may not always be the case. How do we discern when a passage may be a word from the Lord despite it having no connection to the text in its original context? How do we discern legitimate prophecy from false prophecy in our context today?

WHAT DO I DO NOW?

While the study of the prophetic texts encourages us to be attentive to God's voice today, especially through the reading of Scripture, it also highlights the need for discernment. Like the situation that Deuteronomy 18 addresses, not all claims to hear from God may be legitimate. As in the Old Testament, all prophetic messages today must be judged and tested so that we can hold on to what is good (1 Thess. 5:19–22). First John 4:1 instructs Christians: "Do not believe every spirit, but test the spirits to see whether they are from God, because many false prophets have gone out into the world." So how do we practice such discernment? There are two tests we can use to prayerfully guide us in this process. First, we test any prophetic word against the Bible. Scripture was inspired by the Holy Spirit and is our highest authority for faith and practice (2 Tim. 3:16; 2 Pet. 1:21). It is the standard by which we assess all other doctrine and experience. Prophecy and other revelatory experiences, while inspired by the Spirit, do not carry the same authority as Scripture but must be measured by their theological consistency with the Scriptures.[14]

Similarly, while Scripture is universal in its authority and application, prophecy and spiritual insight are "designed by God to speak *ad hoc*, to specific people at specific times in specific situations."[15] This point is particularly pertinent in the example of Goldingay described above. We must differentiate between the meaning inherent in the text in its own time and place (referring to the original context) and the many meanings or the limitless significance that can result when we read it in new contexts.[16] So the meaning of the text in new contexts must be tested for its theological consistency with the whole of Scripture.

14. Cecil M. Robeck, "The Gift of Prophecy and the All-Sufficiency of Scripture," in Graves, *Strangers to Fire*, 455.
15. Robeck, "Gift of Prophecy," 456.
16. Goldingay, "Hearing God Speak from the First Testament," 69.

Second, we apply the character test of Deuteronomy 18:22. As noted above, the test of character provides additional criteria for determining the legitimacy of a prophet and the message they bring. Do the messenger and particularly the message motivate and foster love for Christ (1 Cor. 12:1–7)? These tests are true even if someone brings a text from Scripture as a prophetic message or word from God for us today. Similarly, to extend this test from Deuteronomy to the recipient as part of the prophetic community, does the prophetic word foster in the recipient the peace of God (Phil. 4:7) and a greater love for Christ and others?

After we have asked these two key questions in the process of discernment, a response is required. As the Deuteronomy text reminds us, once discerned as from God, the prophetic message requires obedience. May we respond to God's will and way in our lives as Isaiah did: "Then I heard the voice of the Lord saying, 'Whom shall I send? And who will go for us?' And I said, 'Here am I. Send me!'" (Isa. 6:8).

PRAYER

> My Lord, here I am. Send me!
> I ask for your grace to be attentive to your voice today, as well as to walk in discernment through your Holy Spirit.
> May my life be submitted to you, that I may see through your eyes, so that I can faithfully and lovingly represent you to this world.
> Amen.

TOPICS FOR REVIEW

1. What are the main similarities and differences between prophecy in the Old Testament and in the New Testament?
2. Why was false prophecy and divination so attractive to the ancient Israelites?
3. Why do you think the abuse of power and social injustice are such important issues for the Old Testament prophets? Are these issues still relevant today?
4. How should we use the prophetic literature in contemporary preaching?

11

READING THE NEW TESTAMENT LETTERS

In this chapter, you should expect to learn the following:

- ▶ Key features of the letters of the New Testament
- ▶ The importance of the context of the early church
- ▶ How to apply the New Testament letters for today

There is neither Jew nor Gentile, neither slave nor free, nor is there male and female, for you are all one in Christ Jesus.

—Gal. 3:28

Paul travels through Galatia (central Anatolia, in modern-day Turkey) on his first missionary journey in Acts 13–14 and plants churches in the region, particularly among Gentile converts. However, after Paul leaves Galatia, false teachers arrive who teach the Galatians that they need to follow the law—especially circumcision and the Jewish food laws—in order to join the new covenant community. When Paul hears about this false teaching, he becomes furious. He immediately writes a letter to the Galatians addressing

Figure 11.1. Early Christian fresco of a female figure holding a chalice during an agape feast, Catacomb of Saints Peter and Marcellinus, Rome, Italy

this issue. He argues in his letter that to return to the law is to return to slavery.[1] He says the law was given to show people their sins; it was a caretaker until Christ came. But now that we have faith in Christ, we no longer need the law. Now, we are to "live by the Spirit" and "keep in step with the Spirit" (Gal. 5:25) and to exhibit the fruit of the Spirit in our lives (5:22–23).

In Galatians 3:28, Paul emphasizes the acceptance of all people as children of God based on faith in Jesus Christ. In our baptism into Christ, all social and cultural barriers that previously divided people—barriers based on gender, race, or class—are removed. Instead, Paul affirms that believers have died to these old discordant categories and have risen in Christ as a new creation, newly identifying as part of God's family. All believers are children of God; there is no favoritism or privileging of one person or group over another. We all have a new solidarity as kin.[2] Paul earlier has argued in this same letter that our acceptance is based not on our good works or keeping the law but on faith in Christ Jesus alone (3:10–13).

1. Michael J. Gorman, *Apostle of the Crucified Lord: A Theological Introduction to Paul and His Letters*, 2nd ed. (Grand Rapids: Eerdmans, 2017), 370.
2. Dorothy A. Lee, *The Ministry of Women in the New Testament: Reclaiming the Biblical Vision for Church Leadership* (Grand Rapids: Baker Academic, 2021), 114.

This excerpt of Paul's letter has had an enormous, liberating impact throughout history, particularly among marginalized groups, particularly women. While the role of women's leadership is still a contested issue in some church traditions, this passage particularly (along with many other texts from the Bible) has provided rationale for the acceptance of women in ministry and leadership positions in the church. As Cynthia Long Westfall writes, "It means that in Christian circles we do not make distinctions . . . [or] discriminate on the basis of race, socioeconomic categories, or gender."[3] Human categories of identity are relativized and not to be given priority in the ministry of the church. Note that this truth does not override male and female identities, which are based on the creation narratives (e.g., Gen. 1:27), but it does override categories based on human-made cultural, religious, and political identities.[4] This truth of the gospel has very practical implications for the Christian community and relationships, both in Galatia and today. The historic artwork in figure 11.1, depicting a woman participating in and perhaps even leading a Christian meeting, highlights one such implication of this passage. In this picture, women and men, young and old, are all seated equally at a round table and sharing together in a fellowship meal. While the agape meal (or "love feast") as a ritual event was a later development in the Christian tradition, it began as a communal meal not unlike the community fellowship depicted in Acts 2:46–47, following the outpouring of the Spirit at Pentecost.

In this chapter, we will look at the conventions of ancient letter writers as well as the occasional nature of the letters of the New Testament. To analyze the structure of these letters, we will utilize the book of Romans as a case study, which concludes with Paul's commendations of female coworkers. We will also focus on the topic of women ministers as we explore how to read the New Testament letters in their original context and how to apply them to our lives today. Although there are some difficult texts regarding women in Paul's writings, we can see his overall commitment to living out the implications of Galatians 3:28 in his tasking of women with leadership and ministry roles in the church.

Who Wrote the Letters of the New Testament?

Arguably, the second-most influential person in the New Testament, following Jesus (of course), is the apostle Paul. Over half the book of Acts focuses

3. Cynthia Long Westfall, "Male and Female, One in Christ: Galatians 3:26–29," in *Discovering Biblical Equality: Biblical, Theological, Cultural and Practical Perspectives*, ed. Ronald W. Pierce, Cynthia Long Westfall, and Christa L. McKirland, 3rd ed. (Downers Grove, IL: IVP Academic, 2021), 161.
4. Westfall, "Male and Female," 176.

on his missionary travels, and he is credited with writing almost half of the letters of the New Testament. Paul is such an important figure in Acts that the book recounts his coming to Christ three times (Acts 9:1–19; 22:3–21; 26:2–23). From his testimony, we learn that Paul was born into a Jewish family in Tarsus (in modern-day Turkey) but was brought to Jerusalem, where he studied Jewish law. As a Pharisee, he originally was a fervent opponent of Christianity (Phil. 3:4–6). But after an encounter with the risen Christ on the road to Damascus, he became a believer in Jesus. He then took the message of Jesus to the world as an ambassador. Paul had a reputation among the early churches as "the man who formerly persecuted [them but] is now preaching the faith he once tried to destroy" (Gal. 1:23).

The grouping of letters in the New Testament canon begins with the letters written by Paul to church communities, starting with the longest letter (Romans) and ending with the shortest (2 Thessalonians). Historically speaking, 1 Thessalonians and Galatians were probably the earliest letters written by Paul. The next grouping of letters in the canon is also accredited to Paul, written to individuals such as Timothy and Titus and Philemon. (The letters written to Timothy and Titus are known as the Pastoral Epistles.) These are followed by the General Epistles, sometimes referred to as the Catholic Letters. This does not mean they were written by the pope. "Catholic" means "universal," so these letters are called catholic because they address the whole Christian church. They are the letters of James, Peter, John, and Jude. Arguably, Hebrews also best fits in this category.[5] So along with Paul's letters, the General Epistles were all included in the New Testament canon based on their apostolic authority. Finally, the New Testament canon ends with the Revelation of John, which is an unusual mix of letter, prophecy, and apocalyptic literature.

The Structure of New Testament Letters

The letters of the New Testament generally follow the same basic conventions and structure as other letters written in the Greco-Roman period. You may have noticed above that sometimes the letters are called an "epistle." While this term refers to a literary work in the form of a letter, epistles in the ancient world tended to be longer, formal treatises. Yet as William W. Klein notes, the New Testament letters are more structured and didactic (that is,

---

5. Tradition credits Paul as the author of Hebrews. While Pauline authorship of this letter has long been questioned, it provided the general basis for its inclusion in the canon, along with its sound teaching (see chap. 3).

instructional) than other personal letters. The New Testament letters include theological instruction, ethical principles, and practical guidance to the early church community, so they tend to fit between these two genres.[6] This is why both terms ("epistle" and "letter") are appropriate and often used interchangeably. So let's explore the structure of these letters, using Paul's letter to the Romans as a case study.

The Letter to the Romans is often considered Paul's masterpiece. While Paul had planted many of the churches he wrote to, the Christians in Rome were an exception. Paul had not even visited Rome before he wrote to them (Rom. 1:10). Paul wrote this letter to the Romans from Corinth (16:1; cf. Acts 20:2–3) during his third missionary journey. Paul would later visit Rome as a prisoner, after his fourth missionary journey, as he was held under house arrest (Acts 28:17–30). The church in Rome was a key Christian community in the heart of the Roman Empire. However, it was also struggling with ethnic divisions between Jews and Gentiles. Because of these racial tensions, the Roman church needed ethnic reconciliation. So a key theme of Paul's letter to the Romans is God's grace to Gentiles and Jews alike.[7] The message of Galatians 3:28, that we are all one in Christ, was also desperately needed for this church.

In terms of structure, each New Testament letter generally includes a salutation, a prayer, the reason for writing, the body of the letter, and a closing farewell. Paul's opening salutation to the church in Rome (Rom. 1:1–17) is longer than the greetings of most other letters in the New Testament.[8] Paul identifies himself as the author and greets the church. To introduce his purpose for writing, Paul says, "For I am not ashamed of the gospel, because it is the power of God that brings salvation to everyone who believes: first to the Jew, then to the Gentile" (1:16). Interestingly, Paul does not provide an explicit reason for writing here, and there is much debate about his possible intentions. However, this verse (1:16) emphasizes Paul's major concern for the unity of the Christian community amid cultural diversity.[9]

The body of Paul's letter to the Romans is the bulk of the material (1:18–15:33), though this is usually further divided into subsections. Michael Gorman provides a helpful summary of the body of the letter:

---

6. William W. Klein, Craig L. Blomberg, and Robert L. Hubbard Jr., *Introduction to Biblical Interpretation*, 3rd ed. (Grand Rapids: Zondervan, 2017), 541.

7. Michael J. Gorman, *Romans: A Theological and Pastoral Commentary* (Grand Rapids: Eerdmans, 2022), 25.

8. We adopt here the basic structure of the Letter to the Romans as outlined by Michael Gorman in his commentary. See Gorman, *Romans*, 33–35.

9. Gorman, *Romans*, 27.

Under this banner of God's righteousness, or saving justice, powerfully displayed in the royal Messiah Jesus, the letter proceeds to tell the story of God's faithful response to faithless humanity (chs. 1–4); the resulting new situation for those who are justified by grace through faith, thereby dying and rising with Christ and living in the Spirit (chs. 5–8); the question of the future fate of ethnic Israel in light of the failure of most Jews to accept the gospel (chs. 9–11); the need for the community at Rome to embody this gospel as they live cruciform (cross-shaped) lives of holiness and hospitality (chs. 12–15); and finally, the relationship of all this to God's great story of salvation and Paul's mission within it (chs. 15–16).[10]

What is interesting from this summary is the contextualization of the story of Scripture for the situation of the community in Rome. Despite the rich theological ideas that speak beyond the time and place of the Roman community, the letter is still deeply personal with respect to their context and pastoral needs.

Paul's closing farewell (16:1–27) begins with a commendation of his co-worker Phoebe (16:1–2). She was a leader in the church of Cenchreae (a port town near Corinth) and tasked by Paul to deliver the Letter to the Romans on his behalf. This role usually included reading the letter and explaining its contents to the recipients.[11] Paul also requested the Roman church to provide Phoebe with appropriate hospitality. Paul then greets numerous women and men in the church with whom he is familiar, either personally or by reputation (16:3–15). The list includes twenty-six people (including Phoebe), ten of whom are women, such as Priscilla the teacher (16:3) and Junia the apostle (16:7).[12] All those listed are identified as exemplary believers, and many as model leaders. The list stresses that Paul endorsed both women and men in leadership. So why does Paul greet and commend so many friends in the Roman church? It seems that these people provided real-life examples of a believer embodying the gospel and the teaching that Paul has been expounding for the last fifteen chapters.[13] Paul then closes the letter with some further encouragements, other greetings from friends, and a prayer (16:16–27).

10. Gorman, *Romans*, 36.

11. Michael Gorman describes the ancient practice of letter delivery, noting that whoever took a letter to its recipient(s) was seen as a surrogate for the writer and required to interpret the letter. Michael J. Gorman, *Apostle of the Crucified Lord: A Theological Introduction to Paul and His Letters* (Grand Rapids: Eerdmans, 2017), 103.

12. See Nijay K. Gupta, *Tell Her Story: How Women Led, Taught, and Ministered in the Early Church* (Downers Grove, IL: IVP Academic, 2023), 141–52.

13. Gupta, *Tell Her Story*, 97.

Reading Someone Else's Mail

So are these letters like personal letters we might receive today? While a few of the letters in the New Testament were addressed to individuals, even these functioned differently from a personal letter today. The general purpose of the New Testament letters was to give specific instruction to a church community or individual. Therefore, each letter addressed a unique situation and the challenges faced by a specific recipient, as we have seen with Paul's letter to the Romans. While some letters may have also been relevant to other nearby communities, each letter was initially written for a distinct audience. For this reason, scholars refer to the New Testament letters as "occasional" writings. That is, a particular occasion motivated their writing. The book of Acts helps to provide the general narrative framework for reading the letters. It describes the development of the early church and Paul's journeys, so we can get a basic overview of the background and situation of some of these letters.[14]

However, the comparison to a personal letter can be helpful in guiding us as we read and interpret the epistles. First, upon receiving a letter from a beloved friend, we usually find the time to read it all in one sitting. We do not read a few lines and then leave the rest for the next day. We tend to read it as a whole and interpret the comments in each section in light of the whole letter. Second, because it is written by someone we know well, we understand their comments relating to their own personal situation and context, with which we would be familiar. They do not need to explain background information in the letter because we already know their story. Much knowledge is assumed in written correspondence. Third, the personal letters we receive often respond to some previous communication or encounter with us, which we also intuitively tend to take into consideration when reading their words.

In the same way, first, each letter in the New Testament should be read as a whole, in its entirety. The practice of the early church was to read a full letter aloud during gatherings. Then whoever had delivered the letter (representing the writer) would answer any questions. We have already noted Paul sending the Letter to the Romans by "sister" Phoebe (Rom. 16:1–2), which was comparable to "brother" Tychicus delivering Paul's letter to the Colossians (Col. 4:7). This emphasizes that the New Testament letters were intended to be read in one sitting. Perhaps because we have chapter and verse divisions in our Bibles, we tend to think the letters are meant to be read piecemeal. But this is not the case. Letters are written as a whole document and should be read as such. Subsequently, each section must be read in light of the

14. Walter C. Kaiser Jr. and Moisés Silva, *Introduction to Biblical Hermeneutics: The Search for Meaning*, rev. ed. (Grand Rapids: Zondervan, 2007), 178.

whole and not pulled out in isolation. Sometimes, we like to go back over sections of a letter and reread them. This is helpful. However, each section must be read considering the whole letter and not taken out of its literary context.

Second, we should seek to understand the background of each letter. This includes increasing our knowledge about the Greco-Roman world in which the New Testament letters were written. We have previously referred to this task as exploring the meaning and situation of there-then—the original audience of the letter. However, one of the challenges we face as contemporary readers is that there is often a historical and cultural gap between the New Testament community and us today (as noted in chap. 1). So it is up to us to try and bridge that gap. As noted earlier in this book, there are many great resources we can use to increase our understanding of the ancient world.

Third, we should read the letters knowing that they are part of a wider communication strategy within the early church. Therefore, we need to consider what prompted the writing of each letter, including the questions or concerns that might have already been raised with the writer. For example, Paul's first letter to the Corinthian church says, "Women should remain silent in the churches. They are not allowed to speak, but must be in submission, as the law says. If they want to inquire about something, they should ask their own husbands at home; for it is disgraceful for a woman to speak in the church" (1 Cor. 14:34–35).[15] This passage might initially seem very restrictive of women and their participation in congregations. However, when we read it in light of the whole of Paul's letter to the Corinthians, we see that the whole community (including the women) has been encouraged to pray and prophesy during worship services (11:5; 14:1). The apparent restriction of women (14:34–35) is found in the section of the letter dealing with church order (14:26–40). We also see that throughout the letter Paul is quoting the questions and concerns raised by the Corinthians so he can then address them. There is much assumed knowledge between the writer and the recipients. But from the context, we can determine that Paul seems to be addressing a specific situation at Corinth. That is, there were uneducated women who were talking and asking irrelevant questions, thereby significantly disrupting the service. We can gather this from the context because Paul goes on to tell his readers that women should ask questions of their husbands at home. We know in the Greco-Roman world that almost all women were married and mostly uneducated. Men, who were educated, knew the rules of instruction, but as

---

15. While some scholars consider this text to be a non-Pauline addition because of the textual variant here in some early manuscripts, arguably the majority, including Craig Keener and Dorothy Lee, consider it original. See Lee, *Ministry of Women in the New Testament*, 120.

these women had never been formal students before, they did not know how to learn in this context. Silence and submission were the normal posture of a student in the Greco-Roman world.[16]

So while Paul does not want to stop the women from learning, he also does not want them to disrupt the church service. Therefore, a solution is suggested: the Corinthian women are to learn from their husbands at home. This outcome would prepare these women to be learners and full participants in the church service. Paul's injunction, then, is not a rule for all women of all time to be silent in church; rather, it addresses a specific situation in Corinth. This brief unpacking of 1 Corinthians 14:34–35 emphasizes the importance of reading each section of a letter in light of its literary whole, as well as considering the historical and cultural background of the Greco-Roman world, in order to help us understand the meaning of the passage and its significance for the original audience.

One of the challenges that this discussion highlights is that of applying the message of the New Testament letters—that is, discerning when an issue or principle is relevant only to the recipients of the letter and when it is also applicable to the broader church. That is, while the letters may be time related, when and how might we understand them as timely in the sense of speaking to our community today? To consider the application of these contextually driven instructions for our own time, then, we return to the idea (raised earlier, in chap. 6) of improvisation.

WHAT DO I DO NOW?

Reading a letter in its literary and historical context highlights the background of the Greco-Roman world. It points to the differences between there-then (the place and time of the original recipients) and here-now (the place and time of the church today). Hopefully, what will become apparent is that our world is often very different from the world of Corinth or Rome or whatever group the author has addressed in the letter. Because our culture and society can be so vastly different from that of the biblical world, we cannot just cut-and-paste the text onto our situation. That is, the timelessness of Scripture does not mean that we apply the situation of Rome or a cultural practice of the Greco-Romans to our context today. We live in a different time and a different culture. Yet in some cases, we might find a high level of correspondence

16. See Cynthia Long Westfall, *Paul and Gender: Reclaiming the Apostle's Vision for Men and Women in Christ* (Grand Rapids: Baker Academic, 2016), 240.

between our own world and that of a biblical text. Therefore, the task of application "calls for an integrative act of imaginative improvisation"—placing our situation imaginatively within the world articulated in the biblical text.[17] This does not mean going back to the culture or historical time of the biblical text but continuing the story of the Bible in our own place and time. The concept of improvisation will be further explored in the final chapter of this book.

To improvise is to live consistently with Scripture, not to clone Scripture. Therefore, a key question we must ask as we discern whether a principle drawn from a New Testament letter is appropriate for both there-then and here-now is to consider if the content and contemporary application are consistent with the broader message and story of the Bible. We began the chapter highlighting Paul's key verse in Galatians 3:28, that there should be no human-made distinctions or cultural restrictions for believers based on race, gender, or social class but that we are one in Christ. When discerning if this application of women's leadership was only for the Galatian church or is also appropriate for today, we must ask if this reading is consistent with the broader message of the Bible. What we find is that while there are some verses that seem to restrict the activity of women in the church (such as 1 Cor. 11:2–16 and 1 Tim. 2:11–15), these verses are likely addressing local issues and correcting isolated incidents. Instead, the overarching content of Scripture highlights the redemptive movement toward the full inclusion of women in church ministry. We see this in the repeated encouragement for women to learn (e.g., Jesus's encouragement of Mary in Luke 10:42); the Spirit poured out on sons *and* daughters at Pentecost, giving gifts to both women and men for the building up of Christ's body (Acts 2:1–41; 1 Cor. 12:1–11); the leadership of women recorded in the book of Acts (like Lydia in 16:11–40 and Priscilla teaching Apollos in 18:26); and the example of Paul endorsing numerous women ministers in his letters (like Phoebe and the apostle Junia in Rom. 16). These examples of women ministering and leading in the early church are consistent with teaching elsewhere in Scripture and therefore give us confidence in applying Galatians 3:28 today to see the whole church, including women, active in service and leadership.

However, not only must we be consistent with biblical teaching, but to be truly consistent with Scripture requires us to also be shaped by it. Christ is our model. As 1 John 2:6 says, "Whoever claims to live in him must live as Jesus did." Similarly, Paul's pronouncement that men and women are equal before

---

17. Volker Rabens, "Inspiring Ethics: A Hermeneutical Model for the Dialogue between Biblical Texts and Contemporary Ethics," in *Key Approaches to Biblical Ethics: An Interdisciplinary Dialogue*, ed. Volker Rabens, Jacqueline N. Grey, and Mariam Kamell Kovalishyn (Leiden: Brill, 2021), 114.

God in Christ (Gal. 3:28) reflects the redemptive movement of the Bible, and so it should shape us and our attitudes toward women's participation in the church community. So we the readers must be creative and imaginative—we must improvise while maintaining consistency with the narrative of Scripture. However, to be able to improvise requires us to have a solid grounding in the story and content of Scripture. Through the narrative, we can see the movement toward redemption and the important recurrent themes, such as justice and care for the vulnerable in our communities. The narrative thrust of Scripture, with Christ at its center, leads us to express crucified love in new and creative ways, seeking the well-being and flourishing of our neighbor. Fortunately, we have the Holy Spirit, the Spirit of truth, to help us in this task. As Paul reminds the Galatians, "Since we live by the Spirit, let us keep in step with the Spirit" (Gal. 5:25).

PRAYER

O Lord God, we thank you for all the blessings you have given.

We thank you for your Word. May your Word be made alive in our hearts and minds today.

Thank you, Holy Spirit, for sanctifying our hearts and washing us in your Word.

Fill us with your wisdom. Walk with us as we seek to follow Christ. May we bring him glory.

Ignite in us a passion for truth, and help us to be courageous and obedient to it.

Amen.

TOPICS FOR REVIEW

1. What are some advantages and disadvantages in communicating by letter?
2. How can we know when an instruction in a letter is only for the addressee(s) and when it might be applicable for the church today?
3. In what ways are we required to "improvise" Scripture? What might be some challenges we face today that are not addressed in the Bible? How should we navigate these new challenges?

PART THREE

Reading and Living

12

DAILY BREAD

In this chapter, you should expect to learn the following:

► The purpose of reading the Bible devotionally
► The importance of daily reading habits
► How to use the method of *lectio divina*
► The role of the Holy Spirit in the reading of Scripture

> The LORD said to Moses, "I have heard the grumbling of the Israelites. Tell them, 'At twilight you will eat meat, and in the morning you will be filled with bread. Then you will know that I am the LORD your God.'"
>
> —Exod. 16:11–12

The exodus story describes how the Israelites are miraculously rescued by God from slavery in Egypt. Because the covenant people have been under servitude to Pharaoh, they are not free to worship God (Exod. 1–6). So following the plagues and the institution of the first Passover, Pharaoh releases the people (Exod. 7–12). They are led by Moses out of Egypt, across the Red Sea, and into the desert to worship God (13:1–15:21). Their liberation enables the restoration of right relationship with God, which is later formalized in the covenant and giving of the law (Exod. 19–31). However, it

The Jewish Museum / Wikimedia Commons / Public Domain

Figure 12.1. *The Gathering of Manna,* by James Tissot
(ca. 1896–1902)

is not long after this miraculous exit through the Red Sea, while they are in
the desert, that the people begin to complain. First, they complain about a
lack of water (15:22–27), and then they complain about a lack of bread and
meat (Exod. 16). These are staple food items in their diet.

In the story of Exodus 16, we see that God hears and understands their
distress. Rather than ignoring their physical needs, God responds to their
grumbling with these provisions. What this passage focuses on is the promise
of daily bread (sometimes referred to as "manna"). God says to the people
that an abundance of manna will rain down from heaven—all the bread they
could want, every morning. They are to gather what they need for the day,
trusting in God to supply the bread for them each day (and a double amount
on the sixth day in preparation for the Sabbath). They are not to hoard it or
be greedy. It is a test of sorts, to ensure they learn obedience to God's instructions (16:4) prior to the giving of the law. The manna is also a gift from God

and a reminder of God's attentive care. Each morning, they will "see the glory of the Lord" (16:7) through this provision. The artwork in figure 12.1, by James Tissot, captures the urgency of the people to gather the daily bread. As described in the text, when they first see the manna, they ask, "What is it?" (16:15). The artwork depicts the Israelite men and women kneeling on the earth, desperately gathering the manna.

This experience of God's provision of manna is echoed in the New Testament. We see it reflected in the account of the feeding of the five thousand in John 6:1–15 and the revelation of Jesus as the "bread of life" (John 6:26–59).[1] First, Jesus feeds the crowd in this food crisis by miraculously multiplying the staples of bread and meat (fish). This event, located in the region of Galilee during the festival of the Passover, functions as a sign pointing to Jesus as a prophet greater than Moses. Moses provided bread, but Jesus himself is the "true bread from heaven" who gives life to the world (6:32–33). Jesus continues, "I am the bread of life. Whoever comes to me will never go hungry" (6:35). He then goes on to clarify: "Your ancestors ate the manna in the wilderness, yet they died. But here is the bread that comes down from heaven, which anyone may eat and not die. I am the living bread that came down from heaven. Whoever eats this bread will live forever. This bread is my flesh, which I will give for the life of the world" (6:49–51). Here is an interweaving of ideas: Jesus provides physical bread and is himself the heavenly bread, which is his physical body that we eat to have eternal life. At the Last Supper meal (which takes place during another Passover festival), Jesus breaks bread, symbolizing his body, which will be broken in his death on the cross. As believers, we also participate in this same meal, in which we eat bread and drink wine in remembrance of Christ as a proclamation of his death until his return (1 Cor. 11:23–26).

In this chapter, we will consider the importance of regularly reading the Bible as part of our spiritual life and formation. The phrase "reading the Bible devotionally" refers to a spiritual practice by which we seek to know God through the text. It is like partaking of our daily bread. One way to read the Bible devotionally is to employ the contemplative practice of *lectio divina*, which we will outline for you to practice. Yet it is just a tool and a method to achieve a purpose, which is to meet with God through the reading of his Word. As the Israelites received their "daily bread" by relying on God for their physical needs (and as Jesus taught us to pray in Matt. 6:11), so we are to rely on God for our spiritual nourishment.

1. Peter Enns, *Exodus*, NIV Application Commentary (Grand Rapids: Zondervan, 2000), 334–35.

The Bible as Our Daily Bread

The Word of God provides us with our own "daily bread." The Bible is more than a historical book or record of past events. God has used Scripture in each generation to mediate life-giving revelation, experience, and understanding.[2] As we read the Bible, it has the capacity to transform us. When the Bible is read from a posture of faith and humility, it can be used by God to speak into our hearts, minds, and lives. God is the primary author of Scripture by inspiring (God-breathing) the words of the human authors. While each book of the Bible was written for a specific audience ("there-then"), it also is God breathed for our world today. As 2 Timothy 3:16–17 reminds us, "All Scripture is God-breathed and is useful for teaching, rebuking, correcting and training in righteousness, so that the servant of God may be thoroughly equipped for every good work." Scripture teaches us how to love and live in imitation of God. It rebukes us by exposing our pride and selfish ambitions. It corrects us by revealing our worries, our anxieties, and our harboring of unforgiveness toward others (or ourselves). It trains us in right living so that we may fulfill our calling as disciples of Christ and children of God. Therefore, the ultimate purpose of reading the Bible is not to know the book but to know the author: God.

This process of spiritual formation is a slow work. It is also a daily activity. Like many aspects of our physical life that need our daily attention, such as good nutrition and regular exercise, so also our spiritual health benefits from daily activity. In the wilderness temptation, while Jesus is fasting, he says, "One does not live by bread alone, but by every word that comes from the mouth of God" (Matt. 4:4 NRSVue). Jesus, the Word incarnate (John 1:1), is our daily staple of bread and the source of our spiritual nourishment. One of the primary ways that Jesus is revealed to us is through the Bible. To know the Bible requires us to read it. To be transformed by the Bible requires us to partake in a steady diet of daily reading.

Consider these verses from the Message version of the Bible: "Don't for a minute let this Book of The Revelation be out of mind. Ponder and meditate on it day and night, making sure you practice everything written in it. Then you'll get where you're going; then you'll succeed" (Josh. 1:8); "You thrill to God's Word, you chew on Scripture day and night" (Ps. 1:2); "By your words I can see where I'm going; they throw a beam of light on my dark path" (Ps. 119:105). The Bible encourages us to cultivate a lifestyle of regular reading of Scripture. It is meant to be not a burdensome chore but a life-giving activity

---

2. William M. Wright IV and Francis Martin, *Encountering the Living God in Scripture: Theological and Philosophical Principles for Interpretation* (Grand Rapids: Baker Academic, 2019), xv–xvi.

that nourishes our whole person. One method used historically in the church to help us read the Bible is the ancient practice of *lectio divina*.

The Method of *Lectio Divina*

The ancient contemplative practice of *lectio divina* (Latin for "divine reading") developed in the context of monasticism and has been practiced by believers for centuries. It is essentially a method of prayerfully meditating on a passage of Scripture for the purpose of communion with God. Angela Lou Harvey describes it as "above all else, reading in a posture of prayer, attuned to the presence of God in the text and ready to listen and respond."[3] One of the first to articulate the process of *lectio divina* was the twelfth-century Carthusian monk Guigo II of Chartreuse. Guigo, inspired by the image of Jacob's ladder (Gen. 28:12), described the process of reading the Bible as climbing a ladder toward heaven to meet with God.[4] The approach has four main stages, with periods of silence between each step.

The first stage is *lectio*, or the slow, careful reading of the passage. In this first step, the reader slowly reads the passage aloud, being attentive to its basic, plain meaning and contemplating the words of the text. At this stage, readers also quiet themselves and prepare their hearts to hear God speak to them. The slow and prayerful contemplation of the text is like pulling off a chunk of delicious bread or tasty food and savoring the first mouthful.[5] "How sweet are your words to my taste, sweeter than honey to my mouth!" (Ps. 119:103).

The second stage is *meditatio*, or meditation. This step requires the reader to study the passage carefully. This includes using our intellectual capacity. That is, we do not ignore all the lessons about context and genre that have been outlined in the previous chapters of this book. As Eugene Peterson writes, "The more we are 'in context' when language is used, the more likely we are to get it."[6] We utilize the tools and skills necessary for understanding a passage in its original context and how it points to Christ. These tools and skills enhance our understanding of the Bible. But we do not leave the text in the past. It is a living book. Its significance is more than just its historical record; we want to be spiritually enriched by meditating on the meaning of the passage. Perhaps we may also notice some literary techniques used. Similarly, we

---

3. Angela Lou Harvey, *Spiritual Reading: A Study of the Christian Practice of Reading Scripture* (Eugene, OR: Cascade Books, 2015), 14.
4. Wright and Martin, *Encountering the Living God in Scripture*, 3.
5. Wright and Martin, *Encountering the Living God in Scripture*, 3–4.
6. Eugene H. Peterson, *Eat This Book: A Conversation in the Art of Spiritual Reading* (London: Hodder & Stoughton, 2006), 86.

might note a phrase or key word that stands out, and so we meditate on that word. This meditative process is like chewing on the food, as a cow chews grass, over and over. As John of Patmos says, "Whoever has ears, let them hear what the Spirit says to the churches" (Rev. 2:7, 11, 17, 29; 3:6, 13, 22).[7]

Third, the reader turns to their heart for *oratio* (to speak, pray). For Guigo, this stage is like tasting the flavor of the morsel of food.[8] The reader then speaks with God, requesting greater understanding and asking God to speak to them through the passage. The reader desires God's love to be known and to increase in them. As the psalmist says, "As the deer pants for streams of water, so my soul pants for you, my God" (Ps. 42:1). This step requires a posture of openness to experience and hearing God address us through a word or phrase,[9] including the probing of our dark secrets. Sometimes, the Holy Spirit reveals our own failings or sins, for which we must repent. This step then allows our heart to respond to the passage and what God might be revealing in contemplative prayer.

This leads to the final stage: *contemplatio* (contemplation). The culmination of this reading practice is where the reader sits in silent prayer, simply resting in the peace and presence of God. Words are no longer needed. For Guigo, the final step is the swallowing of the food and enjoying its goodness and nourishment.

Guigo reflects on the experience of the soul during this entire process:

> When you break for me the bread of sacred Scripture, you have shown yourself to me in that breaking of bread, and the more I see you, the more I long to see you, no more from without, in the rind of the letter, but within, in the letter's hidden meaning. . . . So give me, Lord, some pledge of what I hope to inherit, at least one drop of heavenly rain with which to refresh my thirst, for I am on fire with love.[10]

The movement of the whole practice of *lectio divina* is from the head to the heart. It guides us toward a prayerful response. If you would like to try this method of devotional reading, a good passage to begin with is Psalm 63:1–8. In fact, the book of Psalms is ideal for this practice because its metaphors provide rich expression of our union with God.[11]

---

7. Peterson, *Eat This Book*, 87.

8. Wright and Martin, *Encountering the Living God in Scripture*, 4.

9. Marcus J. Borg, *Reading the Bible Again for the First Time: Taking the Bible Seriously but Not Literally* (New York: HarperCollins, 2001), 39.

10. Quoted in Wright and Martin, *Encountering the Living God in Scripture*, 4–5.

11. Thanks to Dr. Robyn Wrigley-Carr for her reflections on *lectio divina*, which are utilized in this section.

Yet the practice of *lectio divina* is not a religious formula or mechanical procedure. It is a dynamic activity and so can be practiced in a way that is messy, playful, and muddled. Yet it aims to lead readers into the mystery of union with God. While *lectio divina* is a deeply personal reading activity, it is not individualistic. Peterson notes, it is "a way of reading that intends the fusion of the entire biblical story and my story."[12] By implication, we are joined with countless other believers, past and present, who have also been fused to God's story. Similarly, while this practice does not bypass our minds, it is not just an intellectual exercise to accumulate knowledge. Marcus Borg writes of this practice, "The purpose of the practice is not to read or hear the Bible for information or content. Rather, the purpose is to listen for the Spirit of God speaking through the words of the biblical text."[13] Yet how does the Bible facilitate an encounter with the living God? Just how does the Spirit work in and through the Bible?

The Role of the Holy Spirit in Reading Scripture

The Holy Spirit is active in every step of reading Scripture. Just as the Spirit was present with the biblical authors when they wrote their books and letters, the Spirit is also present with believers when they read the Word of God today (as noted previously). The Bible is a human product—it is created; into it, the breath of God was breathed, and it continues to inspire the breath of life. As the ultimate author of the Bible, God speaks to us through his Word. Beth Felker Jones writes, "When we recognize the Scriptures as the Word of God, we are recognizing a reliable connection between these texts and the God whom we meet and know there."[14] God's Word is living and powerful; it transforms human lives and reveals God's purposes for creation.

To help articulate the reading experience, Rickie D. Moore uses the analogy of an altar.[15] The altar in the Old Testament narrative is a sacred space where people meet with God, often when making sacrifices. The Bible is like an altar because it is the sacred space where we meet with God, and we are altered. This does not necessarily mean that we have mountaintop experiences every time we open our Bibles. Instead, it involves yielding ourselves to hear from God in the sacred space of the Word. As William Wright observes, "To

12. Peterson, *Eat This Book*, 90.
13. Borg, *Reading the Bible Again*, 38.
14. Beth Felker Jones, *Practicing Christian Doctrine: An Introduction to Thinking and Living Theologically* (Grand Rapids: Baker Academic, 2014), 41.
15. Rickie D. Moore, "Altar Hermeneutics: Reflections on Pentecostal Biblical Interpretation," *Pneuma* 38, nos. 1–2 (2016): 148–59.

understand the sacred Scripture . . . is to receive a penetrating insight into these divine realities, to have a genuine faith-experience of them, and to have one's mind and heart touched by them."[16] Scripture mediates the divine realities and life-giving connection with God in the present. When we meet with God at the altar of the holy Bible, God affirms and encourages us, speaks truth afresh to us, corrects and guides us, treasures us, and calls us to respond in personal obedience. The Holy Spirit inspires the words we read in our Bible to be real and life-giving for each one of us as we live in the community of Christ. This leads to transformation. The Spirit is the transcendent yet intimately present source for our ongoing revelatory understanding of the Bible.[17]

Similarly, another analogy, used by Cheryl Bridges Johns, is the role of the Holy Spirit at creation.[18] In Genesis 1:1–2, the Holy Spirit hovers over the barren waters, like a bird spreading her wings. The uncreated Creator Spirit broods over the created emptiness of creation. Then, as the word of God is spoken, the Creator Spirit reaches out to transform the empty creation by forming it and filling it through his life-giving power (1:2). In a similar way, the Creator Spirit takes the created Scripture and spreads his wings, filling our impoverished thinking with a deeper understanding of God's Word.[19] The Holy Spirit leads people into a richer knowledge of the mystery of Christ and helps us to live out this transforming power in our lives.[20] This mystery continually invites us into the deeper life and to drink of God. "I want to drink God, deep drafts of God. I'm thirsty for God-alive" (Ps. 42:1 Message).

Revelation does not rely exclusively on the human intellect as it results in a sense of "knowing." The Hebrew term "to know" (*yada'*) is a relational term, often used as a euphemism for sexual intimacy. It refers to a knowing that is "more by heart than by mind."[21] When we read the Bible, God awakens in us a love for him and others. Revelation mediated by Scripture is relational in that it results in relational knowledge. The Spirit is the chief agent of this revelation (Isa. 11:2).[22] Paul writes, "I keep asking that the God of our Lord Jesus Christ, the glorious Father, may give you the Spirit of wisdom and

---

16. Wright and Martin, *Encountering the Living God in Scripture*, 222.

17. Wright and Martin, *Encountering the Living God in Scripture*, 123.

18. Cheryl Bridges Johns, "Grieving, Brooding, and Transforming: The Spirit, the Bible, and Gender," in *Grieving, Brooding, and Transforming: The Spirit, the Bible, and Gender*, ed. Cheryl Bridges Johns and Lisa P. Stephenson (Leiden: Brill, 2021), 15.

19. Johns, "Grieving, Brooding, and Transforming," 16–17.

20. Wright and Martin, *Encountering the Living God in Scripture*, 231.

21. Cheryl Bridges Johns and Jackie D. Johns, "Yielding to the Spirit: A Pentecostal Approach to Group Bible Study," *Journal of Pentecostal Theology* 1 (1992): 112.

22. Craig S. Keener, *Spirit Hermeneutics: Reading Scripture in Light of Pentecost* (Grand Rapids: Eerdmans, 2016), 161.

revelation, so that you may know him better" (Eph. 1:17). The purpose of the revelation of Scripture is to know God better. The relational dependence of the Spirit on the Father and Son (and vice versa) overflows into our revelatory experiences to unite us in participation with the triune God.

WHAT DO I DO NOW?

As the psalmist says, "Your word is a lamp for my feet, a light on my path" (Ps. 119:105). Like a spotlight illuminating a path or road so that we can see and walk clearly in the right direction, the Spirit illuminates the words of the Bible for us. Scripture forms us and guides us along our journey of life. It shapes us and our passions, which inform our behavior. The Bible is to be lived. Peterson encourages us to "live what you read. We read the Bible in order to live the word of God."[23] Yet as noted above, the purpose of the Bible involves more than just providing moral guidance or cognitive information about God.

The telos, or end goal, of the Bible is to reveal God and to allow us to participate in the life of God. The Eastern Orthodox community has developed a particular way of understanding this concept. Called *theōsis*, it refers to deification or divine transformation, such that we become like God. That is, we are drawn "toward the fullness of God and our own fullness in God."[24] As we read and obey the Bible, the intention is for us to become more and more like Christ, for us to participate more and more in the divine life. Chris E. W. Green writes, "Scripture, read with and in the Spirit, actually works to conform us to Christ, materializing his character in us, incorporating us into his identity."[25] Coming to know Jesus, which we do when we read the Bible, is becoming more like Jesus. Yet all of this requires us to read, study, and apply the Bible diligently. The Bible is a gift from God, for us to know him and the salvation he offers us. It is the place we can encounter God. So if we want God to transform us, we must read the Bible. We need to study it carefully, attending to the words of someone we love, patiently listening in anticipation for our loved one's voice and words, inspired by and illuminated by the Spirit.

23. Peterson, *Eat This Book*, 84.
24. Chris E. W. Green, *Sanctifying Interpretation: Vocation, Holiness, and Scripture*, 2nd ed. (Cleveland, TN: CPT, 2020), xv.
25. Green, *Sanctifying Interpretation*, 135.

PRAYER

Most holy God, draw me, weak as I am, after yourself. I yield myself to you.

I surrender to you my hopes, my dreams, my ambitions.

Holy Spirit, giver of life, come and infuse me with your transformative grace.

Come, sweet Spirit. Regenerate and renew my heart.

I am yours. For the glory of God.

Amen.

TOPICS FOR REVIEW

1. In what ways is the Bible like our daily bread?
2. Have you tried using *lectio divina* or a similar approach for your devotional reading of the Bible? What was it like? What are some of the benefits of devotional reading?
3. How would you explain to a non-Christian the value of reading your Bible?

13

LIVING THE WORD

In this chapter, you should expect to learn the following:

- ▶ The difference between meaning and significance
- ▶ The importance of transitioning from there-then to here-now
- ▶ The necessity of application
- ▶ Common mistakes in application
- ▶ Personal aspects of application, both inward and outward

Your word is a lamp for my feet, a light on my path.
—Ps. 119:105

In parts 1 and 2, this book has explored the foundations of biblical interpretation and the importance of reading according to the genre of texts.
However, hermeneutically, these by themselves do not complete the task. As
the verse from Psalm 119 suggests, God's Word is a light for our feet so that
we can move forward. We are to apply and faithfully implement the message
of the Bible. Actions are integral to the whole hermeneutical process. We have
also previously discussed the role of the Holy Spirit inspiring the writers of
Scripture and how the Spirit also illuminates the biblical text for readers as
we journey in our Christian walk. The light of God's Word provides wisdom

Public Domain

Figure 13.1. *The Holy Spirit Descends on the Apostles and the Virgin,* by Sanvala, Mughal, India

and guidance in our daily lives. Even when the path is slippery and dark, Scripture shows us the way.[1]

Likewise, as can be observed in the painting shown in figure 13.1 depicting the outpouring of the Spirit on the day of Pentecost (Acts 2), the Spirit was poured out so that the believers would "receive power" (1:8). This was an empowerment for witness, for service. The Spirit's guidance leads us to action. As noted previously, hermeneutics includes moving the biblical message from

1. Federico G. Villanueva, *Psalms 73–150*, Asia Bible Commentary Series (Cumbria, UK: Langham, 2022), 346.

the there-then into the here-now. The hermeneutical task is not complete until it moves into relevance and application for our lives today.

Meaning and Significance for Today

One of the challenges in modern hermeneutics is the discernment of the relationship between "meaning" and "significance." On the one hand, we can ask, How is the text meaningful? One aspect of this question implies, What did the text mean to the original audience(s)? This is a key question we have been exploring throughout the book. However, it also can be asked, What does the text mean to *us*? This explores our personal responses to a passage. Thus, there is a distinction between "meaning" and "significance." That is, the original *meaning* of the text (whichever biblical text is referred to) should be clearly differentiated from the contemporary *significance* for us, as noted in chapter 4. So there is a meaning (or set of meanings) that depends on the original context of the writer, including their known intent, the genre of the text, and the original audience(s). But there are also multiple possible significances, which depend on the varying life situations, cultures, and the like of the contemporary audience. This leads us into the importance of application as part of the hermeneutical process.

Transitioning from There-Then to Here-Now

As noted in chapter 1, an important part of biblical exegesis is to interpret the text in its original contexts—grammatically, literarily, and rhetorically, as well as sociohistorically and culturally. We have identified that as the core of the exegetical process. For example, what did Paul mean in 1 Corinthians 2:1–5 as he wrote to the Corinthian congregation? Or what did Isaiah mean in his oracle of Isaiah 9:1–7? Understanding a passage within its original context (there-then) is the first part of the hermeneutical process. However, that process also includes a consideration of the implications of the passage for the contemporary context. Once we have deduced what the text means in its original context(s), we then appropriate it for the here-now. This is where you can really see both the art and the science of biblical interpretation at work.[2] As any good translator knows, the science of translation involves the direct, word-for-word translation of a text from one language to another. Yet the art

2. Kevin J. Vanhoozer's *The Drama of Doctrine: A Canonical-Linguistic Approach to Christian Theology* (Louisville: Westminster John Knox, 2005) aids in understanding this interplay. Special thanks to Robert Eby for bringing this to our attention.

of translation entails communicating the linguistic and cultural nuances or subtle differences of a text in the recipient language, rather than awkwardly translating word for word only. The interplay takes experience and skill. For anyone who has worked cross-culturally or cross-linguistically, the ability to bridge the gap of language and context is challenging; yet it can be developed through experience and practice. In the same way, we are to "translate" the biblical text from its original context to our contexts today.

The ultimate goal, then, is to move from the original meaning (by the authors and as understood by the audiences through the text) to its significance for us today. To do this well, we need to pay attention to two main aspects. One, we need to understand the original contexts of the biblical text (what it meant there-then), and two, we need to understand our own contexts well (in order to move to the text's significance for us today, the here-now).

Applying the Bible

Some may ask, Why bother with applying the biblical text in the first place?[3] Certainly, there is a role for understanding the Bible in its cultural-sociohistorical and literary contexts. While some scholars may see the value of exegesis in and of itself, there are several reasons why application is necessary. First, as followers of God, we are to observe or obey his Word. As Psalm 119:105 suggests, we cannot fully walk the path of obedience if we do not have the light of Scripture to show us the way. Obedience to God and God's Word is not negotiable. Matthew 28:20 records Jesus giving us a commission to teach the nations to obey everything he has commanded us. It is impossible for us to truly teach obedience if we are not being obedient ourselves. Further, Jesus himself, in the conclusion of the Sermon on the Mount, equates following his teachings with a "wise man who built his house on the rock" (Matt. 7:24). That is, if we read the Bible but do not put it into practice, our life is built on an unstable foundation. But if we read the Bible and put it into practice, our life is built on a firm foundation. Scripture is chock full of injunctions to follow God's commands, learn from his Word, and walk in

---

3. There are many good works on application; see especially J. Scott Duvall and J. Daniel Hays, *Grasping God's Word: A Hands-On Approach to Reading, Interpreting, and Applying the Bible*, 4th ed. (Grand Rapids: Zondervan, 2020), 239–54, and William W. Klein, Craig L. Blomberg, and Robert L. Hubbard Jr., *Introduction to Biblical Interpretation*, 3rd ed. (Grand Rapids: Zondervan, 2017), 602–36. In systematic theology, there is a subfield sometimes called Christian living, which connects theology to application in biblical interpretation. See J. Rodman Williams, *Renewal Theology*, vol. 2, *Salvation, the Holy Spirit, and Christian Living* (Grand Rapids: Zondervan, 1990), 411–45.

obedience. However, we cannot obey what we do not know. Therefore, the underlying assumption in this discussion of application is that we are actively reading the Bible.

Second, the Bible also notes the ongoing importance of its message (in both the Old and New Testaments), stressing that the principles and lessons found throughout the story of redemption should be intentionally taught to future generations. Paul, for instance, in 2 Timothy 1:5 encourages Timothy to continue in the faith he has learned from his grandmother, Lois, and mother, Eunice. Paul then proceeds in 2:2 to tell Timothy that the sound doctrine he received is to be passed on to future generations. What Paul has taught Timothy ("in the presence of many witnesses") he is to "entrust to reliable people," who in turn are to teach others. This multigenerational outlook highlights the importance of discipleship and our responsibility to teach future generations God's Word. The commission to make disciples of and teach future generations (Matt. 28:19–20) results in multiple generations worshiping together. Exemplified by Timothy's family, a multigenerational outlook envisions extended families loving God and serving him together. This is also reflected in Peter's citation of Joel's prophecy (Acts 2:17–21) that sons and daughters, young and old, male and female—the whole community—can be empowered and used by the Spirit at the same time. The multigenerational nature of biblical teaching also highlights that the Bible is relevant and can be applied in each new context and throughout all generations. As chapter 3 has demonstrated, the church has read, treasured, and interpreted the Bible across the centuries, and it will continue to do so in the future. Thus, as each generation applies the Bible to ever-changing contexts, they demonstrate its ongoing relevance.

Third, the Bible stresses the importance of moving from pure theoretical engagement to practical action and behavior. The book of James emphasizes that faith without deeds is worthless. James views the Bible as central to this task of ensuring that faith is applied. He says that it is not enough to only be hearers of the Word; we must be doers as well (James 1:22–25). Our knowledge must move from our heads to our hearts and to our hands. That is, our faith requires action if it is to be embedded within our whole person. Otherwise, it is as fleeting as looking in a mirror. But when we apply our faith, we move from theory to practice. Faith in God and his Word is irrelevant without action—thus, we are expected to express our faith in good works.

A final note regarding application is that a certain process takes place when we read Scripture consistently. When we come to the Bible as readers or listeners, it informs and transforms us. The ongoing interplay between the reader and the Bible is highlighted by the *hermeneutical circle* (see fig. 13.2).

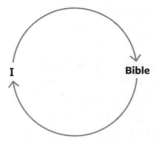

Figure 13.2. The hermeneutical circle / Paul Lewis

The *hermeneutical circle* can also be seen through the process of me, as a reader, with my preunderstanding in place coming to Scripture with an exegetical focus on the text. Through theological reflection I move to application, which in turn informs my new preunderstanding (see fig. 13.3). Theological reflection (and implementation) moves us forward. So the basic hermeneutical circle, from the Bible to me and back again, is an ongoing and involved interaction.

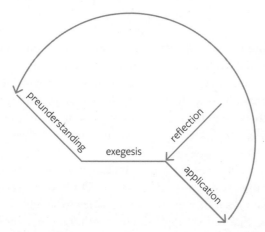

Figure 13.3. The revised hermeneutical circle / Paul Lewis

As noted above, when we come repeatedly to the Bible, it can inform and transform us by the power of the Holy Spirit through the Word. The ongoing engagement with the biblical text should move us from information gathering to transformation, growth, and development. This transformational process of our preunderstanding and our very lives forms us, so that we are slightly different the next time we come to the text. We continue to be changed and informed through our ongoing engagement with the Bible, and this is what makes reading Scripture so dynamic and exciting. The ongoing nature of this process moves us from a static hermeneutical circle to a dynamic *hermeneutical spiral* (see fig. 13.4).[4] While in principle the spiral shows the ongoing dynamism of this process, we are aware that not all spirals are progressive; some may be lateral, and others may decline. To ensure that we don't take an off-ramp (such as going off on a weird theological tangent) or stall ourselves (such as getting stuck in an ethical dilemma), we need others to help us move forward in our interpretive journey. As emphasized throughout this book, it is essential that we read in community. Thus, the hermeneutical community—local, global, and historical—and the biblical text in its historical and literary contexts are needed as guardrails and aids to ensure the hermeneutical spiral continues in a progressive manner.

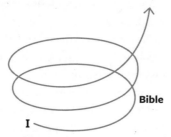

Figure 13.4. The hermeneutical spiral / Paul Lewis

Common Mistakes in Application

There are several common mistakes when it comes to application.[5] The most common is the neglect of the original context, which leads to conflating our own situation with that of the biblical text. This can cause us to confuse the historical environment of the biblical passage with our own, so that there is a disconnect between the historical or literary context of the passage and its meaning, on the one hand, and the implementation or significance of the passage today, on the other. This can be seen in the prevalent usage of what I (Paul) call "refrigerator theology." This term comes from the common practice of printing a verse or part of a verse on a magnet so it can be stuck to a refrigerator, where it can be frequently seen (which in and of itself is fine); yet it is then used out of context in one's immediate situation or applied too broadly. An example is Philippians 4:13, which states, "I can do all things

4. This is the underlying premise of Grant R. Osborne, *The Hermeneutical Spiral: A Comprehensive Introduction to Biblical Interpretation*, rev. ed. (Downers Grove, IL: IVP Academic, 2006).

5. Certain points in this section are highlighted in Klein, Blomberg, and Hubbard, *Introduction to Biblical Interpretation*, 605–9.

through Christ who strengthens me" (NKJV). Within context, this verse is about Paul at times having financial abundance and at other times going hungry; in other words, he can enjoy plenty and endure scarcity "through Christ who strengthens [him]." No matter what economic situation (good or bad) comes his way, Paul is strengthened by Christ. Over the years, however, I have seen this passage used as self-encouragement for a wide variety of modern activities with personal benefit—such as becoming an Olympic ice skater. Certainly, in the whole counsel of God, several themes can be included in this verse—such as Christ empowering us to follow his will or to overcome temptation—but it does not include everything!

Along similar lines, some believers create a different form of this mistake. Over the years, they have highlighted or underlined verses in their Bible, but now they have gotten to the point where they look at only those passages that have been highlighted, to the neglect of the rest of the text. In other words, they neglect to read the verse in its literary context. By pulling these verses out of context, we can miss their meaning, which can lead to faulty application. We can also miss important lessons by reading out of context, such as learning from Philippians 4:13 the value of contentment. In doing so, we can stagnate our growth (and our progress in the hermeneutical spiral) because we read the passage the same way each time without developing our understanding or our character.

Another common mistake in application is found in parts of the world where cultures are decidedly closer to the cultures of the Bible than most Western contexts. Being similar is not equivalent to being the same. Accordingly, some may falsely assume that cultural similarity means that similar practices function the same way or have the same relevance today. For example, in some contexts, a woman is required to wear a scarf to cover her head in church, even though the practice in those contexts emerged from historical and religious origins very different from those of the Bible. Similarly, modern practices can sometimes mirror biblical ones. However, this is more often than not accidental—perhaps a relic of an earlier adaptation of the Judeo-Christian heritage—and should not necessarily be seen as a pattern. An example is the use of tambourines in some church worship services. The other extreme is to assume that since the biblical context or meaning is so different, there must therefore be no relevance for today. This is also a fallacy.

Inward Application

While application is key, much of it is internal to the life of the believer. The Christian life is a journey of following Christ. Whereas part of the inner journey is conforming to Jesus Christ—*conformitas Christi*—it is also true that we are called to imitate Christ—*imitatio Christi*. We must intentionally seek to mirror Christ's life, which includes following Christ concretely in the rough and tumble, sinful world in which we exist, taking up our cross daily. As we learned from the story of Scripture in chapter 6, humanity was originally made in the image of God. But we tainted that image through our rejection of God. Through Jesus, God in the flesh, that image is being restored. But it requires us to be transformed. This is the process of becoming Christlike.

The Bible plays a special role in our calling to imitate Christ and to undergo this transformational process. Paul tells us in Romans that we are "predestined to be conformed to the image of his Son" (8:29). Yet how do we conform to the image of the Son? Paul gives the answer in Romans 12:1–2: "Therefore, I urge you, brothers and sisters, in view of God's mercy, to offer your bodies as a living sacrifice, holy and pleasing to God—this is your true and proper worship. Do not conform to the pattern of this world, but be transformed by the renewing of your mind. Then you will be able to test and approve what God's will is—his good, pleasing and perfect will."

Paul begins here by recognizing that inner transformation is part of our worship but also connected to our bodies. Our inner transformation is enacted and embodied as we walk the life of faith. In fact, worship "results in an altered perception of reality."[6] As part of ongoing spiritual growth, the progressive nature of our biblical understanding and the associated modifications of our preunderstanding lead to an expanded (and at times corrected) perspective about God, his goodness, his grace, his love, his mercy, and so much more. This naturally leads to an attitude of and need for worship. God deserves our worship, and our self-reflection, which comes from his Word and his presence, naturally leads to worship. So a part of our following Christ is worship and a doxological life—that is, a life of worship.

Paul continues to tell us in Romans 12 that we are to reject the old patterns of our thinking and, correspondingly, to renew our minds. This transformation has both natural and supernatural dynamics.[7] Some of this growth can be part of our natural maturation process; however, realization of the full potential can only result from the Spirit's presence and guidance. Similarly, the renewing of our minds is both a physical and a spiritual task. It has a physiological basis, as new neural pathways are developed in our

6. Cheryl Bridges Johns, *Pentecostal Formation: A Pedagogy among the Oppressed*, Journal of Pentecostal Theology Supplement Series 2 (Sheffield: Sheffield Academic, 1993), 89.

7. For a developmental lens on this point, see James E. Loder, *The Logic of the Spirit: Human Development in Theological Perspective* (San Francisco: Jossey-Bass, 1998).

brains.[8] New habits and new ways of thinking are formed. Yet renewal is also spiritual, because the Holy Spirit works in our hearts, wills, and minds to transform us into the image of Christ (2 Cor. 3:17–18). This part of the process is where the Bible is particularly helpful. How do we develop healthy patterns of thinking? We read the Bible. How do we know what it means to be Christlike? The Bible tells us so. As we renew our minds, we are able to discern God's will for our lives.

It is important to be reminded once more that our pursuit of God and his will is conducted most effectively and fruitfully within the community of faith. A local Christian community inspires, challenges, and pulls us forward as we individually, collectively, and institutionally follow Christ. Within the community and by the personal indwelling of the Holy Spirit, the fruit of the Holy Spirit (Gal. 5:22–23) is embedded and embodied in each person. We cannot love, forgive, or be patient in isolation; such fruit is developed in community. This Spirit-empowered implementation of our biblical reading is meant to be fleshed out in daily life. As such, it is not for special events or special occasions only; rather, it is also inclusive of every moment of every day. The fruit of the Holy Spirit then becomes an outward expression of the internal work of character formation and our transformation into Christlikeness.[9] Therefore, as we engage the Bible and apply it, we are transformed internally, and we exhibit this change in our external character and worship.

This leads us to the final aspect of our internal spiritual growth and application of the Bible, which concerns our moral life or our ethics. "Ethics," essentially, is seeking to do the right thing. It concerns living faithfully to God in our decision-making. Yet while ethics definitely does have an outward, behavioral component, it is equally true that ethics involves internal growth in our spiritual lives (e.g., seeking after God's holiness and righteousness).

8. See Caroline Leaf, *Switch on Your Brain: The Key to Peak Happiness, Thinking, and Health* (Grand Rapids: Baker Books, 2013).

9. On the Holy Spirit in the moral life, see Henlee H. Barnette, *Introducing Christian Ethics* (Nashville: Broadman, 1961), 87–97; Leon O. Hynson, "The Church and Social Transformation: An Ethics of the Spirit," *Wesleyan Theological Journal* 11 (1976): 49–61; L. Gregory Jones, *Transformed Judgment: Toward a Trinitarian Account of the Moral Life* (Notre Dame, IN: University of Notre Dame Press, 1990); and Paul W. Lewis, "A Pneumatological Approach to Virtue Ethics," *Asian Journal of Pentecostal Studies* 1, no. 1 (1998): 42–61. For various discussions of the Spirit's role in social ethics, see Samuel Solivan, *Spirit, Pathos and Liberation: Toward an Hispanic Pentecostal Theology*, Journal of Pentecostal Theology Supplement Series 14 (Sheffield: Sheffield Academic, 1998); Eldin Villafañe, *The Liberating Spirit: Toward an Hispanic American Pentecostal Social Ethic*, 2nd ed. (Grand Rapids: Eerdmans, 1993); and Matthias Wenk, *Community-Forming Power: The Socio-Ethical Role of the Spirit in Luke-Acts*, Journal of Pentecostal Theology Supplement Series 19 (Sheffield: Sheffield Academic, 2000), among many others.

These are foundational theological concepts that are developed in the Bible and that inform our ethical decision-making. As we interpret the Bible, apply it, and live it, we reflect the values of Scripture in our moral lives. We demonstrate an authentic consistency between what we believe and our actions. So applying the Bible is central to the development of our internal life in God.

Outward Application

Personal application of the Bible also has outward dynamics and implications for our life of faith. First, as noted above, ethical living is expressed through our personal conduct and activities. While moral formation does have an internal aspect, it is also seen externally in one's behavior and deeds. In an analogous way, as God demonstrates himself in word and deed, so are we to express his presence in our lives through our words and deeds. Again, how do we learn of God's words and deeds? We read the Bible. We progress in our hermeneutical spiral and become formed by Scripture. The Bible, then, provides the foundational principles for our ethical decision-making, which we apply to our particular contexts and cultures. While character is universal (based on God's character, such as his love and justice), actions and applications can be very culturally tied and contextually driven. This point does not diminish the importance of appropriate actions or the principles that underpin those actions, but it is crucial that our ethical decisions are based on solid exegesis.

A key outward application emphasized in the Great Commission of Matthew 28 is the proclamation of the gospel. Similarly, the words of Jesus recorded in Acts 1:8 instruct us to "be [his] witnesses."[10] The interpretation of the biblical text helps us understand both the message, the "good news," and the need to proclaim it. Proclamation does not necessarily require some formalized preaching venue (although it can include this).[11] Proclamation can occur in all kinds of venues or environs with any number of hearers. It occurs wherever one can be a witness to others (individually or corporately), pointing to the good news of Christ. It is also expressed in both word and deed. The biblical message highlights the necessity of not only being receivers of the good news but also serving as conduits for others. Therefore, proclamation and witness are a necessary part of our outward application of the Bible.

10. This emphasis is unpacked in more detail in Paul W. Lewis, "Reconsidering Certain Popular Interpretations of Acts 1:8," *Spirit and Church* 8 (2016): 3–16.

11. There are many fine works on preaching as pulpit ministry, such as Sidney Greidanus, *The Modern Preacher and the Ancient Text: Interpreting and Preaching Biblical Literature* (Grand Rapids: Eerdmans, 1988).

Connected to proclamation is the importance of applying the biblical message through teaching. As with proclamation, teaching venues can vary from formal to informal. Still, just as we are to be conduits of divine grace in proclamation, so are we to pass on what we learn via instruction. As noted above, Paul instructs Timothy (in 2 Tim. 2:2) to teach "reliable people" what he has learned, who in turn will pass it on to others. All believers are on a journey, which means that everyone has someone ahead of them and someone behind them. Accordingly, we can mentor or teach while also being taught by others. This is the gift of community; we learn and teach in turn. Related to this concept is the key application of mentoring or discipleship. Matthew 28:19–20 (noted above) uses only one verb for this task. That is, to "make disciples" is the primary task; "going," "teaching," and "baptizing" are all participles used to express the activity of discipling. Discipling is intentional; it imparts a moral vision and a new hope as it guides followers of Jesus, by the Holy Spirit, into Christ-inspired decision-making.[12] Not only are we called to be Christ's disciples, but we are also called to disciple others.[13]

Another external aspect of application is pastoral care and concern. While many automatically assume that such care pertains to the ministerial vocation only, biblically speaking, all members of the church are called to care for one another. The Bible instructs us to "carry each other's burdens" (Gal. 6:2), to "love one another" (e.g., John 13:34–35; 1 Thess. 4:9; 1 Pet. 3:8; 1 John 3:11, 23; 4:7, 11), and so on. The New Testament is full of these expressions. A key focus in the Scriptures, then, is that we provide care for one another; the application of this injunction is an expression of our love for one another.

While interpersonal care and concern are clear applications of the biblical message, it is also true that social concern (or social justice) is found throughout the biblical text. The Old and New Testaments alike highlight the centrality of taking care of the poor, widows, orphans, strangers, and the marginalized in our midst. Not only are they on the heart and mind of God; they are also our neighbors, to whom we are called to demonstrate kindness (Mark 12:31). Jesus himself, in Matthew 25:31–46, stresses that those who take care of the needs of the marginalized are clearly followers of God. Therefore, works of compassion are also to be on our operational agenda as we seek to apply God's Word to our lives.

---

12. Joe Trull, "The Right Thing to Do: How Do You Decide?," *Theological Educator* 45 (1992): 74–76.

13. There are numerous good works on discipleship; however, a pivotal one that is theologically and practically robust is Dietrich Bonhoeffer, *The Cost of Discipleship*, trans. R. H. Fuller, rev. ed. (New York: Macmillan, 1959), esp. chaps. 1–5.

As we have seen throughout this book, applying the Bible personally, both internally and externally, is a key part of the hermeneutical process. Yet how do we know we are applying the Bible adequately? William Klein, Craig Blomberg, and Robert Hubbard Jr., in their book *Introduction to Biblical Interpretation*, highlight certain queries that can help safeguard our applications.[14] The first is to ask, What was the originally intended application of the text? The second is to ask, Is that application transferable over the centuries to our contexts? If not, then we should identify at least one cross-cultural or cross-historical principle that the text clearly reflects. As a rule of thumb—and as noted in studies of the church growth movement—principles can transfer, but practices do not (if practices transfer, they do so more incidentally than inherently).[15] Once a principle has been identified in the there-then, we can then find a corresponding application that embodies that principle for the here-now.

WHAT DO I DO NOW?

As we reflect on the task of application, it is important, at least in our own minds, to understand the differences between the original *meaning* of the text and its *significance* for us today. Given modern language usage, we may still use the term "meaning" as a synonym for "significance," but by being aware of the differences between these two terms, we remind ourselves that exegetical meaning is different from application.

The second key takeaway is that the full hermeneutical process includes application. It is appropriate and often more practical to first start with exegesis, so as to know what a passage means within its original contexts (the there-then). However, the process eventually needs to transition to our lives today. It should inform our beliefs, conduct, and proclamation. The there-then must move to the here-now—an interaction of the two horizons.

Furthermore, application includes both internal and external components. Both are necessary and should not be neglected, and when both are fleshed out in our lives, they demonstrate growth and feed into our hermeneutical spiral, which, with God's help, incrementally progresses as we become more like Christ. The Bible is truly a lamp for our feet and a light for our path (Ps. 119:105).

14. These questions are taken from Klein, Blomberg, and Hubbard, *Introduction to Biblical Interpretation*, 609–35.

15. Paul W. Lewis, "Church Growth," in *Encyclopedia of Pentecostal and Charismatic Christianity*, ed. Stanley M. Burgess (New York: Routledge, 2006), 100–104.

PRAYER

Lord, we thank you for your Word.
  Help us to be doers of the Word and not just hearers.
  Let our application be based on the "rock" of your teaching.
  And help us apply your Word to our lives so that we can be the
witnesses you have called us to be.
  Amen.

TOPICS FOR REVIEW

1. How does differentiating "meaning" from "significance" help in your own understanding of the Bible, biblical interpretation, and scriptural application?
2. What possible mistakes can you see in the process of applying the truths of the Bible?
3. Do you feel that the internal or the external aspects of application are more difficult? Why?

14

CROSS-CULTURAL HERMENEUTICS

In this chapter, you should expect to learn the following:

▶ The nature of culture
▶ Cross-cultural or missional hermeneutics
▶ Problems related to cross-cultural hermeneutics
▶ The benefits of cross-cultural hermeneutics
▶ How to approach biblical interpretation without study aids

And they sang a new song, saying:

> "You are worthy to take the scroll
>   and to open its seals,
> because you were slain,
>   and with your blood you purchased for God
>   persons from every tribe and language and people and nation.
> You have made them to be a kingdom and priests to serve our God,
>   and they will reign on the earth."

> —Rev. 5:9–10

Throughout church history, the multicultural, multilinguistic nature of the gospel has been recognized. The eighth-century painting represented in figure 14.1 shows the multicultural dynamic of the church (the priest on the

Figure 14.1. Eighth-century Khocho mosaic from Northwest China

left is a Sogdian priest from central Asia, with two Turkish men, possibly Uyghur, and the woman on the right is Chinese).[1] Likewise, there are many Christian manuscripts also found in northwest China that are bilingual, including Bible translations, lectionaries, and the like.[2] The church, from its inception on the day of Pentecost up to today, has engaged in cross-cultural activities and initiatives. Along the same line, Revelation 5:9–10 emphasizes a future time when people from every tribe, language, people, and nation worship God. This will happen only when everyone can know about God,

1. For further commentary on this painting, see Ken Parry, "The Art of the Church of the East in China," in *Jingjiao: The Church of the East in China and Central Asia*, ed. Roman Malek, Collecta Serica (Sankt Augustin, Germany: Institut Monumenta Serica, 2006), 321–39, esp. 324 and fig. 2 on 334; Xiaojing Yan, "The Confluence of East and West in Nestorian Art in China," in *Hidden Treasures and Intercultural Encounters: Studies on East Syriac Christianity in China and Central Asia*, ed. Dietmar W. Winkler and Li Tang (Vienna: LIT, 2009), 283–92, esp. fig. 5 on 391.

2. On this, see Jes P. Asmussen, "The Sogdian and Uighur-Turkish Christian Literature in Central Asia before the Real Rise of Islam: A Survey," in *Indological and Buddhist Studies*, ed. L. A. Hercus et al. (Delhi: Sri Satguru Publications, 1984), 14–16, and Nicholas Sims-Williams, *Iranian Manuscripts in Syriac Script in the Berlin Turfan Collection*, Mitteliranische Handschriften 4 (Stuttgart: Steiner, 2012), 21–48.

understand his ways, and seek him. This truth points to the necessity of missional hermeneutics or cross-cultural hermeneutics.[3]

Cross-Cultural Hermeneutics

In recent years, intercultural, global, and missiological concerns have become pivotal in hermeneutical discussions.[4] We live in a multicultural world, and our engagement with the biblical text should likewise be informed by this reality. Before getting into some of the key components of cross-cultural hermeneutics, we need to first discuss the meaning of the word "culture."

Culture[5]

While there is an important cultural dynamic in biblical interpretation, the role of culture is even more complex when we are bringing an additional culture (or cultures) into the mix. By "culture," I mean "the web of significance human beings weave in order to create meaning."[6] Culture includes a complex conglomerate of customs, knowledge, beliefs (philosophical, religious, and other), worldviews, habits, conduct, and rituals, which has a form of internal coherence and assumed acceptance. Culture is not only a sum of these elements collectively; it also includes an account of how things make sense within the culture. Further, culture is paradigmatic in the sense that all information is filtered and put together a certain way through the

3. On reading the biblical text missiologically, see Craig S. Keener, *Spirit Hermeneutics: Reading Scripture in Light of Pentecost* (Grand Rapids: Eerdmans, 2016), 42–43.

4. Important works along these lines include James V. Brownson, *Speaking the Truth in Love: New Testament Resources for a Missional Hermeneutic*, Christian Mission and Modern Culture (Harrisburg, PA: Trinity Press International, 1998); Gene L. Green, "The Challenge of Global Hermeneutics," in *Global Theology in Evangelical Perspective*, ed. Jeffrey P. Greenman and Gene L. Green (Downers Grove, IL: IVP Academic, 2012), 50–64; Michael A. Rynkiewich, "Proposals for a Missional Hermeneutic: Mapping a Conversation," *Missiology* 39, no. 3 (2011): 309–21; Shawn B. Redford, *Missiological Hermeneutics*, American Society of Missiology Monograph 11 (Eugene, OR: Pickwick, 2012); and Henning Wrogemann, *Intercultural Theology*, vol. 1, *Intercultural Hermeneutics*, trans. Karl E. Böhmer, Missiological Engagements (Downers Grove, IL: IVP Academic, 2016).

5. Parts of this section are adapted from Paul W. Lewis, "Morality in Local and Global Perspectives," in *Christian Morality: An Interdisciplinary Framework for Thinking about Contemporary Moral Issues*, ed. Geoff Sutton and Brandon Schmidly (Eugene, OR: Pickwick, 2016), 155–71.

6. Wanda Deifelt, "Intercultural Ethics: Sameness and Otherness Revisited," *Dialog: A Journal of Theology* 46, no. 2 (2007): 112. Deifelt is interacting with Clifford Geertz, "Thick Description: Toward an Interpretative Theory of Culture," in *The Interpretation of Culture: Selected Essays by Clifford Geertz* (New York: Basic Books, 1973), 5.

lens of a presupposed paradigm. Culture is a dynamic enterprise in which, in one sense, humans are formed by culture, and they are a part of it as well (especially if they are born and raised in it). Yet in another sense, the capacity of people to reach beyond themselves also means that people play a role in shaping their own culture.[7] In recent years, growing globalization and urbanization have demonstrated more clearly the dynamic element of culture, as cultures interact, change, adopt, adapt, and reentrench in our contemporary world.[8]

Cross-cultural hermeneutics operates in a parallel way, as does cross-cultural ethics. Only with the right attitude and in dialogue with others can intercultural ethics and hermeneutics develop. While affirming that Christians exist in cultures, all Christians are also to be countercultural. Allegiance to the kingdom of God requires them to be critics of their own cultures, a process particularly informed by their reading of Scripture. Likewise, as outsiders who cannot fully understand the culture like an insider, cross-cultural workers (e.g., missionaries) can provide insight(s) into an insider's "blind spots."[9] Thus, there will always be a need for missionaries and cross-cultural hermeneutics.[10] Likewise, we always need to inform our hermeneutics with global and historical Christian perspectives.

Cross-Cultural or Missional Hermeneutics

For this chapter, we will use "cross-cultural hermeneutics" and "missional hermeneutics" somewhat interchangeably. They both highlight the importance of engaging directly with others across cultural barriers. Cross-cultural hermeneutics highlights the cultural barrier that needs to be crossed, whereas missional hermeneutics emphasizes the purpose and goal of this process (tied to God's mission reaching out to a lost and dying world). In other words, the former focuses on the how of this process, and the latter on the why, yet the two overlap significantly. Using the SMCR communication model (see chap. 4), we can properly implement our role as a sender of a message via a channel, yet receivers may still not readily understand.

Missional hermeneutics has two objectives. First, the communication from the sender(s) should be appropriate for an understanding of the biblical text by

7. Some would call it "transcending themselves"; see Deifelt, "Intercultural Ethics," 112.
8. Deifelt, "Intercultural Ethics," 112–19.
9. This can include Westerners coming from literary cultures and engaging those from an oral culture. See Walter Ong, *Orality and Literacy: Technologizing of the Word* (London: Routledge, 1982).
10. David C. Kelly, "Cross-Cultural Communication and Ethics," *Missiology* 6, no. 3 (1978): 312–13.

the recipients within their context. Second, the recipients should be equipped and enabled so that they can become good hermeneuts themselves.

As for the first objective, for cross-cultural hermeneutics to work, three stages are needed. The first two are tied to what we have already discussed. We start with the exegesis of a passage, focusing on the there-then interpretation of the biblical message within its original context. Second, we then translate that message for the here-now—that is, the interpreter's (or missionary's) own cultural context. The additional piece is to then become a sender to a different cultural recipient and to focus on the there-now proclamation in a third cultural context (see fig. 14.2). This can also be called the third horizon.[11] Therefore, there are three horizons in the task of interpretation when we are engaging a third culture: the horizon of the text, the horizon of the interpreter, and the horizon of the recipient (see chap. 4). Every cross-cultural interpretation involves the interaction of these three horizons. However, once the recipient is equipped to directly interpret the Bible for themselves, then she or he engages only two horizons.

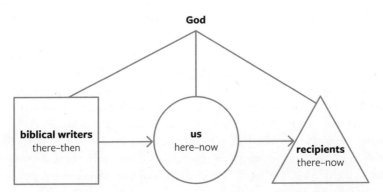

Figure 14.2. From there-then through here-now to there-now / Paul Lewis

11. This has become a common term for hermeneutical issues related to the contextualization of the gospel into another culture. A few of the many works on the topic of contextualization are Stephan B. Bevans, *An Introduction to Theology in Global Perspective* (Maryknoll, NY: Orbis Books, 2009); A. Scott Moreau, *Contextualization in World Missions: Mapping and Assessing Evangelical Models* (Grand Rapids: Kregel, 2012); and Craig Ott and Stephen J. Strauss, with Timothy C. Tennent, *Encountering Theology of Mission: Biblical Foundations, Historical Developments, and Contemporary Issues* (Grand Rapids: Baker Academic, 2010). See these classic texts on the "third horizon": D. A. Carson, "Church and Mission: Reflections on Contextualization and the Third Horizon," in *The Church in the Bible and the World*, ed. D. A. Carson (Grand Rapids: Baker, 1987), esp. 218–19 (213–57); Harvie M. Conn, *Eternal Word and Changing Worlds: Theology, Anthropology, and Mission in Trialogue* (Grand Rapids: Zondervan, 1992), 188–90; and Dean Fleming, "The Third Horizon: A Wesleyan Contribution to the Contextualization Debate," *Wesleyan Theological Journal* 30, no. 2 (1995): 139–63.

In order for a missionary to do his or her job well, they need to be competent in a variety of areas. First, the exegete working in a cross-cultural setting must be solidly familiar with the exegetical tools for interpreting the Bible from within its *original* context. So a familiarity with the art and science of hermeneutics, as well as the appropriate tools, is necessary. Second, while "translating" the message into one's here-now is a goal, this can be done only with a critical awareness of one's *own* cultural context. This is key, since we are called to follow Christ and since we are also called to be critics of our own culture. The third step for a robust cross-cultural hermeneutic is to incorporate astute insight into and awareness of the *recipient's* context and culture.[12] It goes without saying that this is a really involved task. The tendency of some missionaries is to not investigate the original contexts or the recipient contexts well. While we cannot be experts at everything, doing all three tasks effectively should still be the goal.

This also leads to the second objective. In a missional context (and any cross-cultural context), the recipients should get to a place where they themselves can interpret Scripture directly. Paul in 1 Corinthians 11:1 instructs, "Follow my example, as I follow the example of Christ." This verse highlights an important consideration. The Corinthians needed to follow Paul as he followed Christ. It was Christ in Paul that was to be their focus. An important corollary is that only if they had a close and personal relationship with Christ could they discern Christ in Paul from Paul himself. Similarly, a genuine cross-cultural hermeneutic must always have as an objective that the recipients move from this three-stage process (or the three horizons) to their own two-stage process: there-then to here-now (see fig. 14.3). This must always be the end goal. Cross-cultural hermeneutics is not only about transferring content, techniques, and methods; it is also about leading the recipients into their own understanding of their role in their own hermeneutical process.

Cross-cultural hermeneutics has frequently been called *ethnohermeneutics*. As Larry W. Caldwell notes, "There is a need to further explore hermeneutics directed specifically towards how to interpret the Bible from one culture to the next, from one people group, or ethnic group, to another."[13] Part of Caldwell's concern is that Western-based hermeneutical methods have often been promoted as universal, whereas they are *just* that—Western. As Daniel A.

---

12. A theology developed in a recipient culture is called a contextual theology. See Stephen B. Bevans, *Models of Contextual Theology*, rev. ed., Faith and Culture (Maryknoll, NY: Orbis Books, 2002), as a helpful survey of various models.

13. Larry Caldwell, "Toward the New Discipline of Ethnohermeneutics: Questioning the Relevancy of Western Hermeneutical Methods in the Asian Context," *Journal of Asian Mission* 1, no. 1 (1999): 23.

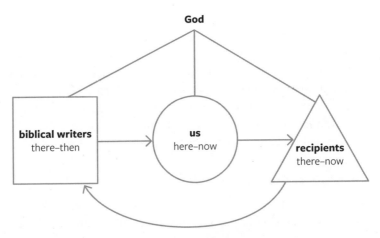

Figure 14.3. Moving from three horizons to two horizons / Paul Lewis

Tappeiner states, Caldwell's "call to ethnohermeneutics seems to result from some kind of confusion between the missiological task of contextualizing the supracultural truth to various cultures, and the theological task of determining the content of that supracultural truth and its significance for today."[14] The missionary's contextualization task and the theologian's theologizing task, while complementary, should not be conflated. Equally, there is a fine line between contextualizing the Christian message within a recipient cultural context and adapting the message based on the recipient culture alone.

Problems Related to Cross-Cultural Hermeneutics

While cross-cultural hermeneutics has some distinct positive elements, there are some potentially negative issues that need to be brought to the forefront. First, as was noted above, in order for cross-cultural hermeneutics to flourish, there needs to be a proper understanding of each of the three horizons: the horizon of the text (which includes its historical and literary contexts), the horizon of the interpreter (us and our cultural contexts, preunderstandings, and biases), and the horizon of the recipient cultural contexts. This is a difficult task, and it is frequently not done well. The original contexts can be

14. Daniel A. Tappeiner, "A Response to Caldwell's Trumpet Call to Ethnohermeneutics," *Journal of Asian Mission* 1, no. 2 (1999): 231. See the response by James R. Whelchel, "Ethnohermeneutics: A Response," *Journal of Asian Mission* 2, no. 1 (2000): 125–33, as well as the reply by Larry Caldwell, "A Response to the Response of Tappeiner and Whelchel to Ethnohermeneutics," *Journal of Asian Mission* 2, no. 1 (2000): 135–44. See also William Patrick Brooks, "Critiquing Ethnohermeneutics Theories: A Call for an Author-Oriented Approach to Cross-Cultural Biblical Interpretation" (PhD diss., Southern Baptist Theological Seminary, 2011), esp. 103–20.

neglected, our own biases can be glossed over, and the target contexts can be ignored. In this case, the recipients will suffer from missionary malpractice.

Second, there is the issue of missionaries as cross-cultural exegetes not equipping the recipients to become appropriate hermeneuts themselves. The missionary or cross-cultural communicator can become a long-term or permanent gatekeeper, not allowing recipients to become their own exegetes and hermeneuts. Most often, this is not intentional, but it can take place due to neglect or issues of power. This can be a big issue in practice and needs to be guarded against.

The Benefits of Cross-Cultural Hermeneutics

There are likewise many positive possibilities for cross-cultural hermeneutics. First, whenever someone engages the biblical text with those of another culture, the potential to learn from each other grows. People from differing contexts can have different blind spots; thus, they can help each other overcome their respective limitations in reading the biblical text. For example, Western readers may discover that they interpret Scripture through the lens of individualism by reading the Bible alongside people from collectivist cultures. Those of differing cultural contexts can provide various insights as well. Further, some people groups "listen" better to literary nuances, whereas others have a rationality that aids in following arguments, and so on. Learning together in community helps everyone grow beyond their own perspectives. In a similar way, engaging the text with others from differing cultures can grant us a better understanding of our own cultures, lenses, and blind spots. For example, interpreters from capitalist cultures might find their emphasis on wealth accumulation challenged by the Bible and other groups that emphasize living simply. We benefit from the interaction as much as, if not more than, the recipients do.

Further, working with others from different cultural perspectives can expand our personal understanding of the biblical text. For instance, numerous biblical passages espouse the need to protect and minister to the strangers in our midst. By engaging in genuine dialogue and studying the Bible together, we can learn how immigrants themselves understand these passages. This can help us in our own Christian life and local Christian community; we "are no longer foreigners and strangers, but fellow citizens with God's people" (Eph. 2:19).

Biblical Interpretation without Study Aids

While English readers are blessed with a wide variety of Bible translations and a vast number of resources with which they can study Scripture, there are thousands of languages still awaiting their first Bible translation. There are also many linguistic groups that have an adequate translation but lack study aids of any kind. Here are some steps to help these groups until they can work in another language with appropriate resources or until quality resources become available in their own tongue.

The first step for those without study aids is to focus on analyzing literary contexts (and cultural-sociohistorical contexts as much as possible). This entails looking at the biblical book in view as a whole. An outline of the text and its content will aid in getting an overview of the book. Further, we need to understand that chapter and verse divisions are aids to our study but are not inspired or original. Sometimes, the big picture helps in understanding a passage. First Corinthians 2:1–5 is an example. Over the years, I have heard some Christians use this passage in support of their conviction that Paul was opposed to sermon preparation and learning. However, in the broader context, 1 Corinthians 1–4 is about divisions in the church in Corinth. Accordingly, 1 Corinthians 2:1–5 is about how Christ has saved the Corinthians through his Spirit; Paul is not diminishing preparation but assuring his readers that their salvation is not due to his rhetoric or eloquence.[15] So seeing the bigger context is important.

Another element of the literary context is the local context—what happens right before or after a passage. An example is Matthew 10:1. Just prior to this verse, in 9:35, Jesus is going around teaching, preaching, and healing in various synagogues. Verse 36 notes that Jesus has compassion on the people since they are like sheep without a shepherd. This leads Jesus, in verses 37–38, to request of the disciples (including us): "Ask the Lord of the harvest, therefore, to send out workers into his harvest field." Matthew 10:1 is where Jesus calls the Twelve and grants them authority to heal and command unclean spirits. In other words, there is a progression from 9:35 to 10:1: (1) Jesus is doing the ministry and healing; (2) he has compassion on the masses; (3) he recognizes the need and requests prayers for laborers; and (4) he calls the Twelve and gives them authority to heal and exorcise evil spirits. The minister pool expands from one to thirteen (the Twelve plus Jesus). To understand some passages, a close engagement with the local context is important.

Beyond this, look at the whole Bible. It is important to test things in light of the whole counsel of God. An understanding of the whole biblical text and its story of redemption is important so as to avoid extremes. Related to this, as highlighted by Martin Luther, Scripture interprets Scripture. Allow

---

15. See, e.g., Gordon D. Fee, *The First Epistle to the Corinthians*, New International Commentary on the New Testament (Grand Rapids: Eerdmans, 1987), 88–97.

the biblical text as a whole to verify understandings of individual passages. Here are a couple of related principles for looking at biblical texts: First, when you are looking at the whole counsel of God, if one passage is unclear on a topic, and another passage is clear, then the clear passage takes priority over the unclear one. Second, pay attention to key theological points that are found in multiple texts, especially throughout the canon. The corollary is to be cautious of something that is unclear or found in only one passage.

Another principle is to read according to genre (narrative, psalms, letters, etc.). There are significant differences between texts according to their genre. The genre determines the reading strategy.[16] (For a discussion of various genres, see chaps. 6–11 above.)

Other considerations have to do with the fundamental attitudes we bring when coming to the biblical text. First, recognize that we all have biases and that we all need God's help in overcoming detrimental blind spots and holding firm to nonnegotiable presuppositions (see chap. 5). Second, we need to allow the Spirit to transform us through his Word, the Scriptures, rather than attempting to transform the text into our image (including our ideologies, lenses, etc.). Third, related to this, we should "listen to the text"[17] and let God speak through the text to us.

There are some additional considerations to entertain as well. As we interpret the text, it is important to be mindful that at times the Bible teaches directly through commands, directions, instructions, and the like, but at other times, it teaches indirectly through examples, such as through the stories and lives of characters (e.g., Abraham, Moses, Paul). And sometimes, these examples are about what *not* to do, or they show the consequences of foolish actions (e.g., Samson, Herod Agrippa of Acts 12). The biblical text is there to teach, and Lord willing, we can learn and grow to be more like Christ.

WHAT DO I DO NOW?

Before getting into a discussion about cross-cultural hermeneutics, one of the key things to consider is the nature of culture. While pertinent to the discussion of the two horizons or the culture of the biblical times contrasted

16. Tremper Longman III and Raymond B. Dillard, *An Introduction to the Old Testament*, 2nd ed. (Grand Rapids: Zondervan, 2006), 31.

17. Even noted Bible scholars have to be reminded of the importance of listening to the text. See William L. Lane, *The Gospel according to Mark*, New International Commentary on the New Testament (Grand Rapids: Eerdmans, 1974), xii. See also F. F. Bruce's note along these lines in his foreword to Lane's commentary, ix.

with our own, culture is especially pertinent to the discussion of missional or cross-cultural hermeneutics.

Cross-cultural hermeneutics is an important aspect of contemporary life. We live in a multicultural world, and engaging cross-culturally and missionally requires one to be aware of the three basic stages required to contextualize the message of the Bible in a recipient culture. This is particularly important in pastoral contexts, such as when preaching or teaching in public. In such settings, there may be many multicultural recipients in a single venue.

We also recognize that cross-cultural hermeneutics has several potential problems, including the malpractice resulting from missing or neglecting one of its three basic elements (the biblical context, our current cultural context, and the recipients' context). Yet cross-cultural hermeneutics also has several worthwhile potentialities, such as when a different perspective helps us see something in the Bible that we previously missed due to our cultural or personal blind spots.

One of the sad dynamics in our world today is that while many people have multiple Bible versions and Bible study resources in their own language (or at least in a language they can understand), many others don't even have the Old or the New Testament in their language. So for those with a Bible yet nothing else—or a bare minimum of resources—we have looked at how to guide their interpretive efforts. The key emphasis is to study the literary context (and as much of the historical context as possible), as well as to interpret within the whole counsel of God and to allow Scripture to interpret Scripture.

PRAYER

Lord, we thank you for your Word and the opportunity to share your gospel with others.

Let me be a good student of your Word, aware of my biases and contexts and attentive of the contexts of those to whom you have called me to proclaim the good news.

Lord, I pray that you will help me model, teach, and proclaim your Word in such a way that those in other cultures can know you and grow on their own.

And help those who do not have a Bible or study aids in their own language to be thoroughly guided by your Spirit so that they may know your Word and follow the whole counsel of God.

Amen.

TOPICS FOR REVIEW

1. What is a good definition of "culture"? What does culture mean to you?
2. Why is cross-cultural or missional hermeneutics important? What are the main features of cross-cultural hermeneutics?
3. Using the SMCR theory (see chap. 4), discuss the complexities of cross-cultural hermeneutics and the third horizon.

15

JOINING THE STORY

This chapter includes a recap of the foundations of biblical interpretation (being PERSONAL), and you should expect to learn the following:

- ▶ How the Bible is God's story, from creation to new creation
- ▶ The now-and-not-yet framework
- ▶ How we participate in God's story of redemption

Anyone who listens to the word but does not do what it says is like someone who looks at his face in a mirror and, after looking at himself, goes away and immediately forgets what he looks like.

—James 1:23–24

As this passage from James highlights, it is not enough to study the Word; study must lead to application. James humorously tells us in this proverb-like saying that applying Scripture reinforces its message—when we apply, we don't forget. Therefore, we are called to be both good listeners and doers; listening to the Word leads to action. Tangentially, the stained glass window shown in figure 15.1 honors the establishment of the Patrician Brothers, but several features need emphasis. First, the Spirit's role in establishing the Word is highlighted. Second, notice how this window connects with the

Andreas F. Borchert / Wikimedia Commons / CC BY-SA 3.0

Figure 15.1. Stained glass window by George Walsh in Church of the Most Holy Rosary, Tullow, Ireland

servant of the Lord. Third, this window shows the movement of the servants to serve others in the application of the Word. All three are necessary in moving forward in the Christlike, Spirit-filled life. As we review the main lessons of this book, our goal is to reinforce the central ideas so you can also put them into practice and not forget them. This reminds us of the very beginning of the book, where we outlined the task of interpretation as PERSONAL. As we conclude, we will review the story of Scripture once more and consider how we join this grand narrative to participate in God's story of redemption.

Being PERSONAL

How do we begin the task of interpreting Scripture? We start with the understanding that biblical interpretation is important, since through the study of Scripture we come to a deeper relationship with and comprehension of God. Yet as we reflect on our role as interpreters, we see that we have our own biases and recognize that there is a gap or a significant distance between our times and biblical times. This is why we need to read Scripture within its own contexts—historical, cultural, literary, grammatical, rhetorical, and linguistic. The biblical texts are historically and culturally situated, and we must read them accordingly.

Likewise, while always starting with and maintaining an attitude of prayer, we need to begin with the right tools: a good Bible translation (and a variety of versions for study), along with some quality Bible dictionaries and wordbooks, handbooks, and atlases (if available). These tools help us in the task of exegesis, which is exploring what a passage means there-then. We begin with the basic components of a biblical passage itself: we focus on key words, the flow of sentences, the paragraphing, and the overall discourse and argumentation. These are the fundamental steps we need to take in order to start the wonderful adventure of biblical interpretation.

We have outlined the interpretive task with the acronym PERSONAL, so that the task can be more readily remembered. While we encourage beginners to adopt this approach, it is really for everyone to use in an ongoing way. Similarly, while we outline this approach using certain steps, the stages overlap. Prayer, for instance, should be part of the beginning of the process, consistent throughout, and part of application and implementation. Other aspects are accumulative, such as applying the text as part of one's hermeneutical spiral. Over years of study, you will be increasingly informed and formed by your ongoing understanding and application of the Bible. However, none of us ever arrive at an end point; there are always new insights to glean and new resources to consult. Biblical interpretation, if done well, is a lifelong pursuit. So as James advises, let's look in the mirror of this book once more to remind us of the key steps for biblical interpretation—the steps of being PERSONAL.

1. **Pray.**
   ○ Start with prayer. Ask God to help you be receptive to what he would like you to learn.
   ○ Maintain an attitude of prayer, asking God to guide you by his Spirit throughout the process.
2. **Evaluate** yourself.
   ○ Be aware of your own biases and preunderstanding.
   ○ Note the negotiable versus nonnegotiable elements (see chap. 5).
   ○ Be a student of your own cultural context. What are your cultural blind spots? What are your personal blind spots?
3. **Read** in context.
   ○ The first context to identify is the original context of the text. This refers to understanding the context of the original audience, the

there-then. It includes the historical situation as well as the cultural and social world of the community relevant to the passage.

- The second context is the literary context. Assumed here is that each passage uses a particular genre. Most genres found in the Bible have been explored in part 2. We need to identify the type of literature being used—such as poetry, letter, proverb, or historical narrative—so we can read the literary context accordingly.
- The literary context includes, first, the words and grammar of the passage we are studying. The second layer is how the passage fits in the larger structure of the chapter and book.

4. **Seek** meaning—note the key details of the passage and what it is communicating.
- Consider the words and phrases of the passage.
- Look over and even diagram the passage's sentences, seeing connections from the immediate context and the rest of the book.
- Look at place names, people, and themes.
- Next, seek out available resources, such as Bible dictionaries, wordbooks, handbooks, and atlases, to understand the passage and the places, people, and events that it refers to. (Dig deep, and learn as much as you can at this stage, not only for present purposes but also for future usage.)

5. **Observe** with your head and your heart.
- First, what did this passage mean for the original audience—there-then? Meditate on the passage with the original context in mind.
  - What is the apparent reason for the writing of this passage? How do the context and genre inform your understanding?
  - What are the concerns of the author?
- Second, turn toward your heart. "Open yourself to the costly demand of the text and commit yourself to repentance and change in the light of it."[1] What does this passage mean for you—here-now?

6. **Note** your ideas about the meaning of the passage in your own words. Write out a summary of your ideas.
- Continue to note how others understand this passage within its historical context. Note some ideas from quality commentaries (three or four is fine).

1. John Goldingay, *Models for Interpretation of Scripture* (Grand Rapids: Eerdmans, 1995), 286.

- Do these commentaries offer any additional insights?
- Is there a consensus among the commentaries?
- Do you need to make any adjustments to your own summary?
- Finally, consider how your local, global, and historical community of faith has understood the passage. (This step may be labor intensive, but even just some basic time and energy will return some significant results.)

7. **Apply**—put the Word into action.
   - The above process should lead to theological reflection—Where do you go from here? And it should lead to (silent) prayer, allowing the presence of God to touch your heart and mind.
   - After this, consider: What is at least one application or key lesson for the week? How can you verify whether you have implemented this insight?
     - Internally, how does this impact your walk with the Lord?
     - Externally, what actions or expressions need to take place?
   - Also consider: How has this process led to an understanding of the biblical text that is new or is deeper than the one you had when you read the same text the last time? (How does it help you in the hermeneutical spiral? How does it inform your preunderstanding?)
   - Conclude the application portion with prayer, asking for God's guidance and empowerment.

8. **Live** and share.
   - In our living, we move from initial actions to ongoing habits that are second nature and that inform our dispositions.
     - Our thoughts, affections, experiences, and ethics become more Christlike.
     - This process combines our lifelong learning with our being conformed into the image of Christ.
     - It also modifies our preunderstanding, which can influence our next engagement with the text.
   - Associated with living is sharing, which has three aspects to it.
     - First, we share as part of a community of faith, interacting with fellow believers both to discover what they see in the text and to assist them in their understanding of the passage.
     - Second, beyond the community of faith, we share with nonbelievers as witnesses to the truth.

- ▪ Third, we share to help our own growth. As James 1:23–24 says, as we do, we remember.
  - ○ We can also share in cross-cultural situations. Engaging with others from different cultures can broaden our outlook and help us overcome our own blind spots.

Making our reading PERSONAL ensures that our interpretation of the Bible is built on a solid foundation. The significance of a passage in our here-now is founded on our exegetical analysis of the there-then. As the Holy Spirit inspired the original writers and editors, so the Spirit illuminates the same text for us today. As the psalmist says, "Your word is a lamp for my feet, a light on my path" (Ps. 119:105). Like a spotlight illuminating a path or road so we can see and walk clearly in the right direction, the Spirit illuminates the words of the Bible for us. Scripture forms us and guides us in our journey of faith. It shapes us and our passions, which inform our behavior. The Bible is to be lived. Yet as noted previously, the purpose of the Bible involves more than just providing moral guidance or cognitive information about God.

The telos, or end goal, of the Bible is to reveal God and to allow us to participate in the life of God. As we read and obey the Bible, the intention is for us to become more like Christ and to participate in the divine life. Knowing Jesus, which occurs when we read the Bible, should result in us becoming more like Jesus. Yet this requires us to read, study, and apply the Bible diligently. Scripture is a gift from God. It is the place we can encounter God. So if we want God to transform us, we must read the Bible. Yet as we read the Bible, we soon realize it is not a compendium of random books; rather, it tells a story. It tells us God's story of redemption. This story moves from creation to new creation. The narrative of the Bible has a telos.

The Bible: God's Story of Redemption

One feature of a story is that it moves through time. It starts with a beginning. Usually, at the beginning of a story, there is some kind of complication or problem that propels the plot forward. Then the story moves to a middle, which involves the messiness of the conflict. When we are in the middle of a story, we can sometimes wonder how the story will unravel and resolve. Then the story moves to the ending. For Christians, the end of the story of the Bible presents a glorious vision of restoration and hope. Titus 2:13 says, "We wait for the blessed hope—the appearing of the glory of our great God and Savior, Jesus Christ." The study of end times is called "eschatology," which derives from the Greek combination of *eschatos* (meaning "last things") and *logos* (meaning "word")—so we get *eschatologia*, or words on the last things. But to understand the end of the story, we need to go back to the beginning, because the story of the Bible moves from creation to new creation. As we have noted, our human story starts in Genesis.

The first words of the Bible tell us that "in the beginning," God has already been in existence. God always was and is—he is the eternal Creator of the world. God's eternal existence, all-sufficient and sovereign power, and unchallenged majesty remind us that God is distinct from creation. Genesis also tells that when God creates the world, he establishes humanity as his stewards and custodians to care for creation (Gen. 1:28; 2:15). However, humanity rejects God's rulership (Gen. 3), and thereby, all that is under human authority is impacted. This includes the earth and nonhuman communities (3:17–19). Human greed and sin distort God's good creation. Sin distorts our humanity so that we become selfish and self-serving. So this is the beginning of the story of Scripture.

The Old Testament proceeds to tell the story of redemption, focusing on Israel and God's revelation to that historic community. The Old Testament follows Israel's testimony of trying to live faithfully to their covenant agreement with God, established at the exodus. The covenant identified Israel as God's treasured people (Exod. 19). They were to be a light to the nations, living in the land of promise. Although they were established in the land and given requirements for worship and leadership, they repeatedly rejected God and failed to keep the covenant. The prophets warned them of the consequences of such behavior. Yet, despite Israel's failure to keep the covenant, resulting in exile, God was faithful to them. Although they returned to the land following exile, they remained under foreign occupation. In their longing for the promised messiah, we see that their story points to the coming of Jesus Christ, whom Christians identify as the fulfilment of Israel's longing and the climax to their story.

The middle of the Bible's story of redemption is marked by the coming of Christ: his life, death, and especially his resurrection. Christ's coming, which we celebrate at Christmas, is good news for all people and all of creation. Jesus is the light of the world. There is much darkness in our world. Many of us have experienced an interior darkness when we have looked inside our souls—a darkness into which Jesus can and has shined a light. In John 8:12, he says: "I am the light of the world. Whoever follows me will never walk in darkness, but will have the light of life." Jesus is the center of the story of salvation. This center is not necessarily the middle in terms of chronology, but theologically, Christ's death and resurrection are the climax of the story of Scripture. His first coming propels the story toward the end as we await his second coming.

Scripture tells us that, in order to atone for our sins and reconcile us to God, Jesus had to embrace our sinful human condition, yet he himself was without sin (Heb. 2:17). The Son of God became fully human in the incarnation (John 1:1; 1 John 4:10). By his suffering on the cross, he took our place and paid the price for our sins (Rom. 6:23). Jesus gave his own life as a ransom for many (Matt. 20:28; Mark 10:45; 1 Tim. 2:6; 1 Pet. 1:18–19). God's salvation includes the world—the cosmos (2 Cor. 5:19). However, Romans 8 tells us that all of creation is groaning and suffering as it eagerly awaits the fulfilment of God's redemption. God's story of redemption is not just about saving a person's soul. It is about the redemption of all creation. This is the salvation that is now revealed to us in Jesus Christ but that is also yet to be fully revealed.

Where is the story of the Bible headed? It moves from creation to new creation. God's work in the whole world is moving ultimately toward a redeemed future. The story of Scripture ends with restoration. This current world will be transformed into a radically new creation, as described in Revelation 21.

Still, the end of the story does include the sobering reality that at the end of time, there will be a reckoning based on whether we have acknowledged and lived according to the lordship of Christ. In John 14:6, Jesus says, "I am the way and the truth and the life. No one comes to the Father except through me." Our actions, decisions, and lives in the present—especially our responses to Jesus's invitation for new life—have future consequences regarding our eternal destiny. But we are not at the end of history yet. The story has not finished. The end of the story envisions a renewed creation. This gives us great hope for the future.

So we know the start of God's story—a good creation marred by sin. We know the ending—a redeemed future. And we know how we get there—through faith in Jesus Christ. What, then, do we do in the present, in the here-now? We live in this gap between the middle of the story and the end of the story. Although Jesus has redeemed us, we are clearly still stained by sin in the present. We all make mistakes and choose our own selfish ways, even when we do not want to. There is still much pain and suffering in our world. If Christ reconciles us with God through his death and resurrection, then why is this world still unreconciled, as evidenced by war, corruption, and pandemics? If the new creation is a glorious transformation of our world, then why do we not see it now?

We live in a tension. It is a practical tension but also a theological tension. Scholars call it the "now but not yet" situation.

The Now-and-Not-Yet Framework

We can sometimes wonder, If Jesus conquered sin and death on the cross, then why is there still suffering in the world? Why is there still evil and corruption?

This question was a dilemma for the earliest Christians as well. They thought the Messiah would come and expel the Romans, who had colonized Israel, and restore the kingdom to Israel. They thought it would be an immediate rollout—that the Messiah would bring about the transition from the past and present evil age to the brand-new, restored, glorious age to come. Sometimes, however, the solutions are not what people expect.

Instead, what was expected as an immediate rollout has been and will continue to be rolled out over the period between the first and second comings of Christ. Some things occur immediately (such as our restored relationship with God and our regeneration by the Spirit), but some things are still to be put right. Yet even these realities yet to be fulfilled have been in a sense achieved because of Jesus's work on the cross.

So we live in this in-between time. It is called the now-and-not-yet. We live in this tension between the now and the not yet, or the yet to come. For example, let's think about salvation. If you have confessed Jesus as Lord, then you are already saved. You are assured of your salvation. Paul says in Ephesians 2:8, "For it is by grace *you have been saved*, through faith—and this is not from yourselves, it is the gift of God."[2] We are saved. However, Paul also says in Philippians 2:12–13, "Therefore, my dear friends, as you have always obeyed—not only in my presence, but now much more in my absence—*continue to work out your salvation* with fear and trembling, for it is God who works in you to will and to act in order to fulfill his good purpose." Wait, which is it? Are we saved already, or are we being saved? And then Paul says in Romans 5:9, "Since we have now been justified by his blood, how much more *shall we be saved* from God's wrath through him!" Which is it? Are we saved? Or being saved? Or will we be saved?

The answer is that it is all three, all at once. This is the now-and-not-yet tension. We were saved when we gave our hearts to Jesus (in the past). But we work out our salvation in the present, in the process of sanctification, which is the process of becoming like Jesus. This means that once we are saved, we are not to live like our old selves but to live as though our salvation means something. We work out our salvation (in the present). But then we will be saved at the end of time, when history comes to an end, and we go to be with the Lord forever. That is, we will be saved (in the future).

---

2. Emphasis has been added here and in the quotations that follow in this paragraph.

This same framework can extend to many of the blessings and hopes that we have in Jesus, based on the atoning work of Christ on the cross. These include healing. We are encouraged to pray for healing (in the present). We pray actively in faith for the healing of our bodies. Yet healing is also a signpost that points to the not yet. Healing the sick is one of the "signs and wonders" that often accompany the proclamation of the gospel, especially as described in the book of Acts. But sometimes we pray and people are not healed (in the present). What do we do? Healing in the now is a foretaste of what is to come in the eschaton. So we continue to pray, but we also recognize that healing sometimes does not occur in our lifetime. Sometimes, healing is only provided in the time yet to come. Healing in such cases is provided in the future, in heaven, when our bodies will be transformed. Ultimate healing is provided in the time to come, when, as Revelation 21:4 says, "[God] will wipe every tear from their eyes. There will be no more death or mourning or crying or pain, for the old order of things has passed away."

The Christian life, then, is shaped by the assurance we have now in Christ, but it is also shaped by this future hope of the time yet to come. What implications does this have for our lives today? Eugene Peterson writes, "The biblical story invites us in as participants in something larger than our sin-defined needs, into something truer than our culture-stunted ambitions. We enter these stories and recognize ourselves as participants, whether willing or unwilling, in the life of God."[3] We participate in God's story of redemption. Fortunately, God has given us the Holy Spirit to help us in this journey.

WHAT DO I DO NOW? JOIN THE STORY!

How do we participate in the story of Scripture? New Testament scholar N. T. Wright uses an analogy we will adopt to help us understand how we are part of this living story today. Wright likens the story of redemption to a five-act Shakespearean play.[4] Every Shakespearean play has five acts. But imagine that a lost play written by Shakespeare was recently discovered—a play that no one has ever heard of or read before. The problem, though, is that the play only has four acts. The last act of the play, the fifth act, was lost or never written.

---

3. Eugene H. Peterson, *Eat This Book: A Conversation in the Art of Spiritual Reading* (London: Hodder & Stoughton, 2006), 41.
4. N. T. Wright, "How Can the Bible Be Authoritative? (The Laing Lecture for 1989)," *Vox Evangelica* 21 (1991): 7–32, also at https://ntwrightpage.com/2016/07/12/how-can-the-bible-be -authoritative.

Yet this mostly finished Shakespearean play is brilliant. Everyone wants to see it performed. So what does a theater company do?

The actors play out the first four acts according to the script, which is like Scripture. The script of the first four acts, in this analogy, is the story of Scripture. The first four acts can be described as (1) creation and the fall of humanity into sin; (2) God's covenant with Abraham and focus on ancient Israel; (3) the coming of Jesus, his death, and his resurrection; and (4) Pentecost and the birth of the church. But then the story stops. The last act is missing. There is no script for the last act. However, we are given a glimpse of the ending by the story. The story of Scripture will conclude when history is finalized, as anticipated in the book of Revelation. We know how God's story of redemption ends. It concludes with God's intervention in history. It ends when Christ returns to judge the living and the dead. The ending of history closes with the renewal of creation, when believers will be with God forever.

In this analogy, we are the actors of this theater company. We must play out the end of the story of Scripture. However, we must be consistent with all that has gone before in the story. We must live consistently with the message and teachings of the Bible. Yet we must move the story forward toward its ending—new creation. But we have no script. This requires us to improvise. To improvise requires us to know the story well. We must know what has happened in the first four acts of the story (Scripture) to move the story to its conclusion. This is how we are called to live in this now-and-not-yet period. We stay true to the script of Scripture. We keep faithful to God and the story so far. But we also act now with the end in mind, to see the story through to its conclusion.

We are part of this story. We are called to live consistently with Scripture in the present context of the not yet. However, we must not "cut and paste" the there-then world of the biblical text onto ours, because we live in a different time and different context. Instead, we must be consistent with what Scripture teaches us and with the end of the story to which the Bible points. We participate in this story by being led by the Spirit of God. We must be led by the Spirit in order to improvise our part of the story, as we live out the gospel in our changing world. We must be "carried along by the Holy Spirit" (2 Pet. 1:21). This is why we desperately need the discernment of the Holy Spirit to guide us, lead us, and help us in this life of faith. It is also why we need to be anchored in a faith community to provide support, encouragement, and advice along the way. The Spirit-filled life is a Spirit-led life.

Therefore, the Bible is central to our faith and applicable to our daily lives. Scripture reveals the good news of God's salvation for this world. The story of God's redemptive activity is recorded in the history of Old Testament Israel, revealed in Jesus Christ, and outworked in the New Testament church. We continue this story. May we live faithfully to the story of Scripture in whatever new contexts and situations we face. We hope that you will embrace, with the Bible as your anchor, this opportunity to participate in God's story of redemption.

PRAYER

Lord, we thank you for your Word, the opportunity to study your Word, and the ability to see you through your Word.
"Lord, grant [that] I may receive an awareness of the power that is within [your Scripture]."[5]
And let me have the enablement and empowerment to be your hands extended, your word vocalized, and your presence incarnate in this lost and dying world.
Amen.

TOPICS FOR REVIEW

1. What has stood out to you most from this introduction to biblical interpretation?
2. What has been the most challenging concept for you from this book?
3. In what ways are we required to "improvise" Scripture? What are some challenges we face today that are not addressed in the Bible? How should we navigate these challenges?
4. Have you felt the nudging or presence of the Spirit as you read the Bible? How should you respond?
5. How do we join God's story of redemption today?

---

5. St. Isaac of Syria, *Daily Readings with St. Isaac of Syria*, ed. A. M. Allchin, trans. Sebastian Brock (Springfield, IL: Templegate, 1989), 75.

RECOMMENDED RESOURCES

Bartholomew, Craig G., and Michael W. Goheen. *The Drama of Scripture: Finding Our Place in the Biblical Story*. 3rd ed. Grand Rapids: Baker Academic, 2024.

Bauckham, Richard. *The Bible in the Contemporary World: Hermeneutical Ventures*. Grand Rapids: Eerdmans, 2015.

Bray, Gerald. *Biblical Interpretation: Past and Present*. Downers Grove, IL: InterVarsity, 1996.

Brown, Jeannine K. *Scripture as Communication: Introducing Biblical Hermeneutics*. 2nd ed. Grand Rapids: Baker Academic, 2021.

Caldwell, Larry. *Doing Bible Interpretation!* Sioux Falls, SD: Lazy Oak, 2016.

Dockery, David S., Kenneth A. Mathews, and Robert B. Sloan, eds. *Foundations for Biblical Interpretation*. Nashville: Broadman & Holman, 1994.

Duvall, J. Scott, and J. Daniel Hays. *Grasping God's Word: A Hands-On Approach to Reading, Interpreting, and Applying the Bible*. 4th ed. Grand Rapids: Zondervan, 2020.

Fee, Gordon D. *New Testament Exegesis: A Handbook for Students and Pastors*. 3rd ed. Louisville: Westminster John Knox, 2002.

Fee, Gordon D., and Douglas Stuart. *How to Read the Bible for All Its Worth*. 4th ed. Grand Rapids: Zondervan Academic, 2014.

Goldingay, John. *Models for Interpretation of Scripture*. Grand Rapids: Eerdmans, 1995.

Grant, Robert M. *A Short History of the Interpretation of the Bible*. With David Tracy. Rev. ed. Philadelphia: Fortress, 1984.

Grey, Jacqueline. *Three's a Crowd: Pentecostalism, Hermeneutics, and the Old Testament*. Eugene, OR: Pickwick, 2011.

Kaiser, Walter C., Jr., and Moisés Silva. *Introduction to Biblical Hermeneutics: The Search for Meaning*. Rev. ed. Grand Rapids: Zondervan, 2007.

Keener, Craig S. *Spirit Hermeneutics: Reading Scripture in Light of Pentecost*. Grand Rapids: Eerdmans, 2016.

Klein, William W., Craig L. Blomberg, and Robert L. Hubbard Jr. *Introduction to Biblical Interpretation*. 3rd ed. Grand Rapids: Zondervan, 2017.

Osborne, Grant R. *The Hermeneutical Spiral: A Comprehensive Introduction to Biblical Interpretation*. Rev. ed. Downers Grove, IL: IVP Academic, 2006.

Peterson, Eugene H. *Eat This Book: The Art of Spiritual Reading*. London: Hodder & Stoughton, 2006.

Ramm, Bernard. *Protestant Biblical Interpretation*. Grand Rapids: Baker, 1970.

Redford, Shawn B. *Missiological Hermeneutics: Biblical Interpretation for the Global Church*. American Society of Missiology Monograph Series 11. Eugene, OR: Pickwick, 2012.

Stuart, Douglas. *Old Testament Exegesis: A Handbook for Students and Pastors*. 5th ed. Louisville: Westminster John Knox, 2022.

Vanhoozer, Kevin J. *Is There a Meaning in This Text? The Bible, the Reader, and the Morality of Literary Knowledge*. Grand Rapids: Zondervan, 1998.

Wrogemann, Henning. *Intercultural Theology*. Vol. 1, *Intercultural Hermeneutics*, translated by Karl E. Böhmer. Missiological Engagements 1. Downers Grove, IL: IVP Academic, 2016.

Wyckoff, John W. *Pneuma and Logos: The Role of the Spirit in Biblical Hermeneutics*. Eugene, OR: Wipf & Stock, 2010.

INDEX